Footing with
Sir Richard's Ghost

Patricia Glyn

For the Glyns, past and present,
and for the aboriginal dogs of Africa

Author's Note

The spellings of names and places in Richard Glyn's diary have been modernised and corrected for the sake of accuracy and consistency. It is clear from The Diary, and other journals of the time, that the words 'Zulu,' 'black,' 'native,' 'nigger' and 'kaffir' were used, interchangeably, to denote African people and not necessarily in an insulting or derogatory manner. Nonetheless, some of those words are – understandably – deeply offensive to readers today, and I have opted to replace these with less demeaning alternatives, albeit at the risk of losing some of the authenticity of the voice of the original writer/s. There is also much debate at present as to whether the aboriginal people of the African continent should be called 'Bushmen' or 'San' and here I have deferred to the opinion of experts who speak their language, study their culture and travel with them. These men and women tell me that the 'first people' of Africa are happy to be known as 'Bushmen' because the word 'San' is a Nama term denoting, sometimes pejoratively, 'bush dweller'.

Every effort has been made to trace the copyright holders of images reproduced in this publication, but where this has proved impossible the publishers would be grateful to hear from any person/s in a position to convey information in this regard.

SHARP

Copyright © 2006 Published Edition Patricia Glyn
Copyright © 2006 Text Patricia Glyn

First edition, second impression 2006
Published by Sharp Sharp Media (Pty) Ltd
48 Rothesay Ave
Craighall Park
Johannesburg
South Africa, 2196

ISBN: 0-620-36401-7

Publisher: Zann Hoad
Editor: Sean Fraser
Design and Layout: MANIK Design Studio
Printed and bound by Creda Communications (Pty) Ltd

To contact the author:
Patricia Glyn
P O Box 81400
Parkhurst
South Africa, 2120
email: patriciaglyn@wol.co.za
tel: +27 82 881 8550 mobile
    +27 11 501 2230 fax

Table of contents

Acknowledgements

The very long list of people at the end of this book is testimony to the tremendous support I received before, during and after my journey. Those listed are the friends and family members, experts and academics, acquaintances and strangers who provided me with every conceivable type of assistance from the time I first dreamt of embarking on the walk to the moment I wrote the last word of this book. They gave me advice and information; lent me books and found maps; offered us camp sites along the road and opened their homes to my crew; drove hundreds of kilometres to bring us treats and supplies, and solved problems for us back home; listened to my rants and my ecstasies on the phone, and wrote e-mails of love and encouragement. As trite as it may sound, without their contribution, both my walk and the account of it within these pages could not have been a success, and I am deeply grateful to them all.

I would, however, like to express my special thanks to some of the people mentioned in that list. My aunt, Mevagh Glyn, not only gave me a copy of Sir Richard's diary, but the encouragement to put on his mantle and take to the road. During the scary days that followed my decision to shadow my ancestor, author Tim Couzens read the journal that so mystified and confused me, made invaluable notes on it and – most importantly – bolstered my confidence by saying, 'You not only *can* do this, but you *must*.'

In the months that followed, I was taken under the wing of many other academics, experts and enthusiastic amateurs in the fascinating field of southern African history. They soon proved that I was a minnow among whales and that I had a lot to learn. But with their time and patient tutelage, I have gleaned what I hope is sufficient to the task of writing about Richard's expedition, the sport of hunting, the land he traversed and the people he encountered. So, thank you for advice given and research done by Mike Main, Jane and Vincent Carruthers, Izak Barnard, Roger Webster, Arto Toivonen, Ivor Sander, Mike Callender, Alec Campbell, Len Wigg and the late Sir Christopher Davson.

My love and thanks also go to Sir Richard Lindsay Glyn for his enthusiastic support of my 'mission', his hospitality at Gaunts House, the inspiring letters he sent to me while I was on the road and his permission to publish extracts from the precious diary of which he is custodian.

While I was getting fit for walking, my mother, Norma, was too – but on a pair of crutches after a hip operation. She gave me unqualified moral support, despite great discomfort and pain, and despite the fact that my frenetic expedition preparations made it impossible for me to help her through this taxing time. I'd like to thank my sister, Shirley, for undertaking that task so competently, and for the many matters she attended to on my behalf during my absence from home.

For the many people who came to the Victoria Falls to welcome us at the end of our journey – notably my 93-year-old uncle, Ronald Glyn – I will always have a special place in my heart. Thank you.

David Livingstone once said, 'I think I would rather cross the African continent again than undertake to write another book,' and I certainly concur with his sentiments. The publishing process is not an easy one, and it is not one I'd be quick to repeat. But I had help in this exhausting business from people whose judgement I trust and whose professionalism I admire – thank you to my picture researcher, Ruth Muller; my editor, Sean Fraser; my publisher, Zann Hoad, and my book designers Manik Design. It was a great pleasure working with all of you.

To the little team that battled through rain, wind, deep sand and thornveld with me for four and a half months, I owe deep and lasting gratitude. My backup crew, comprising John Kerr, Louis Changuion and Sue Oxborrow coped with a gruelling schedule, difficult working conditions and an exacting leader. Film-makers Karin Slater, Franci Cronjé and Phil Vail had to put up with a camera-suspicious subject whom they often had to follow on foot in hot, back-breaking conditions. Tapiwa and Mpho trusted me when they had no idea what they'd face around the next bend in the road or where they would next lay their heads to rest. Thank you all for joining me on this extraordinary odyssey and for teaching me so much about life and myself.

My sincere appreciation goes also to my sponsors: Discovery Health, Isuzu, Front Runner, Oztent, Cape Union Mart, Garmin, CLAW, IFAW and Hill's.

And, lastly, thank you to the one person without whose help I would most surely not have come through the agony of writing this book with my sanity intact. As my personal assistant, Internet researcher, general factotum and patient friend, Sue Oxborrow bolstered me through the hardest test of my life to date. She remains what I first dubbed her on The Blue Cross Challenge – a 'Second To None.'

Map of the Journey

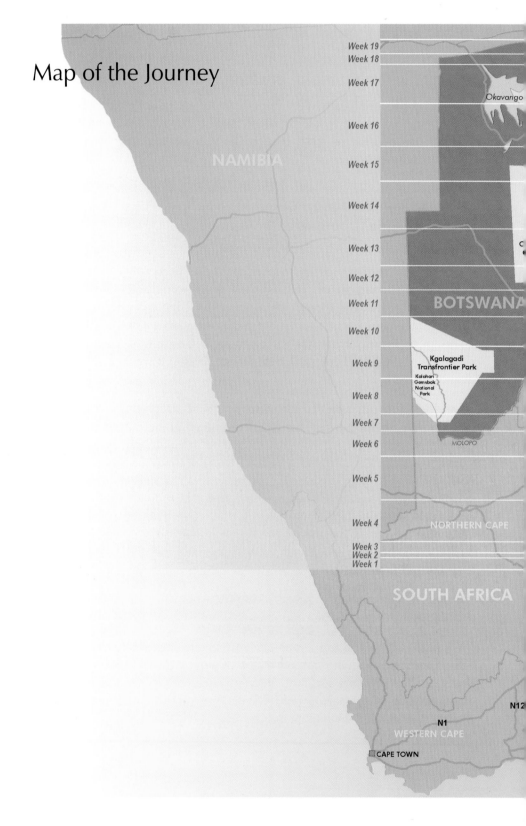

Week 19
Week 18
Week 17
Okavango
Week 16
Week 15

NAMIBIA

Week 14
Week 13
Week 12
Week 11

BOTSWANA

Week 10
Week 9
Kgalagadi
Transfrontier Park
Kalahari
Gemsbok
National
Park
Week 8
Week 7
Week 6
MOLOPO
Week 5
Week 4

NORTHERN CAPE

Week 3
Week 2
Week 1

SOUTH AFRICA

N12
N1
WESTERN CAPE
CAPE TOWN

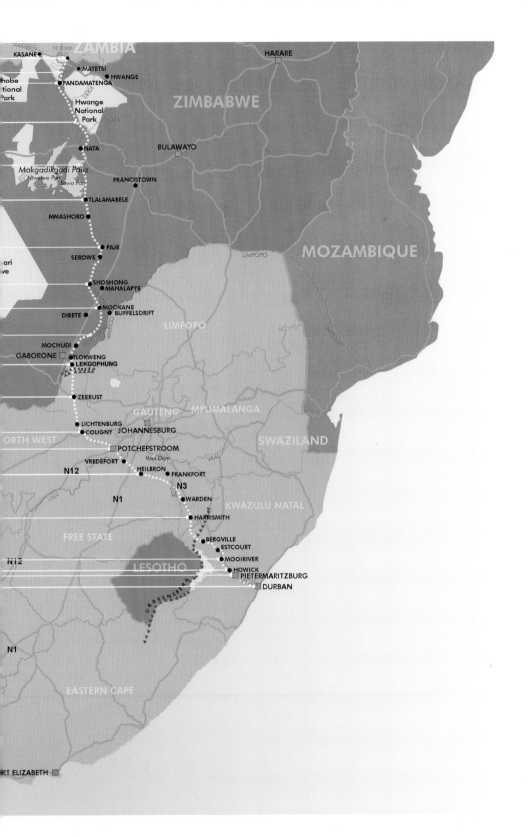

The Call of the Ancestors

Sir Richard George Glyn, 1831–1918

The Diary. Sir Richard's Diary. I heard about it as a child and grew up on snippets about its author. 'This is a precious piece of Africana literature,' explained Dad, 'and it describes your ancestor's journey through Africa when it was still a very dangerous place, full of wild animals and hostile tribes. Sir Richard George Glyn was his name and he was your great-great-grand uncle. In 1863, he set out from Durban by ox wagon and became one of the first white men after David Livingstone to reach the Victoria Falls. But he nearly died along the way – such a brave chap.'

More I didn't know, or care to know. I didn't read the journal, nor did I bother to find out more about the man – what little Dad told me was enough to provide fuel for my schoolgirl imaginings and grist for many a playground boast.

'Well *my* ancestor was an explorer, so there! Bet you don't have one of those in *your* family. When I'm big I'm gonna be one too.'

Later I came to learn that I was fortunate in having not only Richard, but a heaven's worth of well-documented ancestral stars to follow in my destiny-sail, should I wish to. The begetters, who in part made me what I am, have been the subject of numerous books and memoirs, some of them cloying hagiographies, others pedestal-toppling critiques. If these are to be believed, there is no shortage of Glyns to serve both as models and warnings.

What luck. After all, you can't choose your parents, as the saying goes. And it follows that you can't choose their parents either – or, in turn, theirs. But they were there at my birth, these whispering progenitors who launched me into life on a raft of genes I can't escape and exploits I can't erase. Which of them shall I navigate by?

Several of their portraits grace the chandeliered rooms of Gaunts House, Dorset – the only one of the Glyns' stately homes still in family hands.

Gaunts House, Dorset. Built in 1809...

Solid citizens they were by reputation, and mighty solid they look as they stare down upon climbers of the mansion's staircase, some of them imperious, others mildly embarrassed by their high-day regalia and powdered wigs. Their generous girths are brocaded, their chunky calves wrapped in white stockings, but as I gaze back at their well-fed faces I cannot summon the notion that they are my bloodstock, my kin. Even the paintings of their women fail to evoke

... and enlarged in 1887

my simpatico, their pale and gentle forms so unlike my robust femininity. After five generations in Africa, my branch of the ancestral tree has bent to different breezes and I must face the fact that I lack both the wherewithal and the inclination to follow in the footsteps of my banking, soldiering, politicking, bewitching forebears. All of them, that is, bar one: the man pictured at the summit of the staircase, stiff-spined on a glossy horse and surrounded by excited hunting hounds – Sir Richard George Glyn.

Over the past decade, my activities have pointed me, increasingly, in the direction of this man, he of The Diary and hero of an odyssey to the heart of Africa 142 years ago. It is quite common, I am told, for men and women in their forties to develop an interest in pursuits that test their physical stamina, no doubt in some deep-seated but futile attempt to stem the tide of ageing. So of late I have been pitching my strength against rivers, mountains and long roads and found great enjoyment in these trials. In fact, I have become somewhat addicted to the intense joy and profound insights that come with extreme exertion – well, extreme by my 'unsporty' standards. I have climbed Mount Kilimanjaro twice, had a good stab at Mount Aconcagua (the highest peak in the southern hemisphere), walked 500 kilometres from the lowest to the highest points of Zimbabwe and spent three months on an expedition to Mount Everest, reporting from Base Camp on a South African team's efforts to stand on top of the world. My low threshold of boredom has been assuaged by these trips and my even lower threshold of tolerance for city life satisfied by the break from shopping malls and walled suburban enclosures.

When I returned from Everest in May 2003, I struggled to settle down, and hoped that one day I would find some new adventure which excited my curiosity and tested my mettle. I gave my next 'project' little serious consideration in the ensuing year, but for some reason I kept thinking about Richard's journal. What sort of man was its author? And what had he encountered on his expedition through Africa? Was he like me – restless and inquisitive? I really wanted to know and badgered my aunt, Mevagh Glyn, to find me a copy of the manuscript. When at last she presented me with one, it lay on my bedside table for months, the last thing I saw before I closed my eyes at night, and the first upon waking every morning. Then, one Sunday in spring 2004, I settled down on my veranda and decided to read it from cover to cover. Whoever my grandfather had employed to transcribe the diary over a century ago clearly had a stubborn old typewriter to contend with because it

Richard Glyn and his wife Geraldine, prior to a hunt at Gaunts House

was full of spelling mistakes and typographical errors. But it made for riveting reading. I found myself both transfixed and horrified by this tale of extreme hardship and great bravery. It described brutal hunts, appalling thirst and gruelling passage through uncharted territory. It told of desertion and mutiny, blunders and accidents. It also depicted a land I hardly recognised, a land teeming with wildlife, uninvaded by alien vegetation, its rivers undammed and its indigenous people still living with their customs largely intact.

I closed the book that day and vowed to walk their route. 'Do it,' urged my sister Shirley in response to my starry-eyed pledge. 'You're quite mad, of course, but I know you can do it. Why *walk* it, though?'

Why indeed? After all, the old party covered a distance of nearly 2 200 kilometres and it took them four and a half months to get from Durban to the Victoria Falls. For the test, of course, the test of my mental and physical strength. For the peaceful meditation that walking provides. For the close observation of sights, smells and sounds for which one has time on foot. For the casual encounters one has on the road. For the hell of it.

I had decided on my next adventure: nearly five months' break from the mundane responsibilities of Johannesburg life in a slow traverse of my beloved subcontinent. Only as I drifted off to sleep that night did I realise that it was 24 October, the anniversary of my Dad's death 19 years previously. Surely that must be a good omen.

But on that momentous day I was determined to mimic Richard's journey as closely as I could. I wouldn't use oxen and horses for the expedition because I couldn't face the prospect of them dying on me, as they had on him, but I would do my level best to stick to his timetable and reach the Falls on exactly the same day as he had, 22 July. But, if I wanted to leave Durban on 16 March, as indicated by the diary, there was a great deal of work to do within a very short space of time. I had precisely five months to find sponsors for the trip, back-up vehicles and crew, film-makers to document the journey, camping equipment and provisions. I would have to investigate the long-disused 19th-century travellers' routes to the interior of Africa and, most importantly, learn more about Richard and his two travelling companions, Henry St George Osborne and the man known simply as 'Bob'.

Ancestral seeds

The Glyns' 'Adam' was a chieftain living in North Wales in AD500. Little information about him survives, nor about the next dozen or so generations of the family, but there are written accounts about the exploits of a ninth-century Glyn prince by the name of Cilmin Troed-ddu. Legend has it that Cilmin stole a neighbouring giant's book of spells and, while fleeing from his pursuer, fell into the boundary brook near Glynllivon. The black waters stained one of his lower legs, resulting in an affliction that has been pictured on the Glyn coat-of-arms ever since.

But his descendants, it seems, concentrated their efforts on generating good fortune rather than pilfering it. They founded, in 1753, one of England's earliest and most lucrative private banks: Vere, Glyn & Hallifax. At least six generations of my forebears spent their productive years in this Lombard Street monument to enterprise and The Empire, their quills scratching away in leather-bound ledgers, quietly recording their mounting investments. The bank financed the silk trade, funded railroads, fostered colonial development, forged valuable alliances and helped the family acquire some of England's and Wales' gracious county seats. In fact, the Glyns' ability to accumulate wealth remained one of their singular talents for centuries – talents that have, so far, singularly failed me.

Along with these riches came another pre-eminent ability that also appears to have eluded me – political nous. Truth be told, the early Glyns were quite infallible in their ability to read the tea leaves of fast-changing monarchical fortunes. One biographer describes them as having 'a particular capacity for weighing possibilities'. Take barrister John Glyn, for instance, whose shameless floor-crossing would cause even a South African parliamentarian to blush. During the politically precarious mid-1600s, when the struggle between King and Parliament was at its most furious and it became clear that Charles I was about to lose his head, John managed to distance himself from royal affiliations. So much so that he came to occupy the position of Lord Chief Justice for arch antimonarchist Oliver Cromwell – an allegiance that saw him committed to The Tower for high treason. A year of confinement amid those mouldy old walls no doubt gave him sufficient time to read some pretty bald writing upon them, and to deftly turn his coat. Within the space of a year, our John had managed to get himself restored to his seat as MP for Westminster, curry favour with the new king, Charles II, and be knighted for his efforts. Mind you, at the coronation he was – to many minds, including that of the famous diarist Samuel Pepys – soundly punished for his unfashionable associations. John got horribly drunk and, in the midst of the procession, he fell off his horse – an incident that will echo loudly for readers familiar with the Eugene Terre'Blanche story.

The Glyn womenfolk, poor creatures, are lauded in the biographies largely for the spouses they scooped, the dowries they fetched and the children they birthed. Catherine Glyn must rank as the most successful husband-hunter of them all, having bagged the famous Liberal statesman William Gladstone in the early 1800s. Mind you, it could be argued that he was the luckier of the two in the match. Catherine was heiress to a fortune, there being no son and heir to the wealthy Welsh branch of the family and the subsequent Gladstone fortunes were founded on her dowry. By the next century, there are faint glimmers of emancipation evident in the distaff lineage, with a couple of lady authors and a successful composer, Margaret Glyn, who wrote no fewer than six symphonies. Somewhat alarmingly for the few of us Glyn girls who have yet to 'settle down', the family has also produced dozens of dames who died old maids, so those of us with many fields of wild oats to sow prefer to regard the Titian-haired Elinor as our mentor. She wasn't born a Glyn, but later generations share her genes and, after all, who could resist claiming a relative for whom the following rhyme was penned:

In the late 19th century Elinor collected admirers like other women of her time collected crockery. She is credited with having invented (as well as embodied) the term 'it' for that indefinable, irresistible charm that makes a woman attractive to the opposite sex. And she is reputed to have enthusiastically explored 'it' in both her private life and a series of – by contemporary standards – scandalous novels. Word spread that Elinor and her heroines liked casting their 'it' spells on exotic animal hides and she became the recipient of no fewer than seven such pelts from far-flung corners of The Empire. One came from Lord Milner, Governor of the Cape, another from Marquess Curzon, Viceroy of India and yet another from (allegedly) King Edward VII.

But the origin of the myth about Elinor's sexual habits is poignant to say the least. Desperate to save her failing marriage to the neglectful, spendthrift Clayton Glyn, she bought a tiger skin in a hotel gift shop and took it upstairs

Would you like to sin

with Elinor Glyn

on a tiger skin?

Or would you prefer

to err with her

on some other fur?

Elinor Glyn

to their room, where she says she 'lay on it and caressed its fur, looking, I imagine, much as my caricaturists have portrayed me ever since. Instead of being impressed with my charms, Clayton laughed so heartily at me that I was snubbed and never reclined on tigers again.' How hurtful. How deeply humiliating. And this from a man whom she had supported financially for years through her books and later through some Hollywood films, which she either wrote, directed or starred in. Although she began writing in the Victorian era, her books became very popular in the 1920s and her book *It* was adapted into a film in 1927, starring herself, Clara Bow and Antonio Moreno.

If I had any, I fear my caricaturists would be swift to point out that I should fight shy of laying claim to Elinor's genes. After all, I am not nearly as prolific an author, I have never supported a man financially (let alone a recalcitrant husband) and my pillow prowess has, to date, garnered me gifts more in the order of second-hand bath mats than tiger skins.

Most of the Glyns, however, will be remembered by history as unshakeable pillars of respectability. Few scandals rocked their pedigreed boat and even fewer black sheep roamed their massive estates. As bankers, vicars, lawmen and soldiers, they proved their loyalty to Crown and country and were rewarded for their services with several knighthoods, three baronetcies and a peerage. Two of them became Lord Mayors of London and one was aide-de-camp to Queen Victoria.

The family sent their sons into battle on foreign fields, from where they returned glorious and decorated. No fewer than five Glyns were officers in the Crimean War; Colonel (later Lieutenant-General) Richard Thomas Glyn was second in command to Lord Chelmsford at Isandlwana; General Sir Julius Richard Glyn, KCB, fought in the South African Frontier Wars and the Indian Mutiny; Lieutenant-General Sir John Plumptree Carr Glyn, KCB, served in the Crimean and Ashanti Wars. All in all, I was born into one hell of a family, and if traditional African people are correct about the ancestors being one's guides and judges through life, I am surely not lacking in supervision.

Colonel (later Lieutenant-General)
Richard Thomas Glyn

The Expedition

The campaign room – my kitchen

So what route did they take to the far interior of the 'dark' continent, these three men, Richard Glyn, Henry St George Osborne and the mysterious Bob? Sir Richard's diary gave scant clues for my historically untrained eye. In it, he mentioned a few towns that are extant today. Pietermaritzburg, Harrismith and Potchefstroom I knew, of course, as well as some of the natural wonders they passed, like the Drakensberg mountain range in KwaZulu-Natal. But the rest of his writing described a kind of pan-to-pan, kraal-to-kraal odyssey through near-virgin territory. Who were these African 'chiefs' they met? Where were these hills and those wells? Was this an old spelling of that… or that? I had no idea, so I spent the next few months, between November 2004 and February 2005, being guided by historians who helped me make at least some sense of the antiquated references in the journal. I pored over Victorian maps, I read accounts of early exploration, hunting and trading on the subcontinent and I drove hundreds of kilometres to find experts in local terrain and topography. And what I learnt from these generous folk is that the old party, like all travellers of the time, had to follow the great river systems of our subcontinent in order to water their livestock every two or three days. Broadly speaking, the old wagon routes were parallel to the Umgeni, Wilge and Vaal rivers in South Africa; the Ngotwane, Bonwapitse and Nata in Botswana, and the Deka and Matetsi in Zimbabwe. Today a few of these old trails are tarred, some have become dirt roads and many have completely disappeared under thornveld and plough.

Now that appealed to me enormously, because it meant that my journey would be a mix of urban, rural and bush walk – a kind of increasingly remote passage into the wilderness of southern Africa. Sometimes I would follow their exact path, sometimes I would have to take pragmatic diversions to avoid hopping over dozens of farm fences, and sometimes I'd have to crash through the bush on game and livestock tracks. I was now confident that I could mimic their journey with about 80 per cent accuracy. What an adventure.

And what excitement, too, when I was informed by one of the history gurus – author, Tim Couzens, whose research techniques are far better honed than mine – that Bob was, in fact, Richard's younger brother. 'Not possible,' I said. 'He isn't mentioned in any of the family biographies, nor in any of the commentaries on the diary.' But true enough, there he was, cited for the 1863 journey in EC Tabler's book *Pioneers of Rhodesia* (Struik, Cape Town, 1966).

GLYN, ROBERT CARR (1833–1867). Sportsman. A brother of Sir R. Glyn, who served in the Crimea as a captain in the 85th Regiment.

No one in the family had known this, evidently. I hurried to the genealogy and, sure enough, there he was again, his life unremarked upon except for its entrance and exit. Robert had died at the age of 33, single and without issue, only four years after returning from his great African adventure. Why? Of what?

Sir Richard Lindsay Glyn with his African cousins

This was just one of several mysteries I felt compelled to solve, so next I headed for England and Gaunts House where the current head of our family, Sir Richard Lindsay Glyn, opened his heart to my quest and his library to my enquiry. Richard (you'll have gathered that many Glyns are so named) is a tall, gentle man who has largely devoted his life to far less temporal pursuits than mine. He is a spiritual seeker, educator, designer and farmer who lives quietly in a farmhouse on the estate, having transformed the stately home into a retreat for those with similarly metaphysical interests. I was grateful for his tolerance of my fascination with an ancestor who, like me, explored life and the self so differently – through physical quests in rough climes.

My sister, Shirley, and I sat in Richard's homely kitchen on a bleak January afternoon, sipping tea and sharing stories with our distant cousin about separate lives on separate continents, all the while trying to hide our feverish desire to see the original of the precious journal I was soon to shadow. Finally he said: 'Close your eyes and put out your hands.' I felt a warm, heavy volume descend into them. 'Okay – open up.' A dark-brown book lay in my hands, its cover looking so different from what I'd imagined.

The Diary. Ah, the Diary

Dad had told me, all those decades before, that the diary was bound in the ear of one of the elephants Richard shot at Victoria Falls, but that sad piece of memorabilia had been expertly worked into a smooth and supple cover, hardly reminiscent of the rough, veined skin that had fanned the massive head of its original owner.

Inside were pages of light blue paper, each covered with neat, forward-slanting handwriting. The words read almost exactly the same as my typed version, of course, but told me so much more about their author. Here was the work of a meticulous man, anxious to record the minutiae of his exciting journey for those who would never travel so far. In ordered columns he'd detailed the provisions his wagons carried, the temperatures and rainfall he'd experienced and the game he'd shot. Pasted throughout, with the endearing care of a child on a school project, were photographs and sketches. I could have wept. I had had no idea that the journal was illustrated, but now found myself staring at an image of the old hunters, exhausted and weather-beaten after their sojourn in the wilderness.

The 1863 party Back row: (L–R) James Gifford, Guy, Kean
Front row: (L–R) Richard Glyn, Robert Glyn, Henry St George Osborne

Richard is small and awkward, Robert well built and innocent-looking, Henry confident and handsome. Standing behind them is James Gifford, the expedition's young manager, who had been engaged in Durban along with Guy and Kean, the Glyns' 'servants'. Further on in the book is a blurry photograph of the party's black staff, crouched in front of a wagon, eating from a communal pot. They look resentful and morose (see page 57). Another picture shows the outspanned wagons; yet another, some tribesmen they met along the way. Robert's sketches of natural phenomena are also scattered through the pages. They reveal how impressed he was by the strange baobab, the awesome Drakensberg and the astounding Victoria Falls. The diary looked like a kind of *Boys' Own* camping manual – a factual, unemotional account of Victorian derring-do under Africa's wide skies.

'And you know he left a map, don't you?' said Richard.

'*A map?*' I gasped. 'I've spent *months* trying to find their route and now you tell me there's a *map?*'

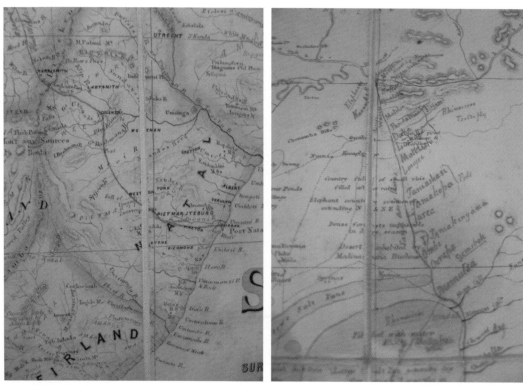

Sections of Richard's map

Pioneering photography

Readers may be surprised to learn that photographs are included in Richard's diary, but by the middle of the 19th century, both the art and science of photography had made great strides since the invention of Calotype processes in the 1830s. Dr AD Bensusan's research for the Africana Society (*Africana Notes and News*, June 1963, Vol 15 No 6) shows that there were no fewer than seven professional photographers working in Durban and Pietermaritzburg at the time when Richard and his party visited the colony, some of them operating out of private homes.

It is likely that one of these men took pictures of Richard's expedition both prior to departure and on their return from the wilderness, but as my ancestors clearly did not take a camera with them on their trip, one cannot rule out the possibility that the photographs of African people in The Diary were purchased from a photographer's collection. Dr Bensusan's fascinating book *History of Photography in Africa* (Howard Timmins, Cape Town, 1966) reveals that at the time, settlers in the province favoured Cartes-de-visite, small portraits pasted on a card, which they often sent 'home' to family in England as mementoes of their loved-ones in the Colony. Those photographers working in studios would probably have captured their images using chemicals like silver salts on paper in a positive/negative process, but early travellers who ventured onto the road with their cameras had to use glass plates in the so-called 'wet collodion process'. One can only marvel at their ingenuity and persistence in trying to capture images in the very rough conditions of life on safari. Their equipment was often damaged in the wagons, their working conditions hot, dusty and bright, and their African subjects often

Baines' sketch of Chapman at work

extremely suspicious of the large box and the black curtain under which the operator worked.

The first photographs to be taken by explorers were captured on David Livingstone's notoriously fractious trip from the mouth of the Zambezi to the Victoria Falls between 1858 and 1863. His brother, Charles', photographic experiments were described with disdain by the great man himself, as they were by John Kirk, the expedition's doctor and an enthusiastic photographer himself. But the party's now-famous artist, Thomas Baines, not only helped Charles take photos but frequently painted and sketched him at work. When Baines eventually left the expedition after he'd been accused of stealing, he joined up with James Chapman on an expedition to the Victoria Falls between 1860 and 1863. Several of Baines' sketches survive of Chapman's struggles to prepare his plates and, in turn, there are two photographs by Chapman depicting Baines at work. Sadly, though, Chapman failed to photograph the famous object of his quest, which he reached in August 1862. In his Introduction to *Travels into the Interior of South Africa* (Bell and Daldy, London, 1868), Chapman wrote: '... everywhere the spray drenched me and poured abundance of cold comfort upon all my hopes ... my efforts at photographing the Falls have proved complete failures (for some cause inexplicable to myself), I have resolved to turn my back on this locality.'

Sure enough, there at the back of The Diary was a coloured chart of our subcontinent, which brought me as close to tears as the diary itself. I unfolded its neatly creased quarters to find a spidery, brown-ink line snaking between the Victoria Falls and Durban. In the desert areas, the ink was smudged with what looked like sweat and there were notes along the way of the game they'd shot and the interesting features they'd passed. The magic of their expedition was all there – a tender reminiscence of an exciting time, marked by a feint line across a forbidding landscape. Studying it, I came to realise, however, that while the map solved some important questions about their routing, it was too large in scale to throw light on the finer details of their navigation. So my gruelling work of the previous months had not altogether been in vain.

What else I could glean about 'my' adventurers during our brief stay at Gaunts House was frustratingly little. Of Richard's personality there was virtually no record. His granddaughter Philippa remembers having heard only that he was a small man with a fierce temper who liked riding big horses. Certainly, the family's photographs of him show a clear- but cold-eyed sportsman, slowly changing with time from the young hero of the African odyssey into lord of all he oversaw in those undulating hills of Dorset. His high social standing is celebrated by a shiny brass memorial plaque near the altar of the village church. Robert's plaque, on the other hand, is a modest marble one, tucked away in a cold, dark corner. What had happened to *this* apparently earnest, gentle man? Had he disgraced the family, or had he just died young and untitled? There is only one photo of Robert in the house, other than the one in the diary. It's in an album of his sketches, relegated to an old cardboard box. He loved dogs, that's clear, and horses, and life in the army.

Robert Glyn, 1833–1867

I would have to wait months before finding out more about Robert, just as I would about Henry St George Osborne. The day of my departure from

Durban loomed with much still to be done, so while I headed home to South Africa, the Victorian threesome went shopping:

> *About May /62 having made up our minds that nothing less than the big game of Africa, and if possible the Victoria Falls would satisfy our love of sporting, and travelling, and having taken into partnership Osborne (late Royal Dragoons), we busied ourselves at the London Exhibition by inspecting all guns of all nations, most of which, however, we found could not be tried, or were of too small bore to suit us; at last we settled on getting large Lefacheau breechloaders made by Smith of Davies Street, and Bob and Osborne also ordered magnified Editions of Westley Richards carbine. Our next great point was to select a starting point for our journey, and having picked the brains of all travelled friends, and read all books bearing on the subject, Baldwin's, and the fact of Bob's old regiment (the 85th) being quartered there, made us fix on Natal as the basis of our hunting in preference to the Cape or Walvis Bay.*

Guns galore. 'In numbers we had plenty,' writes Richard. Numbers that would be swelled further in Durban by the purchase of lead, shot, gunpowder and yet more breechloaders. They were setting off with an arsenal capable of wiping out anything from a dormouse to a dinosaur. Pity the game of Africa – the Glyns were coming.

Arming my expedition was, in some ways, a far simpler affair. I would carry only a boat flare and pepper spray in case of trouble, and the only dead animals I anticipated seeing would be those crushed under the wheels of speeding cars along the road. But the rest of my provisions were plentiful and luxurious by comparison with those of the old party. Isuzu provided me with two 4x4s, equipped with fridge, freezer, water tanks, all manner of electronic devices, chargers, lights, tents, mattresses and 18 large boxes that would soon groan with a pantry fit for a five-star safari. Princess Patty was determined not to finish her walk looking like her haggard old ancestors. Poor things, their goodies (sent months ahead of them aboard the *Evangeline* sailing ship) would not arrive in time for their departure from the coast and they would have to exist on very meagre fare, supplemented by their hunts: salt, sugar, coffee, tea, flour, rusks, rice and a few 'preserved provisions'. That was their lot, even if it took them two years to get back to Durban. Worse still, they evidently had no alcohol stashed in secret corners of their wagons. I was not about to try that.

There is an oft-quoted saying among adventurers that pre-expedition preparations are infinitely more stressful than the quest itself, and the two months prior to my D-day proved this to be indeed true. While the English threesome sailed the high seas aboard *The Athens* in an eventless, if hot, journey to South Africa, I finalised my logistics and pounded Johannesburg's streets getting fit for my walk. I had started training almost immediately after committing myself to the adventure, slowly building up my distances to the point where, by January, I was having to get up at 4am to fit in 30 to 40 kilometres of walking before tackling the rest of the day's many chores. Discovery Health's Vitality 10 000 Steps programme was to sponsor my legs and count my steps on their pedometers. The programme is an incentive scheme designed to highlight the great health benefits of walking, and its members are rewarded for clocking up a minimum of 10 000 steps per day (roughly six kilometres). That was far short of what I would have to do daily, of course, and the folk at Discovery had calculated that it would take roughly three million steps for me to reach the Falls. If I had wanted a test, I sure had found one and I was determined not to have my 45-year-old pins give out on me.

I slept only a few hours a night, getting progressively exhausted as I walked, wound up my city life and work, employed a cameraman to record the trip, bought clothing and equipment, found maps for the journey, sourced reference books for our little travelling library and a housesitter to take care of my cats. Via e-mail, I put out word that I was looking for two people to serve as back-up personnel for the walk and waded through the CVs that came in. There were dishearteningly few, but I should have known that the world isn't exactly crawling with grown men and women who have nothing better to do with their time than spend five months looking after me, albeit for a good salary. In an effort to avoid the tempestuous egos and rampant hormones to which the young are prone – and of which I'd had a surfeit at Mount Everest – I had also narrowed the field by insisting that I would only engage people over the age of 35.

The list of skills I required in the chosen twosome was long and varied. I needed self-sufficient people who could, ideally, do everything from fix a vehicle to cook on an open fire, read maps and navigate, know their way around computers and satellite communication and, above all, handle the stresses that inevitably come with travelling in adverse conditions over a long period. Several of the hopefuls were Zimbabwean, so I travelled to Harare to interview them. Only one had the necessary credentials.

John Kerr lives in the sugar-farming district of Triangle, where he runs a small computer business which he could leave in the care of a colleague, should

John Kerr

I take him on board. His resumé revealed that he had lived all over the world, was a qualified commercial pilot and aircraft engineer, and had spent many hours of his spare time rebuilding diesel engines in old Mercedes sedans. John's a quiet, self-effacing man with a crinkly face who arrived at our meeting sporting white jeans, highly polished boots and two Jack Russells, which he clearly adored. His round, brown eyes had seen their fair share of life's punches and his demeanour was earnest. 'How keen are you to join the expedition?' I asked. 'Oh, 120 per cent keen,' was his immediate reply. Well, apart from being impressed by his many skills, I was 120 per cent keen on the fact that he loved his hounds. To my mind, that has always been a predictable indicator of compassion and empathy, and I left Harare a day later having decided that I'd welcome his ship-shape shoes on my trip. In time, his dust-kickers were to become his trademark, perpetually shiny in the face of the relentless heat and grime of Africa.

And if John was 120 per cent keen to join me on my walk, my other prospective back-up was double that. I didn't find him – he found me. Out of the blue, in the midst of my frantic preparations, I got a call from a total stranger. 'Hello, my name is Louis Changuion and I'm phoning to ask if I can join your expedition,' said a deep voice with an Afrikaans accent. 'I'm a walker too, and I recently did 800 kilometres in the footsteps of a 19th-century Roman Catholic priest by the name of Joaquim de Santa Rita Montanha. It was a fantastic trip, from Inhambane in Mozambique to Schoemansdal in South Africa.' I explained as gently as I could that I wanted to walk alone, but that if he was prepared to assist me as researcher and camp hand, we could meet.

A lacklustre airport hotel was the venue for our chat, and a tall, rangy figure made his way down the stairs to greet me in the foyer. Louis is a handsome, bearded man who wears his thick, silver hair in a pony tail. He's a published historian and former lecturer, now retired to the village of Haenertsberg in the Limpopo Province of South Africa. There he lives quietly, writes his books and walks in the nearby hills. Like many mountain folk, he's slow moving and slow talking, but he's as fit as anyone half his age, and he has the free-spirited air of a sixties flower child.

We talked about the joys of walking and exchanged tips about speed, footwear and nutrition. It became clear to me that his odyssey had been a kind of tough but happily chaotic romp with hard-drinking mates, and therefore very different from the one I was now facing. My adventures are my living as much as my pleasure and I knew that this journey would be very hard work. I had to walk over 2 000 kilometres, generate publicity

Louis Changuion

for my sponsors, write for their websites, make a movie of the trip and take photographs for my public-speaking engagements and the press. Nonetheless, Louis' enthusiasm was beguiling and his knowledge of 19th-century South African history would be useful on the trip. He admitted to being unused to household chores and unable to even boil an egg, but he would do whatever I asked of him.

'Can you leave your work and home for nearly five months, though?' I asked.

'Ja, no problem – but I'll miss my dogs.'

Ah, another dog lover. Perfect.

Perfect, because I had decided to take my beloved little dog, Tapiwa, on the trip and I would need help in keeping an eye on him. Richard had brought three Pointers with him from England and it seemed appropriate, not to mention highly enjoyable, to have a canine companion by my side too. Friends said I was mad to contemplate taking Tapiwa along. 'You're going to have such hassles getting that dog into Botswana and Zimbabwe, you know. And you're heading for Big Five territory where dogs are tasty treats for lions and leopards. Do you realise that he might die out there?' Of course I did, but the same could happen to me without due care, and how could I deny him the pleasure of months and months in the great African outdoors he was born to roam? If I had the right crew who were prepared to watch out for him as rigorously as I would, surely he'd survive – and thrive.

I had found Tapiwa (his name is the Shona word for 'gift') in southern Zimbabwe three years before, after taking part in a race called The Blue Cross Challenge. It's a 500 kilometre walk, run or cycle designed not so much to test

Tapiwa

athletic prowess as to raise funds for the animals that suffer so horrendously as a result of Zimbabwe's political turmoil. Along with 13 listeners to my SAfm radio show, I'd battled through the 50-kilometres-per-day trial and we'd managed to raise a lot of money for the local SPCA. Driving towards the Beit Bridge border post on my way home, I spied an emaciated brown puppy grubbing for scraps among the stones on the edge of the tarred road. We'd seen many such pathetic sights along our race route, of course, but somehow this one I couldn't ignore. I stopped the car and gave the little mite some of my picnic sandwiches. He gobbled them up gratefully, then sank back on his haunches and looked up at me as if to say, 'Now what?'

Well, quite. He didn't appear to have an owner, but I knew I wouldn't be able to get him through the border without the proper inoculations, so I flagged down a motorist travelling in the opposite direction and asked him to take the dog to the SPCA kennels in the nearest town, Chiredzi. If they hadn't found a home for him in the next month, I'd come back for him. It was madness – I was in a foreign country, hundreds of kilometres from Johannesburg and it would take considerable effort to get him home. Relatives who were farming in the area kept an eye on Tapiwa in the ensuing weeks but like others enduring the trauma of Robert Mugabe's land grab, they had too much on their plates to contemplate taking in another stray dog. I would have to go back for him.

When I did, I found not one but two skinny puppies sitting in that bleak kennel. By sheer coincidence, the local SPCA inspector had been travelling the same stretch of road two weeks after I'd picked up Tapiwa and seen another pathetic little dog being dragged by a wire around its neck. Its owner turned out to be the man I hadn't seen when I stopped for Tapiwa, and he was furious at having another member of his pack taken from him. 'A white woman was here two weeks ago and took my other dog,' he ranted. So I now found myself the owner of Tapiwa's little sister too. I called her Ningi (a corruption of the Ndebele word for 'many') in remembrance of the thousands like her who face starvation every day in that benighted land.

Ningi didn't make it in the end and died of a liver haemorrhage in her second year, but Taps had become my close buddy and we trained together for our walk along the quiet river banks of Johannesburg's Braamfonteinspruit. It was important for him to be strong, because his little legs were to raise funds for Community Led Animal Welfare, a wonderful organisation headed by a saint called Cora Bailey who works in the poorest of the poor townships around our country. Tapiwa's nutrition on the journey was to be taken care of by Hill's Pet Nutrition, so he too would have nothing but the best during our months on the road.

Fear and doubt began to commandeer my emotions in the last two weeks of my pre-departure labours. Physically, I felt ready for the task ahead, and knew myself to be sufficiently determined to let nothing but serious injury stand in my way of getting to the Falls. But there was so much more to making the expedition a success. For the first time in my life, I was an employer of professional people who would look to me for direction. I would have to provide their food and accommodation, and see to their safety and general wellbeing. The responsibility was intimidating and every day more obstacles were springing up in my face. John was delayed leaving Zimbabwe, my sponsorship funds had not yet come through from Discovery, and Isuzu informed me that, despite their best efforts, only one of the vehicles would be ready for the drive down to Durban. The final blow came when my cameraman dropped out.

I felt like a panic-stricken buck in the sights of Richard's breechloader, too numb to cry and too frozen to flee. With just two weeks to go, I suddenly had no movie of the trip. It wasn't so much that I wanted my mug on the box, but the footage would also be very useful for my presentations about the walk. I reached for the phone and started calling my long list of contacts in the television industry. 'Do you know anyone who isn't on any projects for the next five months and can leave in two weeks?' Not surprisingly, the answer was always 'No' – there was simply not enough notice. But Karin Slater and Franci Cronjé were available for a few weeks at a time and could alternate in coming to join the expedition when we hit exciting places. How they would react to the rigours of long and energetic working days in rough conditions I didn't know, but they were all I could pin down.

The months to come would prove how very lucky I had been to find them. Karin is a tall, tolerant and ever-smiling documentary-filmmaker of international repute and she's filmed in some of the most remote parts of our continent. Her camera work is quiet and unobtrusive, she's immensely sensitive and has an infallible eye for a beautiful shot and a character-revealing moment. A consummate professional, she works hard, thinks on her feet and is utterly dependable. Franci is a new media artist specialising in video and her work has garnered her both prizes and exhibitions. She has a wicked sense of humour, is zany and impish and used to arrive on our trip with tubs of fudge, bright

Karin Slater

orange hair and an eyebrow ring. The proposed TV show about my journey had not been pre-sold to any local or international channels, so I was taking a great risk by investing so much in filming the journey. Initially, I had a historical feature in mind, a kind of visual portrait of two parallel journeys across a much-changed continent, but Karin and Franci soon showed themselves to be interested in a more personal genre of film. The way in which women adventurers like me approach the rigours of an expedition is very different from that of our male counterparts, and my film-makers were anxious to record my emotional, psychological and spiritual changes en route. They hoped to make an intensely female documentary, an exploration of my motives for doing the trip and the stresses I encountered in trying to pull it off. What they required from me was honesty, openness and no-holds-barred access

Franci Cronjé

to my thoughts and feelings along the road. It was asking a lot, especially from someone who has been on the receiving end of savage criticism for some of my previous television programmes, but in the months to come their camera would force me to look at many issues I might otherwise have avoided.

Neither of the girls, though, had their own equipment (as had been my original deal) so I watched forlornly as the last of my savings disappeared on a state-of-the-art camera, microphones and hundreds of video tapes.

With both time and money having by now completely run out, I woke up on the morning of Monday, 14 March, bleary-eyed and fumbling after only one hour's sleep. I locked up my valuables, cuddled the cats one last time and reversed out of the driveway with my team. Ready or not, we had to hit the road for Durban. I was flat broke and at my wits' end.

Hounds of the plains

Zulu-speaking people would possibly call Tapiwa and Ningi 'Isiqha', although the umbrella term 'Africanis' (an amalgamation of the words 'Africana' referring to all things African and 'canis' or dog) has been coined by the Africanis Society of Southern Africa for the many different types of rural aboriginal dogs that roam our continent. The Society is currently conducting extensive DNA research to establish the genetic identity and possible differentiation between dogs from different parts of Africa. The hounds have long been the object of racial prejudice by colonists and foreign settlers in Africa, written off as mangy mongrels and scavengers, shot and poisoned by commercial farmers and spurned by Western dog breeders. But latterly their ancient lineage and superb qualities have been generating considerable interest. Many experts now acknowledge them as being among the oldest dogs in the world and quite possibly the first to have arrived on our continent. Neolithic herders from the Near and Far East were the earliest people to domesticate wolves and they migrated to northern Africa with their dogs (these dogs) about 7 000 years ago. The dogs became much favoured by the Egyptian Pharaohs for their speed and endurance and are pictured in the hieroglyphs. With the great Iron Age movements of 2 000 years ago, the Africanis spread southwards and developed different characteristics according to the climate and terrain in which they settled – long hair for the mountains of Lesotho, for instance, or short legs for the thick undergrowth of the Congo's jungles. Because these dogs have never been subjected to European-style selective breeding, they are marvels of adaptability and natural selection. They have superbly functional physiques, great intelligence and resistance to parasites and disease. After generations of hunting in packs alongside their owners, they bond closely with both humans and each other, can survive on very little food, and are quiet, obedient and good with livestock.

Africanis and proud owners

Durban to Pietermaritzburg

In a spray of sea breath he seemed to come to me

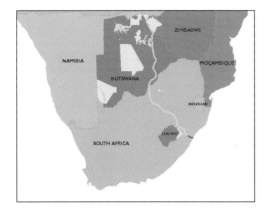

Durban to Pietermaritzburg
96 kilometres
Week 1
16–20 March

Ferbruary, 1863: The Norman, a small rendition of The Athens, took us up to Natal, stopping two days at the sandbank called Port Elizabeth, and passing the lovely coast of the neglected No Man's Land. Crossing the Durban bar in lighters on Sunday March 1ˢᵗ, we landed on the sandy shore of the bay, and put up at Mr Salmon's Hotel, a host as of the year 1860, master of his guests and ruling them with a rod of iron.

Current inhabitants of South Africa's eastern seaboard may smile nostalgically at Richard's description of their coastline. How pristine it must have been in those days, how peaceful and unpopulated. But from the time I first started researching his route and witnessing what had become of the places he described, I was determined not to fall into the futile trap of berating all human development as ugly and wasteful. Sure, there would be many occasions when I'd hang my head in shame over what we've wrought on this continent, but there are an equal number of

Mr Salmon's Hotel, later The Royal

things that have changed for the better. For a start, I'm the independent architect of my own destiny, unlike my Victorian sisters. Had I been alive in the 1860s, I would probably have been relegated to the drawing room of Gaunts House, reading poetry and doing tapestry.

Just what kind of behaviour may have got Farquard Salmon's clientele sent to bed with no dinner is not recorded in Richard's diary. The Royal Hotel, Durban (which it was renamed after a visit in 1860 by Queen Victoria's young son, Alfred) is today a model of low-key, fuss-free hospitality and its management kindly agreed to host my team too. Tapiwa became the first dog in the hotel's history to be allowed into the rooms but came close to becoming their first ever canine casualty when he tried to jump out of a seventh-storey window, chasing after a passing seagull. We dumped our bags in their high-rise rooms and headed out on a hunt for vestiges of the town that greeted my ancestors.

The 'sandy shore' described by Richard is all but fully concreted now and, thankfully, the bare-chested black men employed to piggyback new arrivals across the water from their lighters to terra firma have long since been relieved of their ignominious duties. Up on the ridge above town we found a modest house that is the only private dwelling of the mid-1800s still standing today. It's a tin-roofed bungalow built of mud bricks, nestling incongruously amid the towering apartment blocks that slowly encroached on the subtropical forest that once surrounded it. Locals call it The Elephant House because of the damage its wooden veranda posts sustained from elephants crashing through the dense undergrowth of the Berea in search of food and refuge from early settler guns. In the 19th century it must also have been much-prized by residents seeking refuge from the swampy heat of the town below. In fact, a few dents and scrapes in its structure must have seemed like a small price to pay for the relief it provided from the insectivorous plague to which Mr Salmon's guests were subjected. Within hours of their arrival, Henry and the brothers Glyn must have been scratching themselves silly.

Durban is a paradise of venomous insects: mosquitoes in clouds, dogs black with fleas, oxen minus their ears from ticks, and men driven mad by something like a harvest bug (sandfly). The town is built on a sand flat, on the edge of a bay formed by a high bluff, but unfortunately the bar has seldom more than seven feet of water on it, and the bay itself is nearly dry at low tide. This is one of the great banes of Eastern Africa; for hundreds of miles not a harbour, or even a safe roadstead is to be found. Natal is at present the land of experiment, and thus far to most the land of failure; many have come out expecting to get on without capital, and have had to borrow money at enormous interest, which soon swamped them.

A painting of early Durban by the explorer GF Angus, who visited the settlement in 1849

In 1863, the town was a couple of decades old and only just beginning to outgrow its lawless past as home to shipwreck survivors and intrepid ivory traders. It boasted about 500 mostly wattle-and-daub houses and was populated by a few thousand foreigners, mostly Englishmen, who thrived on petty gossip and even pettier rivalries. In an effort to keep up mother-country standards (and no doubt hold the 'savage' continent at bay), they held regular race meetings and enjoyed the pleasures of a Botanical Garden, a daily newspaper (*The Natal Mercury*) and a little orchestra. And if those entertainments were too tame for some, there was the odd public hanging to look forward to.

Apart from being an entomologist's dream, Durban at the time was also a paradise for bar flies, with as many grubby hotels and taverns as you'd find in a gold-rush camp. And its occupants, newly arrived from England, had plenty of sorrows to drown. Many had been lured to Africa with promises of fertile farms and cheap labour, only to find their allotments too small and the local people unwilling to commit to jobs when they had their own crops to grow and herds to tend. Richard seemed quite moved by his compatriots' futile efforts to build a new life so far from home.

Now he, too, was desperately seeking guides and servants for his expedition and having a devil of a job sourcing them. The town was far from short of transport riders, as hundreds of failed farmers were now trying to make a living by hauling wagonloads to the Free State and Transvaal, but none had been as far as the Zambezi River at the heart of the subcontinent. Eventually, Richard settled for a 26-year-old Scotsman, James Gifford, as headman and overseer. It is quite likely that James's large family had also fallen on hard times and that his father was only too happy to send his young son on a paid trip into the interior with the Glyns. James is described in The Diary as speaking Zulu and a little Dutch, but his ignorance of the most direct road to Potchefstroom would add many extra kilometres onto their (and my) journey in the weeks to come. I had no doubt that his good name would suffer the consequences on ragged days.

Making do largely with what they could get by way of staff and livestock, my ancestors continued to make ready for their journey. Richard picked up a wonderful old 'butcher's hack' called Moonlight for a bargain, but paid double that for Batwing and Birdcatcher, two horses that had done trips with the famous hunter William Baldwin. He was soon to find out that Batwing was 'quite worn out', but that's what happens when you lose your shirt over celebrity memorabilia.

> On Monday, 16 March, the tents for our wagons were finished; tents which were formed of one bit of canvas which went over the top of the wagon, and made pent houses on either side supported by poles, and walled with canvas sides; these we found quite indispensable, for without them we should have had to spend all hot or wet days either in or under the wagons. Our wagons were made heavy but strong, with tyres nearly twice as broad as usual to keep them from cutting deep into the sand. (A mistake.)

The Victorians were ready to depart, 'pent houses' and all. But I wasn't. Perhaps it was my extreme tiredness, but I remained completely disconnected from them and their quest. I am not an overly sentimental woman, nor am

The Expedition Manager

James Gifford

James Gifford was one of 10 children born to Alexander and Mary Gifford, Scottish immigrants who had settled in Natal in 1851. Within the 12 years they had been in the Colony, young James had in fact learnt to speak two African languages (presumably Zulu and Xhosa) and, at the tender age of 19, had been on a hunting trip to Swaziland with William Baldwin (see page 38) which is no doubt why Richard was keen to engage his services. The Giffords' descendant, Delyse Brown, has three letters written by Alexander to his half-brother back in Scotland, one of which comments that at least one of the brave exploits described in Baldwin's book as being his own, had in fact been James's. If so, one wonders why these remained unacknowledged.

From Alexander's letters it becomes clear that James played an essential part in provisioning and managing the Glyn expedition – and that money was no object to Richard and Robert ('They have a very good, very expensive outfit'). Alexander is clearly quite staggered by the quality of the party's wagons and tents, which included 'a large Marquee' for the staff and 'a large travelling carriage built for the purpose (of carrying the horses)' – strangely, this is not mentioned in The Diary. He lists, with amazement, the large number of animals the Glyns purchased, their plentiful provisions and the £1 bonus James was to receive for every elephant they shot, with £30 extra should he manage to get them to the Falls.

But James's inexperience in leading such a trip is made clear in his father's poignant advice on how to traverse the wilderness ahead:

'They will be a year away, they have a large sandy desert to cross, upwards of 200 miles, and not a drop of water, a blade of grass, a tree, or plant, or any kind; I gave James my plan, how to keep the oxen, and horses, likewise donkeys alive.'

Further information about this remarkable young man, who was only 26 when he set out with the Glyns, comes from Shelagh Spencer, who has spent years collecting information about the early foreign settlers of Natal. In *British Settlers – A Biographical Register in Natal 1824–1857* (Vol 7, Natal University Press, 2001) she notes that James's Zulu name was Umgingwayo, which translates as 'He who Swallows' (meaning he who looked after his men in an almost maternal way). Looking at the strength beyond his years evident in his photograph with the hunting party, I had no doubt that the description was apt and that my ancestors were in very good, if very young hands.

I a believer in spirits and after-life entities, so I'm not entirely sure what I was after, but I felt the need for some kind of 'audience' with these men prior to our parallel pilgrimage. Damn it, if I was prepared to walk over 2 000 kilometres with their ghosts, the least they could do was give me a 'Whoo hooo!' Apparently not. They just teased and taunted me, entering and leaving my thoughts according to some arcane and mischievous timetable of which I knew nothing. Where was the sense of purpose and destiny? Where was the excitement at the prospect of four and a half months on the road? Why the feeling that this time I had bitten off more than I could chew and that I might be guilty of hyped-up, self-indulgent trivia?

Most of all, I started to worry about shining a light on the long-gone, private affair of Richard's and Robert's 10-month holiday, 142 years before. Already the publicity machine had made my ancestors' faces known to more people than ever they were during their lifetime. Soon the exploits of three Glyns would be scrutinised, judged and – no doubt – found to be wanting. Should I be doing this to my family?

With only hours to spare before I had to take my first step, I headed for Durban's pier, the point nearest to their anchorage at sea and to The Bluff, the finger of land that had beckoned them ashore. I looked out at the ocean, trying to summon some courage and peace. And there, in a spray of sea breath, he seemed to come to me, the writer of this precious diary, which was all that remained of their 1863 adventure. Richard would help me. Richard would accompany me on a journey that would change me in ways I could only imagine. I collected four mussel shells off the rocks, which I hoped to toss into 'The Smoke That Thunders' at the end of my walk – one for each Glyn and one for

Four mussel shells for the Falls

little Tapiwa. Nearby I found a green stone to use as a marker for the end of each day's trek. All at once I felt relieved and ready. Let it begin.

March 16th: About midday we had packed our very miscellaneous loads and made a start, the Durbanites offering any odds that three greenhorns would never reach the Zambezi. The Berea sand-hill soon tried our spans, mine stuck every 10 yards, and I had constantly to send to Osborne for the loan of his team. Three men flogging hard with huge whips only seemed to make the oxen more obstinate. How I hated them! They would not

The diminutive Baldwin

William Baldwin was a Lancashire lad, born to a family of nine children and put to work at the age of 16 as a clerk in a shipping office. There he quickly discovered that 'quill-driving was not my particular vocation, nor a three-legged stool the exact amount of range to which I was willing to restrict myself through the sunniest part of life' (*African Hunting and Adventure from Natal to The Zambesi*, Richard Bentley & Son, London, 3rd edition, 1894). Despite his diminutive size (5'2"), Baldwin was a highly gifted horseman and enthusiastic sport hunter, and he was soon enticed to Africa by the tales of early travellers about the abundant wildlife of our continent.

William Baldwin

He arrived here in 1851 at the age of 25 and spent several years hunting big game and trading in ivory, penetrating further and further into what is now Botswana before setting his sights on a visit to the Victoria Falls. These he reached, by blunder more than design, on 3 August 1860, becoming the second European to see them, five years after David Livingstone. Baldwin's aforementioned autobiography in turn inspired others, like Frederick Courtney Selous and Richard Glyn, to make their way to Africa, and his name crops up frequently in my ancestor's diary and many works of the period. After 10 years on this continent, Baldwin returned to England, torn between his love of safari life and the painful solitude of so many years alone in the bush. Strangely, he was not much wealthier for the 15 000 hard miles (24 000 kilometres) he'd travelled in pursuit of elephant, because having amassed over 5 000 lb (2 270 kilograms) of ivory, his driver left it hanging in a tree in order to make room for more in the wagons and drove off, never to find it again. Baldwin spent the rest of his life hunting foxes and shooting birds, but in later years accompanied the famous explorer Sir Richard Burton on a trip to Iceland, prospecting for gold.

The old party's wagons and camp

pull together, it was horrid work, and the Zambezi at that rate seemed hopeless. At last however we did reach the top and outspanned … At 3 o'clock it came on to rain hard, the tents sheltered ourselves on one side, and the horses on the other comfortably for a time, but at night the pegs drew out and down came the tents on ourselves and horses, the latter of course broke loose and disappeared in the darkness, the servants however soon recaptured them. Next day it was still raining. Oxen must not treck in rain as their necks get sore, so we were obliged to stay where we were, only riding down to Durban in the afternoon to get grub for ourselves and horses.

How frightfully embarrassing – and I bet Richard's legendary temper was at full throttle! To seasoned locals, his party must have resembled a bunch of schoolboys on their first camping trip. I can see the doubting Thomases now, doubling their bets as they watched this pantomime from a pub at the bottom of the hill, and ruthlessly ribbing the greenies as they slunk in for succour, sopping wet.

Send-off from Durban

Like Richard, I too had those who lacked faith in my mad mission, but with the press conference over, it was time to set out from the front steps of Durban's oldest hotel. Some good folk from a local branch of the 'Walk For Life' exercise programme surrounded me in a blue-and-white guard of honour and we launched ourselves into the oppressive lunchtime heat.

Three quarters of an hour later, we were done for the day. After only 5.18 kilometres, Tapiwa and I stopped in the middle of the old toll bridge over the Berea road, secretly relieved that the ancestors had given us such a short day's walk after all the chaos and tension of the send-off.

In 1863, The Berea provided challenges other than thick mud, as owners of The Elephant House would have known. The ridge's undergrowth was a wild and dangerous tangle of vines, above which big-leaved trees reached for a humid

sky. Richard was deeply impressed by the forest's impenetrability, but over the decades since his visit it has been hacked away to make room for rows and rows of ugly monoliths. If possible, I wanted to sleep in whatever remained of that jungle, and there is one tiny vestige of it left – a place called Burman Bush. Its location in a busy city is betrayed by the persistent drone of traffic on all sides but it was quite wild enough for my tired team. We bailed out of the Isuzus and wearily started setting up our first little camp of the expedition – and it has to be said that the ancestors' inefficiency had nothing on ours. Louis and John wrestled with an unfamiliar mishmash of tent poles and ropes while I tried to sort out equipment

The Berea road out of town – then and now

and provisions that had been haphazardly stuffed into every corner of the vehicles. The little clearing in the trees echoed with refrains like 'Has anyone seen…?', 'Do you know where…?' and 'I've lost my…' Our gas stove was not

yet set up, so – like my soggy forebears – we sent downtown for takeaways. Late that night, I fell into my 'Oztent', burdened by the loneliness of trying to keep everything together but thrilled to have green canvas above my head at last. This little frame would be my and Tapiwa's home for the next four and a half months and I decided that, regardless of whatever plush accom-

My 'wagons'

modation was offered me along the way, I would sleep in it each and every night. It was another way I could mimic the old journey and get a taste of both the discomforts and joys of living outdoors.

Dawn confirmed that we were still far from done with 'civilisation', as Tapiwa and I launched ourselves into a peak-time vomit of exhaust fumes on the province's major roads. We started late because (as I noted in my personal diary) *'our systems aren't slick and folk aren't exactly moving at the speed of light. I can see this will require great patience from me.'* Just how much patience I was not yet to know.

Local drivers gave us no leeway or quarter as we struggled along on the narrow edges of the tarred road, and after a few kilometres Taps was relegated to the vehicle for his own safety. But I had my work cut out for me, because if I wanted to keep to the old party's timetable, I would now have to average 25 to 30 kilometres per day in order to keep up with the wagons. When the old party moved, so would I. When they stopped to rest on Sundays – as everyone did in those religious times – so would I. When they spent time reprovisioning in the few settlements dotted along their route, so would I. Richard, Robert and Henry would dictate both my movements and my route.

The easiest way from the beaches of KwaZulu-Natal to the Great Central African Plateau was first established by the great herds of southern Africa with their infallible sense of contour and navigation. Centuries later, the early peoples of the region, followed by their carts and wagons, deviated little from these ancient pathways along the gentlest ridges and broadest shoulders of the area's hills. Eventually the 19th-century wagon route between the port of Durban and the colony's capital, Pietermaritzburg, was tarred and became famous as the route of South Africa's premier road race, the Comrades Marathon. Heroes of that race will scorn my description of its gradients as gentle, but by comparison with those of modern highways like the N3, they are so, and for me too the road felt far from easy, as I tackled one hill after another for the first few days of my walk. Most of the punishing stretches are named after the early colonisers of the region, so

Early days – dangerous traffic for Taps

I climbed in the company of Mr Cowie, Mr Field and Mr Botha, cursing them by turn for the work-out they were giving my legs, with extra invectives for William Field's brother, John, who was very proud of himself for getting rid of the last two elephants in the Pinetown area in the 1840s. The bones of these great pachyderms were later used by surveyors when they ran short of pegs to mark out new farms in the area – such ironic ignominy.

Such ironic ignominy, too, in the naming of one of the grossest abominations in local architecture I passed. Imagine inheriting paradise valley and naming the white monstrosity that utterly defaces it just that: 'Paradise Valley.' And, tell me, was there a deliberate plan to make Pinetown's main road the ugliest in South Africa? In Richard's time it was a health resort known as the 'Cheltenham of Natal', a haven for Durbanites anxious to escape the heat and insects of the coast and particularly favoured by honeymooners and the health conscious. Nowadays, it's home to indigents with empty eyes and disappointed faces. Local businesses appear to be trying to out-banner each other. What is it about car and tyre customers that they apparently respond only to very loud, very large, very obvious advertising? I sank myself into my headphones and allowed Sting to float me along with his intelligent, sensitive sounds.

The Valley of a Thousand Hills – view from the Comrades route

For days the walk was filled with a series of coincidences that Karin believed to be signs that the ancestors were with me. I'm a tad too cynical to share that view, but certainly there were numerous synchronicities that provided little windows of delight as I laboured away. I stopped for a break under a spreading umThombe tree – a Natal Fig (*Ficus natalensis*) – on Westville's incline where the wagons outspanned for the first time on the road to Pietermaritzburg. An old friend, Oscar Chalupsky (10 times world champion paddler), who had told me about the tree the day before, just happened to pass at that very moment. Another of South Africa's great sportsmen, nine times Comrades champion, Bruce Fordyce, also just happened to call when I was at the bottom of one of his best-loved hills on the race route, Inchanga. (*Ntshangwe* is the Zulu name for a long-bladed knife or a sharp ridge.) 'Enjoy every minute you're out there, *skattie*,' Bruce said, 'I envy you and this will be the greatest adventure of your life to date.' A little earlier I had stopped at the marathon's Wall of Remembrance to pay silent tribute to the many pounding feet and pumping hearts that had done this route so much faster than me. Row upon row of green-and-gold plaques cover the bricks of an embankment at the side of the road, each one marking a brave effort on the tar beneath my feet. Some runners are famous, many not, some are gone, none forgotten. My reverential mood was not shared, however, by two prostitutes sitting under a tree at the end of the wall. '*Eish*, but this heat, it's too much. It keeps clients away,' they moaned. A little old lady with them offered some beaded trinkets for sale and when I declined those, she thought I might like some dagga instead. A large, sweaty man drew up in a bakkie, and I headed on.

The road ran along a high ridge, providing a 360-degree view of lush, green waves of hills – thousands of them, as per the legends. Small villages clung to their sides and well-used paths snaked along their contours. Well-wishers and the simply curious stopped to enquire after my wellbeing or the reason for my being out there alone in the blazing sun. One dear soul, when she heard I was walking to Victoria Falls, said in as patient a tone as she could summon: 'That's very far, you know. Are you from overseas?' Pastor Steven Khoza from the Cato Ridge Apostolic Church stormed down his rural driveway with a jug of iced orange juice, calling out, 'You are a hero, you are a hero!' Steven is an ex-Comrades runner who'd been watching my slow progress up 'his' hill and decided to minister to (no doubt) the slowest ascender of it he'd ever seen.

It became clear almost immediately that we would not be able to sleep on the side of the road at the point where I finished each day's walk – the sites were too busy, too ugly or fenced. Added to that, moving our camp every night was just too energy- and time-consuming, so we started a system whereby Louis would drive about 100 kilometres ahead and find a suitable camp site for the next three or four nights, from where he'd drive me back in the morning to the point where I'd left my stone marker at the end of the previous day's walk.

Driving to the day's start point

For our second night, Oscar organised a treat of a camp site with his friends at Tala Game Reserve in the Camperdown area, where Franci and John cooked while Louis and I started researching the next day's stories. *Don't you ever relax? he says, I've never worked so hard in my life.* We were just getting a measure of how gruelling the journey would be. The sounds of grumpfing wildebeest and ho-ho-ho-ing hippos were all new to Tapiwa, of course, and he spent that night sitting rigid in the corner of my tent, nervously barking warnings to me about 'those things out there, Mum.'

And I was doing some world-class barking of my own – at my well-meaning but hopelessly disorganised crew.

Friday, 18 March.
Too much sun today. And too much time alone without back-up. The morning was a screw-up – we left late, John had to do e-mails and a Pick 'n Pay shop, so I was left on the road for hours and hours without food or water. It took two and a half hours to get me to the starting point, which also pissed me off a treat so I wasted the first part of the walk blowing steam out of my ears.

Saturday, 19 March.
Completely lost it with the crew this am. Was without water for Tapiwa for four hours after getting going. Louis lost a mattress because it wasn't strapped onto the vehicle. My cereal for breakfast wasn't in the van, nothing was packed properly. Cold mince left in last night's cooking pot. Think John was faffing around with gizmos and widgets and forgetting that he and Louis are there to support the walker – that must always be their first priority.

My temper can be a veritable Guy Fawkes display, but it generally ignites as rarely as that annual anniversary. Yet here we were, hardly out of Durban, and I was losing my rag with alarming regularity. What exactly was triggering these episodes worried me intensely as I continued to soldier along the R103.

Comrades on the run

The Comrades Marathon is approximately 90 kilometres long and has been run between Durban and Pietermaritzburg since 1921, with the cities alternating each year as the start and finish points. It is arguably the world's most famous ultra-marathon, renowned for its camaraderie and crowd support, and its traditional send-off is a cock crow rather than a starter's gun. The race was started by Vic Clapham, a veteran of the Great War who wanted to stage a living memorial to the spirit of his fellow soldiers in that conflict, and it has been staged every year since its inception, with the exception of the war years 1941–45.

To date, approximately 75 000 people have entered this gruelling test of mental and physical stamina and among their number have been many inspirational athletes – like Wally Hayward, who ran his last race at the age of 80, five decades since he first entered in 1930. Many people take part despite severe disabilities. Estienne Arndt, for instance, has completed two Comrades despite having an artificial foot, and several blind runners enter each year, guided by 'pilots' linked to them by short ropes. Legend has it that

on seeing one of these blind entrants struggling towards the end of the race, a particularly well-endowed female runner came up next to him and said by way of incentive: 'If you make it, I'll let you touch what you cannot see.'

Only in 1975 were women and black people allowed to enter the marathon, although many had done so unofficially before that date, including the well-known ultra-distance runner Mavis Hutchinson, who completed seven races, and Hoseah 'Hoss' Tjale who completed 13. But possibly the most notorious unofficial entrant was a horse named 'Why Not', which took part in 1925 and came in (only!) an hour and 10 minutes before the first runner. There have been two deaths during the race, but many cases of people having to retire exhausted. One runner was forced to withdraw because his heavily pregnant wife, who was seconding him, found that she had gone into labour mid-race.

Gold medals are awarded to the first 10 runners to cross the finish line, and Alan Robb holds the record for the highest number of these – 12. But the man whose name will always be most closely associated with the Comrades Marathon is its so-called 'king', Bruce Fordyce, nine times winner and holder of 11 gold medals. Few will forget the 1981 race (his first victory), not only for his flying feet and shock of bouncing blond hair, but for the black armband he wore as a mark of protest against the apartheid regime. But perhaps many of his fans are not aware of the contribution Bruce has made to people living along the Comrades' route – notably, the sports facility at the foot of Inchanga Hill, which he raised funds to build while he was Chairman of The Sports Trust.

Heroes one and all – the Comrades Wall of Remembrance

The road winds and twists across the N3 highway like a drunken supermarket trolley, and as the main link with the interior in the old days, it was dotted with inns and staging posts catering to the needs of the hundreds of transport riders taking loads to the Boer republics and beyond. The old watering holes that survive today are much changed and it takes a keen eye to spot them in their guise as farm outhouses and storage barns. We found a couple of them, small buildings with low doorways and tiny windows whose rough-stoned walls had so much to tell, if only they could speak. Mary Thrash, the owner of one such former hostel, reckoned that hers would have been far too insalubrious for the gentlemanly Glyns, but I longed to spend a night or two partying with their rough-and-ready customers of old. The wagon drivers in the heyday of the gold- and diamond-rush were a motley crew, rather like the stagecoach riders of the American Wild West, and they would have arrived at these overnight stops full of exciting stories about what had happened to them, their beasts and their loads along the road to the interior. Highwaymen regularly stole their bullion and lions often attacked their ox teams, so they

Early traders – rough and ready customers for local inns

must have welcomed the safety that the huge outspans offered every 25 to 30 kilometres. Those spots were always located near water on the flattest verges afforded by local terrain, and here man and beast could be rested, watered and fed. Nowadays, they are invariably occupied by chicken farms, the ox dung that fertilised these grassy banks replaced by chicken manure, and the sounds of bellowing beasts substituted by the tortured squawks of thousands of battery hens.

Mary Thrash and her 'insalubrious' inn

It had been decided that after dropping me off for the day's walk, Louis' job would be to find interesting anecdotes and stories from the ancestors' time and from ours to use in both the film and my book. He found a somewhat sobering one in a little village halfway between Durban and Pietermaritzburg.

Just prior to the Glyns' expedition, a great crime had been committed against South Africa, unbeknown to its perpetrator. His name was John Vanderplank and he arrived here from Australia in the late 1830s, settling on a farm he bought and which he called Camperdown. The plywood packing case with which he'd arrived became his home for a few years while he built the grand house that may still be seen in the village today. In fact, legend has it that he often had to dive under the box's lid for protection against the marauding hyenas and leopards of the area. Things went well for Vanderplank in his new home, but the wind blew a treat in the (then) treeless hills of Natal. But John had just the solution. In his pocket, carried all the way from Australia, were the seeds of a tree he'd come across down under and which he thought would make for an ideal windbreak around his box. So he came to plant the first hedge of Black Wattle in South Africa and – unlike in its native country, where it did only moderately well as a stunted shrub – the tree flourished. So much so that soon John was handing out seeds to anyone and everyone who wanted them. In a matter of decades, the Black Wattle had spread as far as the Transvaal and none of its propagators could have known just what a rampant invader it would become, sucking up our precious water, choking our local plants and forever altering our landscape. Ironically, you'd struggle to find a Black Wattle in Camperdown today, but like its ugly sisters, the Silver and Green Wattles, it is always an indicator of the old wagon routes and settlements because it was used for fuel at the ox outspans and eventually for the tanning industry, after its bark was found to have extremely high tannin content.

After their abortive start in Durban, Richard, Robert and Henry took three days to get to Pietermaritzburg, and having lost time looking for echoes of their trip along the road, I had to walk 40 kilometres on the third day in order to get there on schedule. A 12-hour trudge under a killer sun was topped by a late-afternoon climb up the steep hill towards my finish – the former military garrison of Fort Napier. With the sun burning low on the horizon, I fell gratefully against the cool stonework of a surviving bastion from the old army base that had hosted the Victorian threesome during their time in the former capital city. The garrison is now a psychiatric hospital, which some might argue made it a fitting venue for my stay in Pietermaritzburg, but because it houses the criminally insane (among others) it was unsafe for us to stay there. So I hid the stone and headed off by car to our next camp on the shores of Albert Falls Dam, feeling deeply satisfied and content at having reached the first milestone of my journey.

For me, the magic has begun. I can feel the release coming.

Fort Napier's bastion

Pietermaritzburg to Howick

A lengthy halt in the former capital of the Colony

Week 2
21–27 March

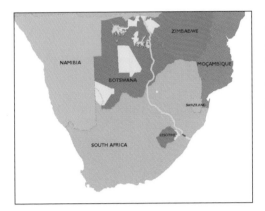

Pietermaritzburg to Howick
28 kilometres
Total: 124
Week 2
21–27 March

The old diary determined that we should stay in Pietermaritzburg for about a week, and I resented such a long halt in our progress so soon after our departure from Durban – doubly so when we came to spend most of our ostensible 'rest' time on mundane chores. My computer crashed, the cellphone went on the blink, we had power troubles and wiring glitches, vehicle niggles and kit shortfalls, all of which required us to leave our peaceful camp on Malcolm and Yolande Falconnier's farm every morning for long, hot days in abominable downtown traffic. If Karin was right and the ancestors were watching this expedition, then I had to assume that we had angered them. But in 1863, the boys were having a simply marvellous time.

March 21st: P'Maritzburg, the seat of government, is a pretty town, backed to the North by high hills, laid out in Dutch style, that is straight streets, green squares, and gutters full of running water with rows of willows and blue gums, both imported trees. Here we finished our equipment, buying nine horses, more oxen, stores, dogs and donkeys. Dined with the 85th and other friends and attended the races, where Bob much distinguished himself by winning the hurdle race on Baldwin's horse Birdcatcher, but overworked himself into a fever which weakened him for a very

20th Regiment of Lancashire Fusiliers on parade, 1870

long time. Osborne also was laid up with it, but managed to get right again just in time to start when everything was ready.

What was wrong with Bob? Like his brother, he was clearly a good rider, but was he unfit? Was he a sickly man with weak lungs or a weak heart? I would have to watch him in the weeks to come.

As former officers in some of Queen Victoria's greatest regiments, Richard, Robert and Henry would have been wined and dined at Fort Napier like visiting royalty. And as sport hunters, they would have found many

Fort Napier in the early days of the Colony

kindred spirits in the Colony, hunting being a prized pursuit among Victorian gentlemen officers and the reason why many sought service in South Africa.

Some less-than-gentlemanly things went on at the Fort, however, as I learned from historian Graham Dominy who joined me on the old parade ground and conjured up the lifestyle of hundreds of bachelors so far from home. His thesis on Fort Napier contains photos of them looking like little toy soldiers in straight lines of red jackets and crisp white pants, but the reality of their existence was far from innocuous. Up there on the hill, excessive and petty punishments were often meted out to soldiers of the rank and file. One commandant notoriously made the troops do route marches around the nearby mountains in a bad storm, then returned them to the Fort to stand for hours at attention in their soggy uniforms, bayonets fixed. What a perfect lightning conductor that turned out to be – a bolt of it fried three of the unfortunates and wounded another 12.

Snobbery and racism underpinned all their dealings with both each other and the townsfolk, drunkenness was rife and, given that officers were not encouraged to marry before the age of 30, you will understand why venereal diseases were widespread. Paul Thompson, an expert on the architecture of the Fort, showed me around the crumbling, neglected buildings from where not a single shot was ever fired in anger. No wonder they were all so bored and the prostitutes so busy. There were perceived threats at the time, of course, from both Boer and Zulu, and tunnels were rumoured to run underground between the Fort and some officials' houses downtown, but no evidence has ever been found of these escape routes. Nor of the ghosts that are alleged to flit along the warrens.

Richard, Robert and Henry – military men

To the sons of Victorian gentlemen, regular employment as we know it today would have been an anathema. Most young men of Richard's, Robert's and Henry's ilk either went into politics, the church or the army. And despite the fact that their father was a highly successful banker, the Glyn brothers had chosen the military as a way of passing their youthful years. At the time of the Africa odyssey, Richard was 33, he had not yet succeeded to the baronetcy (which he was to inherit on his return to England from an uncle who died childless) and had been a soldier in the 1st Royal Dragoons for seven years, rising to the rank of Captain – although it is worth noting that officer status was not earned but purchased in Queen Victoria's army.

Robert's sketch of soldiers of the 85th Regiment of Foot

During this time he had served in the bloody and savage Crimean War, notably at the battles of Balaklava and Inkerman as well as at the Siege of Sevastopol – and had earned medals and clasps for his efforts. How terrible must have been the suffering he endured – and witnessed – in that desperately cold, blunder-ridden, appallingly callous waste of human life. As an officer in the Heavy Brigade at the Battle of Balaklava, I imagine him on his large, jostling horse, his heart racing as he waited for the signal to attack the Russians. Shoulder to shoulder, he would have raced in with his fellows, musket firing, sword cutting and slashing at his Cossack foe in ferocious clashes that left bodies of horses and men everywhere, before retreating to his line. And then he would have watched in horror and silence, as if at a theatrical tragedy, the infamous charge and abominable slaughter of the Light Brigade in the 'Valley of Death', during which 600 men were killed in 25 minutes. He would have seen men die of exposure, malnutrition and illness – four times as many perished from disease as did from enemy action in the Crimea. Did he become inured to such carnage, and indifferent to the bloodshed? And how many men did he kill? I simply don't know.

I do know with some certainty, however, that his brother Robert, three years his junior, witnessed no such mayhem – notwithstanding his time as a boarder at Harrow School, a trial he managed to endure for only one year. Having seen his school programme comprising exclusively of Cicero, Homer and Aristophanes, I can fully appreciate why he left so soon. Robert signed up at the age of 17 for the 85th Regiment of Foot and served 11 years with them and the Royal Fusiliers. His army experience must have been considerably less irksome than Richard's, particularly as he was stationed in Mauritius for three years. The island did, however, endure a major cholera epidemic while he was there and in 1854, 11 000 islanders succumbed to the disease. But the regiment was quick to isolate its men and suffered no losses. Eighteen months later they appeared to have forgotten these lessons and 19 of them died during the next outbreak of the disease. Robert's record of that time survives through his sketches, however, and they show him to have been captivated by the tropics' trees and fruits, people and landscapes. I think he was a sensitive, artistic soul – entirely unsuited to warlike pursuits.

Henry St George Osborne looks to me from his photograph to be something of a hell-raiser and, given his Irish descent, I would think he was fond of a party. At the time of the 1863 expedition, Henry was 24 but no doubt already furiously independent and self-reliant, having been orphaned from the age of eight. He was born in County Meath, Ireland, the son of the 'gentleman' Henry Osborne and his wife Mary, both of whom died of either cholera or typhoid in the great famine of 1848/1849, which claimed one million lives. Where and with whom Henry lived after the loss of his parents is not known, but he joined the Royal Dragoons in 1857 and sold his commission in 1863 to come on holiday to Africa.

When not carousing at the Fort, the three travellers were, like us, provisioning for their trip.

Our stock now consisted of three wagons, with 69 Zulu oxen, 10 horses, about 12 dogs, some English pointers, though pups obliged us to leave one at Durban, and another at Maritzburg, the rest Natal curs, for a sickness had thinned them very much the year before, and we were obliged to be content with any we could get.

14 oxen drew each wagon, the spare ones and the horses were driven behind. The horses we clothed every night, tied them to the wagon wheels, and gave them a feed of mealies (Indian corn) and did not allow them to eat grass early in the morning, when the dew was on it, as that is said to be the cause of the terrible African horse sickness.

Thomas Baines' impression of Pietermaritzburg's Market Square in 1870

Africa's tiny killers

Early explorers of Africa encountered many life-threatening challenges in their efforts to 'civilise' our continent: waterless deserts, impenetrable forests and inhospitable tribes. But the single-most important barrier to the development of the 'far interior' of the continent was insect-borne disease, and ignorance of the cause and treatment of these sicknesses led to many a tragic tale in the annals of 19th-century travellers. The part which malaria played in restricting early white settlers largely to the coastal areas and high ground of Africa is well known, as is the terrible suffering exacted by the disease on early penetrators of its Interior.

They remained ignorant of the fact that mosquitoes were responsible for carrying the disease until 1898 and myths about treatments and prophylactics abounded. But the afflictions which the explorers' livestock endured were legion. The greatest killers among these were nagana, horse sickness, lung sickness and a variety of poisonous plants. Their occurrence and prevalence determined not only *when* people travelled (in the winter, when the insect-vectors were largely dormant) but *where* (largely high-lying or semidesert areas where they didn't proliferate).

A horse dying of horse sickness

African horse sickness is an insect-borne disease that has become a major endemic plague throughout southern Africa, sometimes resulting in prohibitions on the export of our horses and the crippling of our horse-racing industry. One could argue, however, that for the 19th-century inhabitants of our continent who were much more reliant on horses for their transport and hunting, and who didn't have the vaccinations against it that we have today, it was far more devastating. Eduard Mohr, an early German traveller, gives this moving description of the disease and its effect on 19th-century horse owners in the field (*To the Victoria Falls of the Zambesi*, Books of Rhodesia, Bulawayo, 1973): 'The first symptom of this destructive disease is a peculiar trembling of the hind legs in walking; then the eyelids swell so much that the cavity beneath the eyebrows is completely filled in, a bad tumour is formed, and death ensues in about 24 hours. During the rapid, and with but rare exceptions fatal, progress of the disease the horse perspires violently, its skin being covered with a white foam; it neighs piteously, and runs to the cart, trembling violently, as if it would take shelter there, finally falling down dead. One may be a great lover of horses at home, and yet have no sort of idea what a fine hunter becomes to a traveller in the desert. If our faithful four-footed friend, to whose speed alone we owe our safety in many an exciting chase, should die suddenly of this fatal plague, none but a sportsman who has himself had an opportunity of witnessing the achievements of his own horse in the field can realise our grief'. The disease is spread by gnats or midges and it presents as either (or both) an acute pulmonary or more chronic cardiac form of distemper. An infected horse with the pulmonary form of the sickness suffers severe fever, sweating, increasing respiratory distress and mucous discharge from the nose. When symptoms appear, the disease is too far advanced for any treatment and death follows in anything from three hours to four days. The cardiac form of horse sickness results in swelling of the head and neck, but horses sometimes recover. During Richard's time, it was not known what caused the disease – hence the myth that it was brought on by horses eating damp or freshly cut grass or poisonous plants. The early travellers tried everything from 'sweating' the animal, bleeding it, putting on poultices and even dangling a clove of garlic from the bit. Horses that survived an attack were thought to be immune and were called 'salted'. They fetched a high price – often double that paid for an unsalted one – but much fraud was practised in the sale of them because it was extremely difficult to identify those with immunity.

The word *nagana* derives from a Zulu word for a virulent disease transmitted by the tsetse fly and caused by three different parasites that afflict livestock, in particular cattle and horses, as well as humans in the form of 'sleeping sickness'. The areas where it was most prevalent were invariably the low-lying, hot, riverine areas of the tropics, known as 'fly belts' and although the limits of these belts were not sharply defined and varied from season to season, every effort was made to keep domestic animals out of these areas – particularly during daylight hours when the tsetse is most active. Wild animals, although they transmit the disease, do not display any of its symptoms and elephant are reputed to know the areas where they are safe from it. Early signs of nagana were loss of appetite and energy, followed by severe weight loss, bloody faeces and coughing until the animal grew anaemic, too weak to graze and eventually died – sometimes within 10 days, in the case of working oxen. Various repellents were used by early travellers, including smearing their horses and oxen with oil, paraffin and cow dung, but the best treatment (which was not always successful) was to rush the animal out of the 'fly' and give it a lengthy rest and good food. A vaccine has yet to be developed against nagana but there have been successful programmes to eliminate the tsetse fly with pesticides. I read with some horror in the early days of my trip that several early explorers lost their dogs to nagana, and with equal alarm that others inoculated their hounds by giving them dead tsetse flies with their food, which made them very sick but gave them immunity. It is not something I tried.

Lung sickness was introduced to South Africa in an infected bull from Holland that landed in Mossel Bay in 1854, and it developed into a ravaging plague, spread by trek oxen. An estimated 100 000 head of cattle died of the disease within the first two years of its arrival and it killed over 70 per cent of Natal's cattle when it first reached the Colony. And because the Zulu and Swazi peoples' wealth was determined by the number of cattle they owned, it very nearly ruined these groups. Lung sickness presents rather like pneumonia – it is spread by a germ and is highly contagious. Its symptoms are fever, listlessness, coughing and emaciation, and death usually comes within two to three weeks. Quarantine can be used effectively – and indeed saved the Zulus' herds – but because the early transport industry was reliant on oxen, this was not practical in the Colony of Natal and resulted in widespread deaths. Richard mentions in his diary having seen oxen in Durban either minus their tails or having ones 'twisted like a pig's' –a result of inoculation against the disease. The lungs of an infected cow were cut out, post-mortem, and the yellow infected sputum squeezed from them. This was then 'injected' into the tail of a healthy ox through a hole punched in its skin, resulting in immunity, loss of the tail – or death from infection or the disease itself.

At the time, Pietermaritzburg was seen as the last stepping stone to the interior and enemy territory (read Boer states), and its commercial life centred round Market Square. Today, the square is a cacophony of hooting and humanity, but back then it was not that different – a swirling mass of animals and adventurers either gearing up for trips inland or just arriving back from long sojourns in the wilderness. Weather-beaten hunters and traders pulled into town, their wagons laden with hides and ivory, sometimes with terrified wild animals tied to the back as half-tamed pets, chickens in coops slung between the rear wheels, pots and pans clattering on the runner boards and dogs yapping in clouds of red dust.

And the kings of the road at that time were unquestionably the wagon drivers. Bill Bizley of the University of KwaZulu-Natal's English department has made a study of these men, whose remarkable talents made them (in his words) the equivalent of today's horse whisperers. Indeed, their ability to handle livestock was simply astounding. These were the men who could cajole their ox teams through crocodile-infested rivers and comfort them on dark nights in lion country; men who knew their oxen's individual personalities and abilities so well that they could position them perfectly along the *trektou* (the chain in front of a wagon) for optimal performance in different conditions; men who could wield a three-metre whip so accurately that it wouldn't touch a hair on an ox's head, but remind it of its duties with a bullet-like crack; men who could summon an ox by name at an outspan teeming with thousands of beasts, and get it to quietly take up its position in line. And make no mistake, an ox knew not only its name, but several commands and instructions – to *trek* (move), stop, pull left or behave.

River crossings – a great challenge to 19th-century wagon travellers

The wagon drivers, then, were the cornerstone of commerce at the time, and despite being both black and illiterate, they came to occupy a unique place in late 19th-century race relations for the respect they were accorded by their white clients. There are tales of drivers being entertained to tea on colonists' front verandas, which in those most racist of all racist times, was nothing short of revolutionary. Bear in mind that in the 1860s, for instance, local tribesmen were not even allowed to wear their traditional clothing in the centre of Pietermaritzburg. In fact, an enterprising African man set up a business on one of the bridges leading into town where he hired out Western clothing for sixpence a day. His customers would change at the bridge, do their shopping in town and change back into their skins on the way out. My, how things have changed – tell that to a Londoner currently paying a fortune for African-inspired fashion.

Wagon traffic, then, became the great equaliser between black and white out on the road, as owner and driver shared the same trials, sat together around their camp fires and slept but a few feet away from each other. It soon became clear to me that the success of my ancestors' expedition rested on the shoulders of their staff, and I stared again at the diary photo of these men, trying to glean their feelings about their imminent departure from home and hearth for anything up to two years. Certainly they don't look happy, and Richard's opinion of some of them borders on contempt:

The Glyns' staff

Our servants were:

Gifford	*Manager*
Guy	*Bob's servant, a white man who could speak Xhosa*
Kean	*My servant, an old 85th man*
Croome	*A Zulu, Osborne's servant warranted to everything wrong*
Tom	*Ditto, the cook*
Tongwan	*Ditto, a sharp boy of Gifford's*
John	*Ditto, Bob's wagon driver, hired for the trip*
Joe	*A Khoikhoi, my driver*
Boy	*An idiot, Osborne's driver*

Two other Zulus as leaders.

Beasts of burden

The importance of the ox in the development of Africa's hinterland cannot be overstated. Without its strength and labours, few of the goods required for general development, mining and agriculture could have been hauled to the interior and little of Africa's produce exported by return. Several different types of oxen were used in the 19th century, most of them crossbreeds developed by early European settlers when they realised that the cattle they'd shipped over from Europe were dying within weeks of their arrival while the local bovines thrived.

The largest of the region's oxen was the bulky Afrikander – a cross between Dutch and Hottentot cattle, which resulted in one of the continent's new breeds, combining strength, stamina and resistance to most local diseases. The Bechuana (Batswana) people had oxen renowned for their deep red colour, which were similarly large and strong in order to cope with the thirst and deep sand of the interior – Richard and Robert were to use these for the second half of their journey. Then there was (indeed still is) the delightful indigenous Zulu or Nguni ox, which is small, often speckled and extremely hardy. It was well suited to hauling lighter loads at speed and was much used in the early days of the Natal Colony.

The standard number of oxen per span was 14 but that could increase as much as twofold should the terrain or load demand more pulling power. The position of each ox along the *trektou* (trace) had a specific name – known to both driver and animal. *Haaragter*, for instance, would be the right-rear ox, *haarvoor* the right-front and so on. The strongest oxen of the team would be yoked

The mayhem of an uncontrolled descent

to the *disselboom* (draught pole) of the wagon and, because it was immovable, unlike the *trektou*, these creatures were most at risk from injury or death should a wagon overturn under water or fall down a steep slope. The most intelligent oxen of the span, particularly those that responded quickest to directives like '*Hot!*' (left) and '*Haar!*' (right) were put at the front as leaders. Spare oxen were driven behind the wagons.

Early tales are filled with accounts of the drivers' humane and accurate use of their whips but sadly there are also stories of abominable cruelty as oxen were mercilessly beaten, had their tails twisted and sand blown into their eyes. There are even reports of exasperated drivers slashing their ribs and flanks with knives. Similarly, the breaking in of young oxen (to teach them to take the yoke and work in a team) was often a violent and traumatic affair.

The history of naming of these patient, mild bullocks both by early travellers and their descendants makes for interesting reading. Adrian Koopman of the University of KwaZulu-Natal's Zulu department has done a great deal of research into this nomenclature and his inaugural lecture (see Bibliography) reveals that because the dominant language of transport riding was Dutch or Afrikaans, Zulu herdsmen to this day use corruptions or adaptations of the old names for their animals, often without knowing it. Hence we have *Jamludi* from Jan Bloed (for a red-skinned ox), *uLentusi* from Lente Oes (meaning 'spring harvest') or *uVitifuthi* from Witvoet (literally 'white hoof', but commonly 'teacher's pet'). The suffix *-berg* ('mountain') usually referred to a very strong ox, so *Witteberg* would be a strong white ox, *Swartberg,* a black one. And how telling of the state of relations between Boer and Brit in the late 19th century that the two oxen in any span that were the laziest or worst-tempered were invariably named *Engelsman* and *Engeland.*

Several of the Zulu names for oxen (today and in the past) contain fascinating hidden messages within them. The animals are sometimes named in order to accuse a neighbour indirectly of witchcraft (this being a dangerous thing to do to his or her face), the idea being that whenever you call the ox's name, the accused will hear your charge. Hence we have names like *Bahlangene*, meaning 'They are gathered against me'. Adrian writes of having met a Zulu wife who was unhappy with her spouse's gambling habits, and named her cow *uMaliyavuza* ('The money is leaking away'). Her husband promptly acquired an ox of his own, which he named *uMaliyami* ('It's my money').

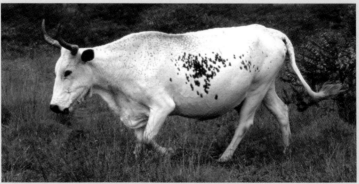

Her name means 'flies in the buttermilk'

In the absence of any further information, I must assume that Guy was an indigent living in the Colony and Kean a demobbed soldier at a loose end, but at least we know what they looked like from the photograph taken with their employers. Arguably the three most important men of the expedition – the wagon drivers John, Joe and Boy – are, however, not pictured anywhere in the diary. How very frustrating. And how sad that the young men who would bravely lead the oxen on foot through Africa are not even named in Richard's staff list. But there are three faces in the staff photo that might well have been those of the 'leaders' – Sabinkosi, Tabata and Skinan. *They* would be my heroes in the months ahead. Only we four would do this journey entirely on foot. My ancestors would ride their horses to the Falls, their staff would bump along on the wagons, but only the *voorlopers* ('front runners') and I would know the rigours of walking over 2 000 kilometres through all sorts of terrain. And I liked that thought – it felt as if my labours would be some kind of restitution for their anonymity in our mutual history. They would work much harder than me, of course, hauling and guiding their teams through rivers, sand and thornveld by ropes made of *riems* (hide thongs) attached to the oxen's horns.

I wanted, if possible, to know more about both their and the drivers' skills and to do that we had to find a span of oxen still in active service today, and after some phoning around we were referred to Pat Colby. Pat is a retired entomologist who farms at nearby Nottingham Road (which was busy wagon country in the old days) and although his ox team is not worked every day, he and his staff can still give a good demonstration of the tremendously hard work involved in 19th-century wagon travel. We headed out into the hills where Pat's voice echoed across the countryside, summoning first his staff and then the oxen. Eventually the impressive animals lumbered in, great chunks of muscle power topped by gleaming scythe-shaped horns. In close proximity they are truly awesome, clearly capable of killing a man with one light toss of their heads. But they are also strangely docile, easily submitting to the will of their handlers. I watched as their necks bent under the yoke, their eyes became dull and their shoulders crumpled in submission.

Pat Colby and John – a lesson in wagon mechanics

After what seemed like a long period of prodding, shoving and roping up, they were at last attached to the wagon and the team moved out – Jan Dube (meaning 'zebra' in Zulu because of his stripes) in the lead, followed by Bloktan ('recovery vehicle'), Kalankal ('crab', after his

The trainee *voorloper*

curling horns) and their forlorn team-mates. But the exercise proved to be something of a bubble-burster after my romantic notions of the relationship between man and beast on the old expeditions. Pat's guys were clearly hung-over and the oxen were recalcitrant and slow to obey. Round and round the farmyard they trundled, the men cussing and the oxen confused. Several times I spied the headman twisting the oxen's tails, this being one of the kinder methods of making a stubborn beast perform when shouts and whip have failed. No doubt the team's lacklustre performance was as a result of them not being put to work every day, but what they did demonstrate beyond question was the enormous effort entailed in traversing just one kilometre of the road. Despite being empty, the wagon was heavy and cumbersome, creaking and clanking with every movement and jolting with every small obstacle in the terrain. Sitting on it for 10 minutes confirmed for me exactly why the Boer women often chose to walk alongside their mobile homes rather than bounce through the byways of our continent – an unsprung wagon is kind to neither kidneys nor mammaries. I also got a taste of toiling on the *riem* like my heroes, the *bamba ntambu* (meaning 'hold the rope' – the Zulu name for what the Dutch called a *voorloper*). Within a few hundred metres, my shoulders felt as if they'd been wrenched out of their sockets and my throat was hoarse from my *hup, hup* encouragements for the oxen to keep moving.

The brakesman at work

Bamba ntambu – young but brave

With great relief we jumped into our very well-sprung Isuzu wagons and headed back to our camp to finish packing for the big move out of Pietermaritzburg the next day.

Friday, 25 March.

Sorted out some stuff and will help the crew get packed tomorrow so that we know exactly where things should go from now on. Then it's up to them because I really don't feel I should be packing up my tent etc. as well as walking and writing and filming and researching. Team happy and calm but we've run out of whiskey! Franci left us today – we'll miss her giggles and her help around camp – and Karin is back, her quiet competence continues to wow me. John is cooking us great meals – he's ingenious and meticulous and (thank goodness) is very clean around camp. We had words when I tried to direct the vehicle load-up, but I wound my neck in when he got shirty. He feels pressurised and I must ease off. Louis is clearly hating doing chores like washing up, but tries to do his bit. And he did sterling work finding info and photos for me in the museums and archives of Pmb.

Truth be told, I had a duty to help sort out the kit, because most of it was mine. Following Richard's lead, I had insisted on keeping 'many useful and useless articles [that resulted in] a rather heavy load for a long journey, but as we had no experience we could hardly tell what was really necessary'. For now, at least, the hairdryer would stay (for high days near electrical sources) along with the soda-making machine for my evening whiskies, my exfoliating cream and a couple of lacy self-indulgences. Poor Isuzus, bearing the brunt of my vanity. They're packed to the gunnels and we haven't even filled our big water tanks yet, nor bought the six weeks' worth of food we're going to need when we're in Botswana, far from resupply.

I stayed up late that night, battling to finish the weekly diary I was writing for my sponsors' websites, car battery and inverter humming away outside the mosquito netting of my tent and my head lamp burning a blue ball onto the computer screen. Trying to write about my walk was already proving to be a much harder task than the actual walking, but at least I had the company of owls and jackals in my toils. Flat-topped acacias cast finger-like shadows across the canvas above my head, while Tapiwa huffed and puffed in his sleep – no doubt dreaming about the buck feeding in the long grass at the edge of our camp. Darling dog nestled in the corner of the tent – so glad to have him to share this adventure. He seems to have finally settled down, accepted that this is his little family, that I will not desert him, that we'll move constantly but that his home will be my tent.

March 26th. Everything that thought could suggest and Natal furnish was now ready, so we started the wagons up the town hill which forms the second step to the South African high level plains… We rode that day to the Umgeni or Howick Falls, a fine waterfall of 340 feet unbroken, quite worthy of Switzerland; the wagonford, or drift, is almost at the edge and in times of flood carts and oxen have been swept over, and made mince of.

Pity the oxen and *voorlopers* getting up that hill – at least on the road I chose to do. Of the three options open to a walker leaving Pietermaritzburg on the old wagon roads, I chose the steep spur used by the Voortrekkers when they first came over the hill now known as World's View into what they hoped would be a place of refuge from British domination. The incline proved to be tough – by far the steepest I had encountered thus far and, because it was again so hot, I left Tapiwa with John. Karin and I got lost in the pine forests on its slopes and were caught up in a manic cross-country cycle race. Only once we'd flopped into the cool shade of a large tree at the top did local history buff Steve Watt tell me that by the 1860s the route would only have been used for descents into town because by then gentler means of departing had been found along the lower gradients of the hill. Typical Patricia – always favouring the nostalgic over the practical. Ah well, I had entertained myself during the slog by imagining the delighted 1838 Boer party, women and children giggling and laughing, the men congratulating each other on what a well-watered, remote garden they had found. Their new home lasted all of five years before the British, their old *wit gevaar* ('white threat'), penetrated their retreat and most of the *trekkers* decided once again on self-imposed exile from Pom domination. Back over the mountains they struggled and into the Free State, where I hoped to meet some of their descendants in the weeks to come.

'Place of the Tall One'

The rest of the day comprised a gentle, 28-kilometre lope to Howick Falls and it felt wonderful to be exercising again after our lengthy halt in the former capital of the Colony. An effusive bunch of friends living in the area lured me into a pleasant pub at the side of the road where we laughed and drank beer until it dawned on me that I was running out of time to get to my destination before nightfall. I wobbled on, singing at the top of my voice with tipply abandon until I eventually sighted the roaring falls that had so impressed Richard. Not being familiar with Swiss cascades, I'm unsure as to whether his description does them any justice, and because the Umgeni River has been dammed since his visit there is much less water now, but the falls certainly deserve the Zulu description of them as KwaNogqaza or 'Place of the Tall One'. A narrow, tumbling sheet of water hurtles over a black-walled precipice into a large pool where a monstrous snake by the name of Inkanyamba waits to consume

The treacherous drift

hapless victims of accident or suicide (so some locals believe). Sadly, there have also been several suicides here and many horses, oxen and riders have met their ends trying to cross the drift just above the falls in the days before the bridge. The most famous case of the 19th century involves the 12-year-old son of the drift's first ferryman, Mr Lodge, a reputedly abusive man who forced the boy to cross the raging river on a client's horse. The child was swept over the cliff to his death and, for the fanciful, the area still resounds with his terrified cries.

Archbell's house, now solar heated

In the grey light of late dusk, I hid my precious stone at the viewing platform above the falls and headed for camp. But we had no camp. The local municipal camp site was full of screaming kids and braai smoke, and I didn't fancy living among caravans for the next few days, so I called Eve and Roland Mazerly, who run a select bed-and-breakfast on a nearby smallholding. I had been referred to Eve during my research of the route because she is knowledgeable about local history and is the great-great-grand niece of William Cornwallis Harris, arguably the greatest of all 19th-century hunters.

Stocklands is a luxurious haven for travellers, so she was breaking all her rules by allowing campers on her manicured lawns. Her pedigreed 'Scottie' dogs yapped their outrage at the *bywoners* (itinerant peasants) defiling their august establishment, but with rain clouds now gathering, we were not to be moved. And a good thing too, as it turned out, because we were on land the early party would definitely have traversed. The small shale cottage not 100 metres from my tent was built by a *trekker* and the stone house added to it was constructed by James Archbell, the Wesleyan missionary who eventually sold his land to the government for the establishment of the village of Howick. Stocklands was a well-known stopover en route to the interior at the time, so Richard, Robert and Henry could well have had as many toots here as we did, huddled under a small square of canvas so hastily erected that it provided little protection from the downpour that greeted our arrival. Weather-wise, it was exactly as it should have been:

Sunday 29th. It rained all day so we were confined to a very comfortable inn.

The greatest hunter-naturalist of them all

William Cornwallis Harris

It seems contradictory to our modern sensibilities that 19th-century hunters were also keen observers (and admirers) of the natural world, but many were, and by far the most talented among them was Captain (later Sir) William Cornwallis Harris. He was an engineer in the Indian Army and during leave from his duties there, he led a hunting expedition from Graaff-Reinet to the Rustenburg area between 1836 and 1837.

The interior of Africa and its game were largely unknown to the outside world at the time, and Cornwallis Harris' descriptions and sketches of the animals that abounded on our plains were the first to captivate the imaginations of Victorian readers. His experiences and watercolours were published in two outstanding works, which remain among the most expensive and sought-after Africana ever printed: *The*

Wild Sports of Southern Africa and *Portraits of the Game and Wild Animals of Southern Africa*. And truly remarkable these works are, filled with wonderment and appreciation:

'Few will deny that to wander through a fairyland of sport, among the independent denizens of the wide wilderness, realising, as it were, a new and fabled creation amid scenes never before paced by civilised foot, is in itself so truly spirit-stirring and romantic, that in spite of the many hardships and privations which are inseparable from a campaign directed against farae naturae, the witchcraft of the desert must prove irresistible.'

In these treasured works, lyrical and descriptive writing is interspersed with poems and hunting anecdotes, detailed accounts of the physiology and character of Africa's fauna and some exquisitely beautiful paintings – all captured in the extreme conditions of life on trek. By his own admission, the watercolours were designed in part to correct and enhance previous illustrations of the continent's wildlife, which had been done from 'mummies and stuffed monstrosities. Widely different, however, is the graceful free-born of the desert, bounding exultingly in light and liberty over his native prairie, from the pampered cripple, pining in sad captivity, with sinews relaxed under the restraint of a prison-house.'

In his book, Cornwallis Harris also provided valuable commentary on the early stages of the Great Trek, and a meeting with Mzilikazi, 'King of the Amazooloo'. He 'discovered' the sable antelope in the Magaliesberg area, and for many years thereafter it was known as the 'Harris buck'.

Howick to Mooi River

Cars coming at me like yellow-orbed creatures

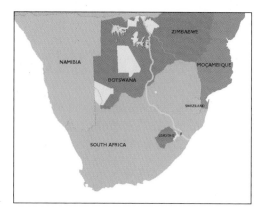

Howick to Mooi River
80 kilometres
Total: 204
Week 3
28 March – 3 April

Not wanting to further compromise Eve and Roland's reputation – or their business – we decided to depart the next day and make our home far enough along the road so as to avoid moving camp for at least five nights. Barry Symons and his family at Mooi River were our new hosts, *typical salt-of-the-earth farmers with simple lives and a kind of peace about them that reminds me of the gracious people of my youth in Zambia.* Our arrival at their farm was christened by another downpour and we were soon slushing around in black, cloying mud, getting soaked to the skin trying to erect our tents. Ah well, let it rain – the old party, too, were being bogged down by it, so I knew I didn't have much walking to do in the next few days. More friends pulled in for a party and in the absence of a fire we dined on their gifts – salads, nougat, whiskey and merriment under dripping tarpaulins. I fell asleep that night to the percussion of raindrops on my little green home and a highly competitive chorus of frogs. The dam outside my front door was a veritable multinational compound for amphibians where at least four different species went about their nocturnal

Elliot Ndlovu and his worried client

courtships with calls ranging from tinkling glass bells to babies' snuffles and even Kreepy Krawly pool cleaners.

Over the next few nights, I got to know those frog calls well as I lay awake worrying about some strange happenings I still battle to explain. With time in hand before we were required to move on, Karin thought it might be interesting to chat to a local *nyanga* (traditional herbalist) about African beliefs in ancestors and journeys of self-discovery like the one I was undertaking. As a committed sceptic about all things spiritual, I was dubious about the merits of the exercise, but agreed to meet with him. So the next day, back to Howick Falls we went, where the engaging Elliot Ndlovu was waiting for us at the platform overlooking the plunging water. He's an amiable man with short, dreadlocked hair and a ready smile, and we chatted about all manner of things that challenged my credulity.

'Inkanyamba (The Great One, who must not be talked about lightly or irreverently) is very, very powerful and much feared in our culture. He can disappear at will and there are no rocks in the pool because he spits them out down river. Our ancestors stay with him and only *sangomas* (mystics and diviners) are allowed there. Your ancestors are with you and they will look after you on your walk. You must trust their guidance,' he said.

'How will I know when they're with me?'
'Oh, you'll know. Strange things will happen when they are around.'

Not being familiar with mystical protocol, I wondered what I was meant to do about my totem. Should I ask him to bless it? I reached down among the leaves where I had left my rock, and scratched around for it. But it was gone. Disappeared, vanished, stolen. A feeling of loss and foreboding swept over me, and I don't mind telling you that this child of a scientific age, this utterly unsuperstitious woman, was unnerved to the point of tears. My talisman was gone. The rock I'd dreamt about hurling into the white spume of Victoria Falls was now (no doubt) at the bottom of this far more modest cascade. How stupid of me to put that kind of temptation in front of inquisitive little boys who were bound to find it at the platform, and how ridiculous to be feeling like this. How ridiculous to be buying into spooks and gobbledygook after all these years of secular education.

Elliot, however, was unconcerned by my loss. 'You shouldn't have been carrying a stone, anyway. You should walk with a stick like the African people do, and tomorrow I'll get one for you. A special stick used by our *thwasas* [initiates into the healing profession] to access the ancestors for guidance. It's a small branch of the coastal silver oak [*Brachylaena discolor*] and it will keep you safe.'

Across the car park, I saw Louis ferreting around in the dust. A few minutes later, he presented me with a small pink chip of concrete on which he'd written 'Howick'. 'Use this as a replacement for your stone,' he said. 'It will bring you luck, I'm sure.' I was touched by his thoughtfulness, particularly as he shared

Healers of the people

The belief in ancestors (*amadlozi*) is seminal to Zulu philosophy and traditional healers such as *isangoma* and *isinyanga* are imbued with special powers in order to contact the spirits on behalf of their patients. The ancestors are thought to act as intermediaries between living people and the Creator, as guides,

Twasas undergoing training

judges and social arbiters in matters of dispute within the family or community. At times, sacrifices are conducted to appeal for the ancestors' help, and instructions from the spirits are often believed to come through dreams.

Isinyanga are usually men and are trained in the curative properties of Africa's many plants, herbs and animal products (*umuthi*). Their internship is roughly three years, but this can be abbreviated in some circumstances if the initiate (*thwasa*) is exceptionally talented. During their 'coming out' or graduation ceremony, *thwasas* will be expected to demonstrate their proficiency by finding objects hidden by their tutor at various points around a house or kraal. The time it takes for them to find the objects indicates the strength of their powers.

Unlike *isinyanga*, who enter the profession by choice (and often in the steps of a family member), *isangoma* are 'called' to become healers by the ancestral spirits, often in a dream. They are diviners and are mostly, but not exclusively, women. They, too, are trained by a senior *isangoma*, but they are 'called' to the profession

by the ancestors and this often exhibits as 'mental illness' or emotional instability. Should a person ignore the ancestors' wishes, the symptoms will continue or worsen. If the 'chosen one' wants to be released from the calling, a goat may be sacrificed in appeasement of the spirits who may, or may not, release the candidate. *Isangoma* communicate with the dead by throwing small bones, shells, stones and other objects onto the ground and the manner in which they land tells the diviner about the underlying causes of a patient's troubles.

The third type of traditional diviner is known as an *umthakathi*. These are sorcerers whose practices are secret and are seldom spoken of in open conversation. Many traditional African people who have adopted the Christian faith believe in *abathandazi*, prophets who are associated with various independent churches but whose healing is done through prayer and sanctification of holy water, rather than through the ancestors or *umuthi*.

Although the coastal silver oak (*iPhahla* in Zulu) is known to be used by traditional healers to communicate with the ancestors, Sendepe Spogte of the Traditional Healers Association tells me that choosing a *thwasa* stick is a very private and special event and is done within the privacy of the apprentice's home. It is not talked about outside the family.

my scepticism about the so-called spirit world. Together we hid the stone in some thick bush where we hoped little hands wouldn't find it.

After a night thrashing around in my sleeping bag, we headed off in the morning for Elliot's herb farm at Estcourt. But the *nyanga* was in a hurry, anxious to hand over the stick as quickly as possible in exchange for the sum of R350. Gone was his all-seeing aura of the day before and in its place was a prosaic, business-like efficiency. And the stick looked puny to me, short and unprepossessing, with three short branches sticking out of one end, rather like a 1940s television aerial. 'We call it the cellphone to the ancestors,' he said, 'and the *thwasas* connect with the spirits through these spikes.'

My new cellphone

To believe or not to believe, that was my dilemma. Well, better to hedge my bets, I figured. If Richard and Robert were around, the last thing I should do was offend them, so I stowed the stick safely next to my pillow and prepared for bed.

The next day, the old party's wagons were once again on the move, and with over 30 kilometres to walk in their wake, we left camp early to drive to my starting point. Forty minutes from camp, Karin pointed the camera at me and asked after the stick. 'Oh God, the stick! I've left the stick. Damn it!' Back we drove and I rushed to my tent – to find the stick gone. Yes, gone. Vanished into thin air and no amount of frantic searching around camp revealed the slightest trace of it.

What. The. Hell. Was. Going. On. Here?

I felt a knot of panic in the pit of my stomach.

'You guys are having me on, aren't you? One of you has hidden it to give me a fright.'

'No one has been near your tent, Tricia,' said John. 'I've been here since you left and I promise I wouldn't do anything so cruel.'

Theories on the stick's disappearance were debated among the four of us, and we eventually settled on Louis' idea – that Tapiwa had eaten it and that he now was my talisman, my connection with the ancestors. He must accompany me all the way to Victoria Falls, come what may.

Well, I thought to myself as we drove off the farm, it's highly unusual for a dog to eat an entire stick and not leave one tiny splinter behind as evidence of its picnic. But I must pull myself together and stop this irrational nonsense. In a gesture of angry defiance, I threw a rotten orange into the pool at the falls, hoping that, unlike stones, some vegetable matter would get stuck in Inkanyamba's gullet, and set off towards the Karkloof mountain range.

> *March 31st. We tried to make an early start, but the oxen (which are always when possible allowed to run loose during the night) had strayed on to Mooi river, so we did not get off till 12 o'clock, the roads still very slippery from the rain. We toiled up the steep Kar Kloof cutting, and in the evening reached Mooi river, where we supped at Whipp's Hotel; today we saw our first antelope, rhebok, and Osborne had a gallop after them, but they were not to be had in that way.*

As I soon found out, not for nothing are the Natal Midlands described as lying in a 'mist belt'. I walked in swirling vapour the whole day, denied the bewitching views for which the region is famous, with cars coming at me like yellow-orbed creatures out of a horror movie fog. Most early travellers

Wagon ways through the Natal Midlands

The *Rooi Gras*, or red grass, of the Natal Midlands offered particularly nutritious grazing for both cattle and horses, so 19th-century wagon travellers often outspanned here. The grass responds well to annual burning and is the reason why early Portuguese navigators called Natal *Terra de Fumos* – on account of the billowing smoke they saw inland. The temperatures around Howick were also warm by comparison with the freezing winds of the Nottingham Ridge where the Glyns were next headed in their slow climb towards the Drakensberg mountains and the central African plateau, so livestock would be given as much time as possible to roam and feed in preparation for the hard toil ahead.

In times of heavy rain, the Curry's Post road was rendered impassable, particularly the notorious Satan Hill, which became a ski slope of slushy mud. (And given that it was common to name stubborn oxen 'Satan', too, that name must have resounded in the surrounding forests more than most.) I'd like to have walked this road because not only was it used by all the famous and infamous tycoons of the 19th century, like Cecil John Rhodes and Barney Barnato, but it's full of transport-riders' inns and military canteens like The Coach House and Old Halliwell. The road became notorious for the highwaymen who held up passing gold and diamond coaches and at one time it was thought that the 'Kruger Millions' were buried somewhere along its edges.

through this area used the historic Curry's Post short cut to Mooi River, but Richard, Robert and Henry had chosen the 'steep Kar Kloof cutting' so I would have to as well, even though it added an extra seven kilometres to my walk. Mick McConnell, whose knowledge of local history is astounding, showed me the way, and certainly the route's Khyber Pass is 'way past shucks' as his wife Gloria puts it. The road winds steeply through Sappi and Mondi country – belts of still and sterile pine forests – and, in the absence of anything but the occasional bird call, I soldiered on to the sounds of Mike and the Mechanics. 'Get

Mick and his Mini

up,' they exhorted, 'do something, get up and take control of your life.' It was our first dirt road of the journey and Tapiwa and I choked on dust from the occasional passing car and struggled to get used to a different road surface underfoot, but at least we were now away from towns and cities. At times there were large boulders at the side of the road, cleared by modern bulldozers, but the route had been the curse of early wagon travellers who expressed great relief in their journals at having passed them. In the late 1800s the route was famous for cattle rustling and gun-running, and the farms nearby still carry the

Afrikaans names given them by their original Boer owners: Heltengracht, Denmagtenburg, Boschhoek. Having settled here in the 1830s, the *trekkers* found themselves too far from markets to practise anything but subsistence farming, and turned to the magnificent Karkloof forests for their income. Hundreds of old, giant yellowwoods, sneezewoods, iron- and red-woods fell to their axes and landed up in houses,

Dirt roads at last

fence posts and wagons. The chains the loggers used to drag these multi-tonne trees ravaged the undergrowth, until the forest began to suffer badly from their onslaught. Eventually the cutting of indigenous trees was banned and thanks to modern land-owners' rigorous protection, the Karkloof is beginning to look like it did 250 years ago – apart, of course, from those sections of it that have been given over to the commercial timber industry.

Ian Player

My reward for going the long way to Mooi River was a meeting with Dr Ian Player, who farms not five minutes from the Karkloof road. He is one of South Africa's greatest conservationists, credited with having led the team that captured and translocated the white rhino – thereby saving it from extinction. But in his youth he was a passionate hunter, compelled to 'kill anything that moved'. Who better, then, to speak to about my ancestors' pursuits in the very place where they saw (and unsuccessfully chased) their first African antelope?

Ian lives quietly in a place he's called Puza Moya (Drink the Spirits) because he believes he was led there by the ancestors. He has the slow, measured speech of a philosopher and the compassionate gaze of a man who has feasted his soul on the wide horizons of Africa and the generosity of her people. For many years he had the great privilege of roaming the bush with a guide by the name of Magqubu Ntombela who not only became his dearest friend, but taught him to track, to listen and to 'read' animals with the kind of sixth sense for which the early inhabitants of Africa are renowned. Over tea in his memorabilia-rich living room, he told me of the sights that would have greeted Richard and his party when they travelled through here. 'The elephant and rhino had already moved on by then, having been routinely hunted for the previous few decades, but there would still have been plenty of rhebok and oribi [the latter are now endangered]. The few Bushmen left in the nearby mountains were regularly raided by Natal Carbineers until they either fled or intermarried with local tribes There are signs of that intermarriage still visible in Howick residents today.'

How astounding that only a short time of foreign occupation had already resulted in the mightiest creatures and its original inhabitants leaving the Colony. We spoke about the innate and insatiable compulsion to kill that all human beings have, now manifest in our collective murder of the earth. And we agreed on the moral dilemmas that hunting presents for people who are quick to criticise it but just as quick to eat meat harvested in the far more brutal abattoir system. The indigenous people of the earth, from Bushman to Sioux, all apologised ritualistically to the animals they killed and Ian believes that when this is not done, the creature's spirit will haunt the hunter forever. So it is that he cannot forget a day in the 1950s when he was taking part in a massive cull of wildebeest, zebra and warthog and found himself down a narrow gorge with a wildebeest at the end of it. The animal gazed at him, unable to escape

Hunting methods of old

The guns used by 19th-century hunters were slow to load and cumbersome to carry. They were also unreliable, inaccurate and considerably weaker than modern weapons. Misfires were commonplace and the hunters had to be in close proximity to their prey for successful kills. The men were often ignorant of where to aim their shots and the literature abounds with accounts of animals' slow and agonised deaths as dozens of small-calibre bullets failed to take effect.

Gordon Cumming, for instance, describes having fired 35 bullets at an elephant (over many hours) before it died; Cornwallis Harris used 27 to kill a black rhino. Richard talks of his party submitting a white rhino to 'regular bombardment, each riding up and firing in turn before he stopped and fell. None of the bullets except those fired at right angles got through the skin and ribs, though some had seven and eight drams of powder behind them and were fired at three yards distance.'

As a result of the poor weaponry, hunting practices of the time relied more on good horsemanship than marksmanship, with men riding close to dangerous game or riding into herds and discharging their breechloaders or muskets at random. The game was also plentiful and, in the very early days, ignorant of the destruction a gun could perpetrate. Once their numbers diminished, the practice of stalking on foot became more common and the ability to track a valued skill. Modern hunters, who largely use the latter method, and contemporary wingshooters, who descry the habit of 'flock shooting' (where the gun opens up on a flock of birds without singling out a specific target) would be horrified by the old hunters' practices. Similarly, shooting game at water holes is frowned upon today, as is shooting at sleeping prey, young animals or pregnant mothers, but it was common in the 1800s. In The Diary, Richard describes Robert firing indiscriminately into a herd of submerged 'seacows' (hippopotamus) until at last one was seen floating downstream. Thomas Baines, in the same manner as his contemporaries, thought nothing of leaving wounded animals to flee without pursuing them to deliver the *coup de grâce*. He describes a buffalo hunt near Victoria Falls thus: 'We fire into them... bullet after bullet stops and heads them off... they take refuge in the palm brake, the wounded lagging in the covert as they go... one with bleeding jaws charges directly at us... still there are others wounded in the brake.'

Giraffe proved to be difficult to hunt on horseback as they were nimble in dense thornveld, capable of out-galloping a steed and of striking out at both horse and hunter with flaying hooves when cornered. It was common for large antelope such as eland to be 'ridden down', in other words pursued on horseback until the animal was so exhausted it could be herded back to the wagons for dispatching in order that the hunters didn't have to cart the meat for miles.

The idea is horrifying to modern readers, but we may perhaps be (reluctantly) admiring of the courage and skill it took to ride closely alongside animals like rhino and buffalo, trying to aim at a moving target from a galloping steed. Both the hunters and their mounts were continually subjected to severe injury (and sometimes death) from falls, faulty weapons and thick clumps of thorns. We might also give cognisance to the terror of having wounded animals turn on their pursuers at very close quarters. This happened to Cornwallis Harris during a rhino hunt and he describes the incident as follows: 'Aroused from a siesta by the smarting of a gun-shot wound, the infuriated animal had pursued his assailant so closely that it became necessary to discharge the second barrel into his mouth.' And on another occasion thus: 'I crawled towards him amongst the grass, and within 40 yards fired two balls into him. He charged up, with his eye flashing fire, and gore streaming from his mouth, to within an arm's length of me. Crouching low... I fortunately eluded his vengeance... [He] soon afterwards dropped down dead.'

From Richard's writing, it becomes clear that he and his party had purchased guns that were too light to bring down big game with ease and it was to take them several weeks before they perfected the skills required to hunt Africa's wildlife, despite being the able horsemen they were.

William Cornwallis Harris's impression of eland being herded back to the wagons

and frozen in its knowledge that its time had come. 'It couldn't get away from me and I've never gotten away from it.'

Felt strangely bereft leaving Ian. It's such a rare gift to have an audience with a sage, and he waved me goodbye with two important pieces of advice. 'Always trust local knowledge on the road ahead' and 'You can never be too detailed in your instructions to your team'.

Was he psychic or something? Already I was struggling under the burden of leading my crew through this great adventure, trying to keep too many balls in the air at the same time and paying the price of assuming that they knew what was required of them.

Once again dear John has got his priorities wrong. He clearly spent the whole day in camp working hard but when we got home at 7pm there was no supper ready. Tapiwa has had a neck massage, however! Must learn to work around J's energy levels. When he's fully charged, he's still at it at midnight (and often gets up at 3am to work). But don't ask him to work beyond his discharge time because he just can't. I worry about his and Louis' stamina, because this is nothing by comparison with what they'll face in Botswana. Louis got news that a good friend has died and he's terribly upset. Very sensitive man, this. He's going to take some time off to go to the funeral.

Tired and tense

John gives Taps a peek

We reached the old Mooi River crossroads the next day, but only after Tapiwa and I had swallowed gallons of dust on the (now dry) roads after a late-afternoon walk. Tall grass on either side of the road is very frustrating for Taps who can't see over it, but smells interesting things beyond. It was lovely to be walking at a different time of day from our usual dawn parade – a contemplative time when birds find their roosts and goats are driven to safety behind locked gates. Silhouetted against the setting sun, the pine trees on the mountain ridges resembled the close-cropped manes of dressage horses.

We were at peace after another glorious day on our astounding continent. And while we headed home, our 1863 adventurers tucked themselves up in bed at John Whipp's Hotel on the banks of the Mooi River. Despite enlisting the help of Isaac Dlamini, who lives within a stone's throw from where it must have been, I could find no evidence of the old inn, but decided that it couldn't have been such a *mooi* (pretty) place for its proprietor, given that he lost two of his children to the river's floodwaters. Like many others who died in the area at that time, the children were buried in the banks of the river and reinterred in consecrated ground once an Anglican church was built nearby. And it seemed to me, as I walked past 'St John's', that many people don't rest easy in their graves here.

Take 'Sam', for instance, a Bushman seized in a raid on cattle rustlers the year before the Glyns came through. He was taken into the employ of Captain William Proudfoot, his captor, but died of tuberculosis and was buried on Craigie Burn farm. Medical science, however, had plans for poor old Sam. The Surveyor-General of Natal had the man's bones exhumed after a couple of decades and sent to an Edinburgh museum for study. But how to get him over there without a bureaucratic stink, if you'll pardon the pun. Well you mark the box 'family silver', don't you see, and dupe a well-meaning lady friend into taking it over as personal luggage, stowed under her bunk in a luxury liner. You could argue that Sam got off lightly by comparison with our more famous Bushman 'specimen' export Sarah Baartman, who had to endure those inquisitive fumblings while still alive. But, unlike Sarah's weary bones, to my knowledge his still lie in an icy Scottish museum, no doubt meticulously tagged but long forgotten.

Life on the road – far more work than play

Mavis Sokhela

Today, Mooi River residents are outraged at another alleged graveyard disturbance, whispers of which reached my ears as I approached town. Boer War graves were allegedly being dug up and reused by residents of the local township of Bruntville, fast running out of burial space for their Aids casualties. Could this possibly be true, I asked of Mavis Sokhela, a bubbly old lady in bright yellow leg-warmers who greeted me at the crossroads. 'Sure,' she said. 'It's true. I'll show you.'

So up the hill we went, to discover that the heroes' graves remain undisturbed, but those of the nearby civilian deceased have got very new, very close neighbours as the cemetery struggles to cope with modern realities. And those realities couldn't be more striking than what I witnessed that Saturday morning. Dozens of township men were spending their weekend digging graves for five of their friends. 'Next weekend,' they said, 'we'll be back to do more.' It's become their off-time pastime, so parties happen more often under the windy gum trees nowadays than they do in local shebeens. I couldn't help wondering what Mary Irene Gilbey and Francis John Carless would feel about the revellers leaning against their gravestones, taking a break between turns at the shovel.

Taking turns at the shovel

Easy week, walk wise, but BIG shock tonight as I calculated just how much walking I had to do in the next week or so. Those wagons will be flying! It's all doable physically, but I have writing and filming to do as well, and the filming is taking the bulk of the time. So far no pain at all in joints or muscles, but must bind my feet with Micropore to prevent blisters.

Mooi River to Harrismith

Meandering in the presence of greatness

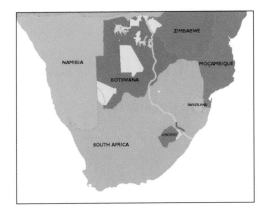

Mooi River to Harrismith
174 kilometres
Total: 377
Week 4
4–10 April

April. We trekked twice, sometimes three times a day, doing about an average of 18 miles [29 kilometres], at a rate of 2¼ [3.6] per hour, crossing several small rivers but shooting nothing, till we came to the Tugela, the largest in Natal, a yellow Tiber-like stream, where we had to swim the oxen and take the wagons over in a punt.

I rose at 5am Monday morning with Richard's timetable uppermost in my mind. This week his wagons seemed to have V8 engines, and I would have to average about 30 kilometres a day for six consecutive days in order to keep up with them. I had trained for these distances and was confident that I would have no muscular or skeletal problems, but The Blue Cross Challenge in Zimbabwe had taught me some hard lessons about what hot road surfaces can do to one's feet. By the end of that race, mine had become a mushy mess resembling steak tartare, with splits and craters so deep I fancied I could see the bones of one of my heels. Determined to avoid that torture again, I hauled out my first-aid kit and wound metres of Micropore plaster around my delicate trotters before setting off.

More biting wind carried me along the old transport track through Weston, an old settlement some two kilometres downstream from the town of Mooi River. Weston had been fairly busy in the 1860s but now comprises only a church, a couple of humble dwellings and a large municipal dump. Plastic bags played unruly kite games in the air and the smell of rotting garbage assaulted my nostrils as I crossed the fast-flowing Mooi River via the Helen Bridge (a national monument), built only three years after 'my' party came through here in order to ease the great problems early travellers encountered getting through the river. The Mooi looks quintessentially English, with grassy banks, poplars and willows, and Tapiwa and I walked parallel to its Arcadian gentleness until we reached the tarred Estcourt road where aggressive truck drivers forced my little companion into the car once again. *How he hates being confined before he's had his daily exercise quota. He stares longingly out of the window at me, and whines when I approach the vehicle.* Gentle rain soaked my back as I followed the ridge-top road. It winds through a series of amusing hillocks that resemble the work of a gargantuan baker who decided just before cooking his bright green buns that he'd lop the tops off all of them. At last I was in archetypal African vegetation – Impressionist

Feet like steak tartare

grasses, delicate daubs of a million golden hues and flat-topped thorn trees from corny bushveld advertisements.

The Mooi is indeed *mooi*

No rest for the 19th-century wagon traveller

Scoffing by moonlight

A day's travel by ox-wagon was broken up into several short treks to avoid tiring the oxen. The treks lasted anything from two to four hours and each was known as a *scoft* or *skof* (from the Dutch word *schoft* meaning 'shift' or 'period of work', and hence the word comes into our lexicon as scoff for a 'meal'). The first was usually at about 4am and was heralded by a crack of the driver's long whip. The *voorloper* then brought in the oxen at a trot and a well-schooled team could be inspanned in a matter of minutes if all staff helped with the noisy process.

Meanwhile, equipment and utensils would be hastily stored in the wagons and, when everything was ready, the driver cracked his whip once again, shouted '*Trek!*' and they were off. If the road was well defined and smooth, a driver could doze until the *scoft* ended. If not, he would arrive at the end of the shift hoarse from continual shouting, and exhausted from constantly having to jump off his seat to prod and cajole the oxen. The last trek of the day finished at about 8 or 9pm, with the heat of the midday hours reserved for resting. Not that the drivers and their staff could rest much even then, because the oxen

had to be outspanned, watered, taken to grazing by the *voorlopers*, treated for illnesses and (at night) protected against nocturnal predators as they slept or ruminated while chained to the *trektou* for safety. During their 'breaks', the staff had their equipment and wagons to fix, whips to mend or grease, wheels to change and wood to gather for fires. The heat of the day provided the best chance for the wagon staff to do chores like bake bread and, for their employers – if they weren't out hunting – to write their diaries while the light was good (as I imagined Richard to be doing.)

Working oxen too hard had fatal consequences. The animals did not perform well when too cold or too hot, their necks developed sores from the wet yokes if they hauled in the rain, and overwork gave them diarrhoea. Too little water made them weak, too much made them sick. In ideal conditions, an ox thrived on one long drink per day, of roughly 10 gallons (45 litres).

The rate of travel was between two and three miles (3.2–4.8 kilometres) an hour, but naturally that depended on the state of the road and the difficulty of the terrain. It is clear from Richard's diary that an average day for his party comprised a distance of between 25 and 35 kilometres.

In the desert or semidesert areas, the oxen would be forced to work for about 18 or 20 hours in every 24, because water holes were few and far between and there was great danger of losing the livestock to thirst if the next water source was not reached in time. Water could not be transported in the wagons in sufficient quantity for the oxen and what was carried was reserved for human consumption. No washing permitted in the 'thirstland'.

At the other extreme, in the rainy months the oxen might have had plentiful water, but the soil was so clogged and heavy that there were sometimes days when a wagon would move as little as a few hundred metres, as the span was outspanned and inspanned dozens of times while the drivers dislocated the wagon and tried to wedge it out of trouble.

Full moon, especially in the summer months, provided the wonderful opportunity of trekking at night – sometimes twice or three times – in order to save the oxen the effects of a scorching African sun. And in areas where the tsetse fly flourished, it was particularly advantageous to move after dark because the fly was not active. The romance of trekking by moonlight had fired my imagination since I first read Richard's diary, and I longed for the time when conditions were suitable for me to mimic their trek by walking at night. I would have four full moons to choose from.

Trekking by moonlight

It was my kind of country and, feeling buoyant and patriotic, I strode confidently into Estcourt, crossing the Bushman's River courtesy of another historic bridge. An angelic face with cupid lips and white teeth bounced along beside me. They belonged to a small boy called Sandile Madlala who was off to town on an errand for his mum, R10 clutched firmly in his little hand. The money was for an electricity card, he told me in perfect English. It would keep the family in light and heat for a week, after which they'd have to use candles again until Dad sent them more money. Ten rand? For a *week*? I would probably spend more than that on Tapiwa's supper. I handed him R20 and we continued up the hill into town, Sandile furtively kissing the note when he thought I wasn't looking. On parting, he drew a sketch for me in my notepad and skipped away into a café to spend R2 on sweets. 'The rest I will give to my mother.'

Humbled by my encounter with Sandile, I rounded a corner into the main street of Estcourt. Bam! Who should I bump straight into? Who should I encounter sitting in his car on the side of the very pavement I was walking, but the one medicine man in the whole of southern Africa I didn't want to see – Elliot Ndlovu. I behaved like a schoolgirl caught bunking out on a Saturday night.

Elliot – apparently unconcerned

'Sorry, Elliot, I've been meaning to tell you, but I was too nervous to call… You know I've, um, lost the stick. It just, er, disappeared on the first night I had it. What do you make of that?'

I thought I caught a glimmer of alarm in his eyes before he hid it in a jovial backslap. 'Don't worry, Patricia. Sticks do sometimes disappear. Phone me tomorrow and I'll tell you why.'

'Why only *tomorrow*?' I muttered to myself as I stumbled out of town. 'I can't wait till tomorrow, damn it – I'm in *agony* here!' Science Child was well and truly rattled.

The terrain on the other side of Estcourt made it clear to me why Richard's wagons now had me bulleting along at hip-waggling speed. Before me lay a broad valley of gently undulating hills that would have provided few obstacles for wheel or ox apart from the Thukela River – until very recently commonly referred to as the Tugela – and there would have been none of the Grand Canyons of soil erosion I was now seeing. Historians would put their money on the fact that the 1863 party crossed the 'yellow Tiber-

Where did they go?

like stream' at a drift near what later became the town of Colenso, but the road to it now is tarred and busy so I decided on a pragmatic diversion, one of several I would take during the course of my walk. The Loskop road, slightly further south, was not only closer to the spectacular mountain range I was now approaching, but it would bring me into greater contact with the people living on its lower reaches. That was the one I would do.

The next day I found myself snaking through an extensive settlement of cheerful, hospitable people, all of them curious as to why I, a white woman, was walking in their midst. The road is named after a flat-topped hill called Loskop (meaning 'loose head'), one of many in South Africa so named because they are separated from the mountain ranges nearest them. Nimrod Mabaso was waiting at the side of the road for a lift into town. 'Our ancestors live at the top of Loskop,' he told me. 'If we can't solve our problems, we go to the chief. If he can't solve them, we go to the mountain, slaughter a goat and talk to our ancestors. If they don't help us, they'll give rewards to our children.' It sounded to me like a somewhat tidy belief system in which the ancestors' intercession could neither be proved nor disproved.

Bonga was running up a hill as part of his soccer training and invited me to join him. Three giggling girls beckoned me to a water pump where they

were lifting 25-litre drums of water onto their skinny necks with astounding strength. Old women beamed at me with pink gums, and two little boys told me the story of their hunting dogs Rex and Tiger. I say 'told me their story', but in truth I could only understand a tenth of it. I'm so ashamed that I don't speak their language. People who speak Zulu (like Karin) inhabit a completely different world from mine – I simply must learn an African language.

And all the time I walked in the presence of greatness – the jagged, imposing amphitheatre that is the Drakensberg, arranged like a protective arm around the left flank of this plain. The mountains provided a graded palette of blues and purples with outlines ranging from comfy mounds to wicked spikes. They're the source of superstitious awe to many, but for a walker at their feet they provided slowly unfolding panoplies of gut-punching wonder. With the sun on my throat in the late afternoon, I fantasised about their peaks, thrust into the skyline. The Boer *trekkers* decided they looked like the back of a dragon. To the Zulus they resembled a barrier of spears. To me they were households built by a rich man for his many wives. Here was Tintwa's home – she was obviously a senior spouse because her establishment is grand and impressive. Nondela must have been a newer acquisition – her establishment is pert and pretty. Another has towering ramparts, yet another fields and gardens.

Tintwa's home (right) and Nondela's cottage (left)

For the *voorlopers* in 1863, though, the sight of this daunting mountain range must have instilled only one feeling – dread. At the time, roughly seven routes had been established through it along the more lengthy spurs of the mountains, mostly by the Voortrekkers trying to get down to the fertile lands I was now traversing. Several of the mountain passes are named after these early penetrators of The Barrier: Van Reenen's, Oliviershoek, De Beer's, Bezuidenhout's. Richard's diary was mum about which one his party used, but at Gaunts House I had seen an old map on which he had re-traced their route when he returned home after his great adventure. It was too large in scale to help solve many of my navigational dilemmas, but the spidery brown-ink line snaking across it was very clear about one thing – he'd used Bezuidenhout's Pass. 'Oh, good choice, Richard,' I thought. 'That pass is still wild

Cutting the back of the Dragon

There are many less well-known passes through the Drakensberg which were forged by early transport riders delivering goods to the Zuid-Afrikaansche Republiek. These men were anxious to avoid the tolls demanded by the Boer government on roads in and out of the province, and every time a new tollgate was erected they found an alternative way through the mountains.

But in the latter part of the 19th century, most of the passes were abandoned in favour of Oliviershoek and in particular, Van Reenen's Pass. Bezuidenhout's fell into a state of disrepair and neglect until it became too dangerous to use and was deproclaimed in 1950. Since then, Adrian Odendaal, who farms on its lower reaches in Natal, occasionally uses the pass to visit his father, who farms at its top in the Free State, and he has plans to allow off-road vehicles the use of its hair-raising road for weekend entertainment. Its steep, rocky inclines will certainly provide them with some excitement.

During the days of South Africa's gold- and diamond-rush, traffic volumes through Van Reenen's Pass swelled enormously. It took the wagon drivers two days to get up the pass and their favourite halfway stop was Wyford Trading Store, where they fed, watered and rested their oxen, and reprovisioned from the shop. In the 1880s and 1890s,

Wyford Farmhouse, once a popular store

its owners recorded as many as 3 000 wagons per month passing their door. With (conservatively) 16 oxen per wagon, that meant a total of 48 000 animals milling around at the outspan in front of their veranda, which must have made for a stupendous amount of cattle dung and may account for the lush, green lawns that one sees there today. The store is now a farmhouse whose owners, Sheila and Stratford Russell,

The view from Wyford in the 1880s

run a lovely weekend getaway below the busy Van Reenen's motorway. Wagon ruts are still visible on the hills above it and they have an early photo of the area showing it to be completely treeless – so different from the way it is now, with its ravines and riverbeds choked by wattle trees and other invaders.

Further up the pass is another famous 19th-century stopover – The Green Lantern Inn – and its owners, Lew and Maria Harris, tell me that it was built in 1892, largely in response to the railway line having been built nearby. The hotel was commandeered by the British for barracks during the Boer War, and in the 1930s it was the venue for the first ever screening of a black-and-white, silent movie in South Africa. The projector can still be seen in the lounge today.

and remote, unlike a couple of the others that have become major trunk roads in the interim. I might even see it in much the same state as you did.'

Closer and closer I got to the pass, walking among the yellow maize and wheat fields of the Geluksburg road and thinking of the strange folk with whom that town will always be associated – The People of the Lost Valley. At the time when Richard, Robert and Henry came through this area, a group of about five *trekker* families came across a magical, banana-shaped valley nearby, accessible only on foot or horseback down a precipitous road. No doubt they were tired of being chased around the continent by both Brit and Black and were attracted to its seclusion, so there they settled. And I mean settled, almost completely cut off from the outside world for about 100 years, until they were discovered by a *Rand Daily Mail* journalist in 1966, living in a kind of weird time warp. Their wattle-and-daub hovels were carved out of the mountain sides, they had no running water, no education, not even candles for after-dark activities. Mind you, nature would have abhorred shining a light on those activities. The handful of families had interbred for four or five generations until they developed the gross features of hill-billies all around the world – flattened noses, stunted limbs and slack-jawed mouths crowded with enormous teeth. Eventually the apartheid government decided that their hideaway must be flushed out and the 'lost ones' wrenched back into the literate world, so they were settled in Geluksburg where the last of them died in 2004.

Meanwhile Elliot Ndlovu, the *nyanga*, had proved difficult to pin down for an appointment regarding the mysterious disappearance of my walking stick. After trying to get hold of him for two days, I began to think he was scared to meet The White Witch who had *vavoomed* his totem. Sitting in the shade of a gum tree on a lunch break, I decided to try his number one last time before I headed up the pass. He answered the call hesitantly.

'Well, Patricia, I have given this some thought and decided that maybe you shouldn't be carrying a stone *or* a stick. I think that you may have something wrong with you. Please go for a cleansing.'

'What's that, for goodness sake?' I asked, getting more and more concerned about the whole business.

'It's a ceremony that only a *sangoma* can perform and I suggest you find one in Harrismith. The ancestors will also tell her what you should be carrying with you to the Victoria Falls.'

I'll probably go out of curiosity more than anything else, and besides, it will make for good movie footage.

April 7h: I overtook the wagons not far from the Drakensberg. Mountains mostly covered with grass, wood (yellow wood) in the ravines and fine bold rocks, often of extraordinary outline at the summit. After vast flogging, and screaming, the wagons were dragged to the top by the united efforts of 2 spans, 26 oxen to each, and we encamped for the night on the last yard of British soil. This is the 3rd and last step to the African plateau whose plains are 596,000 feet [181 650 metres] above the sea. Higher up the mountain range are the coal-beds of Newcastle; gold is also talked of, but is at present only the dream of innkeepers near the place.

Wagons being driven up a pass near Cradock

Sister Shirl

The Pass, The Pass. What a day that was, slowly winding our way up its stony, rutted track, which is now all but impassable for vehicles. Two old friends – Karen Davies and Ingrid Moss – had arrived for a few days' stay along with my sister Shirley, so while she and Ingrid drove the vehicles up the nearby Oliviershoek Pass to the top of the range, Louis (who'd been itching to stretch his legs for nearly a month by now), Karen, Karin and I headed up the ever-deteriorating road towards the skyline. On its lower reaches we met the gentle-spirited Godfrey Mabi – who was still using oxen in exactly the same way as his ancestors had when mine passed through here – and he gave us an impressive display of his oxmanship. Further up the hill, a grey-haired paterfamilias by the name of Obet Ndlovu took one look at Tapiwa and decided he'd make a useful addition to his pack of greyhound-slim hunting dogs. The skin of their last kill was staked out on a fence near his homestead, a jackal destined to be his winter hat. 'You can have that little house dog of mine in exchange for yours.' He looked at me as if I was deranged

Godfrey Mabi

when I tried to explain that my dog was as good as a son to me and that we were not to be parted.

Beautiful groves of indigenous trees nestled in secluded bends of the road and for every 10 metres climbed we were rewarded with new glimpses of the broad valley below – silver streams, verdant riverbeds and

Obet Ndlovu – Tapiwa's new owner?

The Pass, The Pass!

vultures circling below us. It was simply glorious, so quiet and peaceful by comparison with the terrible trouble the Victorians had had getting up it. Louis found evidence of their generation's passage in a few wagon ruts, gouged into the sandstone by lashed wheels straining to hold their grip on the steep incline. And everywhere the voices of the Children of the Mist echoed off the rock faces. The Bushmen of days gone by had proved themselves adept at driving stolen cattle up these seemingly impassable ravines and gorges, reportedly by smearing the path ahead with cow dung to dupe the animals into believing that their kind had been up there before.

We stopped briefly at the top of the pass, on 'the last yard of British soil', before heading down into the Free State. I was overwhelmed with melancholia at the thought that I'd probably never see Bezuidenhout's Pass again in my life and that a quarter of my journey was now over. It was all happening too fast. We are all working so hard that there's no breathing space on this journey. I feel as if it's happening in a dream. Still, a new province lay ahead

The last yard of British soil

and, no doubt, a new adventure for our team. After all, Ex Africa semper aliquid novi.

With the Drakensberg slowly receding behind our backs, we four girls made for the Platberg mountain that guards the town of Harrismith, while Louis and John drove ahead to find our new camp. It's great having old friends here, talking about varsity days and the dreams we'd shared about men and marriage. Nowadays, we face new issues that seem to centre on money and the menopause! My walk is often quite lonely and I've so enjoyed having company for a few days.

Girlfriends

That night we settled on the lawns of a house owned by Andrew and Mel Greene. Their farm is at the base of Rensburg's Kop, an imposing, fissure-faced mountain that is well known in the area as the scene of a ghastly family tragedy long ago. Details of the incident vary – so much so that one could be forgiven for doubting that it happened at all – but, in short, the young Rensburg boy was on top of the koppie when he slipped and fell down one of the many sandstone crevasses that encircle its summit. Badly injured and solidly wedged between vertical stone walls, he lay and whimpered for two days and nights while his Ma and Pa sat at the top, trying everything they could to get him out. Facing a third night in his freezing, lonely cavern, the boy begged his father to put him out of his misery. A shot rang out over the valley, accompanied by the hysterical screaming of Mrs Van Rensburg, and the child's agony was over. Roger Webster's version of the tale in *The Illustrated 'At the Fireside'* (Spearhead, Cape Town 2002), is the one I like best – for its ending. Van Rensburg was tried for manslaughter a while later, but saved any further punishment. The kindly magistrate ended his judgement by quoting a local resident who'd said: 'It is known that the bullet went through the boy's head, but it also went through the man's soul.'

April 8th. Harrismith, the first Boer town, is a miserable place without a tree or ornament of any kind, a few English stores selling the worst goods at the highest prices, or bartering them for wool which the Boer likes better, wheat £2 a sack, English beer 2/6 per bottle.

Richard seemed far from happy with the settlement that awaited him soon after his arrival in the Free State. The town was a mere four years old then, so it could be forgiven its arboreal nudity, if not its entrepreneurial chancers, but my ancestors' decision not to tarry in the town meant that I had little time to see to my business there. And my 'business' once again concerned that blessed stick and the equally blessed stone, so with yet further unwilling suspension of my rational mind, off I went to see a *sangoma* with Joyce Mthembu, the town's tourism officer in tow, as she'd agreed to act as my translator. Makhosi Mthembu (no relation of Joyce) was an enormous woman with loving, round eyes and great folds of flesh around her wrists and ankles. Outside her hut, I was given a towel to wrap around my walking shorts – evidently the ancestors are offended by women wearing anything but skirts. I knelt on a mat, hoping my knees would survive the discomfort, and the ceremony began. Six *thwasas* (initiates in training with the *sangoma*), wearing white headbands and beads in their hair, started singing a song of exquisite beauty, accompanied by the steady beat of drums. Every now and then they broke away from the melody to emit gruff-voiced incantations. Their bodies shook with convulsions and animal-like groans crept from deep within their throats. 'They're calling the spirits,' explained Joyce. Then, all at once, they stopped and silence filled the room. MaMakhosi drew in her breath, lifted her chin heavenward and began petitioning the ancestors, her words flowing with passion and astounding speed. Joyce was finding it hard to keep up. Next I was summoned to sit next to the *sangoma* in the centre of the room. She clasped my hands in hers and started rolling and tossing my body around with strength that took my breath away.

'Your ancestors are proud of you,' she gasped and muttered. 'They are with you and they will make sure that you complete your journey without accident. You are a strong woman. Lucky, too, but you should have done the journey alone.'

Eerie Rensburg's Kop

Does she think I'm Wonder Woman or something? 'That is why you are losing things. You should be carrying a candle and coins, not a stone or a stick. You must light the candle each night and ask for forgiveness for travelling with so many people, and you must throw the coins into the water at the end of your journey.'

Me and the Ma

Her hands moved to my chest and back, which she rubbed ferociously before sitting back and shaking her head.

'You are a very powerful woman. So much power that you could become a *sangoma*.' *But I don't have a healing bone in my body!* 'You must not resist what happens to you at the end of your walk – it will be decided for you by the ancestors.'

On the dusty street outside MaMakhosi's homestead, Joyce and I discussed what had happened.

'Listen to her,' she said. 'I know you don't believe half of that stuff, but even as a modern, educated woman I wouldn't *ever* defy a *sangoma*.'

Certainly, I didn't know what to make of what had transpired in the ceremony, but had come away from the encounter deeply moved by the sincerity and generosity with which help had been offered to me. We headed back into town and bought the small, round candle as instructed, which we took back to the Ma for blessing, along with some water she told me to mix with my drinking water on the road. The coins could be of my choice, but must be silver.

It's late and I must get some sleep – we're moving camp tomorrow and no doubt that'll result in the standard confusion and short tempers. The girls all leave tomorrow and I look forward to have our little three-man (!) team back because we have things to sort out between us. Really can't imagine myself praying to some bloodthirsty Victorians, so have decided to light the candle each night in memory of darling Dad. It's burning as I write this, throwing shadows onto the tent ceiling, my gear strewn all over the show. Still have the Web diary to finish and packing to do. Hell, I hate move-out days!

Harrismith to Heilbron

Endless dunes of khaki and caramel

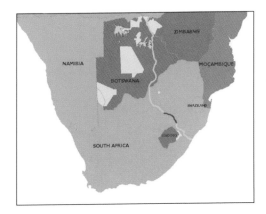

Harrismith to Heilbron
175 kilometres
Total: 552
Week 5
11–17 April

April 9th: We first came to the vast grass plains, which extend all the way to the Vaal River… The whole breadth of the Free State, there is not a bush to be seen, cow dung is the only fuel, which makes cooking very difficult on wet days, and does not suit the temper of our cook…

12th. Cold and damp, not much grub or fire…

13th. Outspanned night in lion order, that is forming a triangle with the wagons, tying the span oxen to the trektou, and putting the loose beasts in the centre.

What a sight those plains must have been – wave upon wave of grassland, endless dunes of khaki and caramel, with the odd cloud casting a dark stain on the buff landscape. And it's still utterly mesmerising to traverse today, despite the subsequent outcrops of alien gums and willows that heralded foreign settlement in the region and defiled its beguiling uniformity. Let no one tell you, however, that the Free State is flat – or windless. Day after 35-kilometre day, I gusted up long inclines and shuffled down their counterparts on roads of hard clay topped by loose pebbles. They give my back hell because I can't get any purchase. Sometimes the stones are so big that I have to weave from side to side on the road to find a more comfortable path. The verges were a bobbing mass of pink and white cosmos blooms that made me feel as if I was caught up in a maniacal advertisement for bathroom freshener. Those flowers would not have been there for the 1863 party, of course, having been introduced to the country in American fodder for horses during the South

Ships on a sea of grass

African War (1899–1902), and they remain an absurd adjunct to this sandy universe. John introduced Taps to horses in a field and I came upon a lovely little scene of this gentle man sitting among the cosmos with these equally gentle creatures all around him. He's a whisperer of sorts, and loves Tapiwa in a way I couldn't have known when I hired him.

The ancestors gave me a lot of extra legwork through the Free State. I suspect that James Gifford, their manager, was unsure of the direct route to their next town, Potchefstroom, and had been told to head north towards what is now the town of Frankfort and a mountain called 'Tafelkop, or Table Hill, a great land

Horse – and dog – whispering

So where did the ancestors go?

mark on these plains'. Our maps confirmed that, by doing so, the party would always have been close to the Wilge River and its tributaries, and with 13 men and about 90 animals to water regularly, that would have been the safest route to take before they met the mighty Vaal River and struck out westwards. Some of the old wagon tracks through the province are now on private land, and because I didn't feel like clambering over farm fences all day long, once again I would have to take some pragmatic decisions and divert slightly from their actual path – such as I knew it. Gifford's routing also meant that I would have to walk an extra 50 kilometres in their wake, but there were many rewards for my efforts. Owls in the sky at dawn, schoolchildren emerging from low, mud houses, cotton-wool lambs with wobbly legs, combine harvesters against a setting sun. Tapiwa and I were now moving through more remote areas than KwaZulu-Natal had provided, signalled (sadly) by more exotic road kills. An aardwolf lay on the side of the road, its eyes pecked out by crows; a giant mongoose hung on a wire fence, looking forlorn and inelegant and a hare had been crushed mid-flight. My little dog's reactions to them were poignant. Gently he sniffed their carcasses, then lay down beside them in what seemed to be a kind of mourning ritual.

With Franci back in the team for a short while, we had an extra driver, so Louis could once again take to the road with me and get some exercise. For several mornings I was entertained by this masterful Afrikaans storyteller in the old Oom Schalk Lourens tradition. The kilometres flew by as his low,

Taps' mourning ritual

melodious tones wove tales about our collective past. With his infallible nose for places of historical import, he found the place where Harrismith was originally situated on a bend in the Meul River and we lunched on sandwiches, surrounded by the cowpats that had so frustrated Richard's cook. I fantasised about asking Louis to attempt some historical recreation by using cattle dung to cook the evening's meal, but bless him, the few suppers he'd produced so far had resembled a cross between a veld fire and a road kill, so I thought it best not to try his ingenuity further.

We waded through the Cornelius River (as the early Glyns did), walked the oldest road in the Free State (as they did), and scanned the horizon every day (no doubt, as they did) for the flat-topped landmark that would herald our turn westwards. And after several long days in the very hot Free State sun, I at last crested a hill and spied Tafelkop's imposing plateau through the haze of a stormy late afternoon. What a thrill. What a hard-earned thrill. First view of Tafelkop! Alerted to it by John's very touching recce maps. They're marked TOH or BOV (Top of Hill or Bottom of Valley) to give me hope on the long inclines. Trouble is there seem to be so many more TOHs than BOVs!

Crossing the Cornelius River

It was time for me to turn west, and for my ancestors to start hunting. At last Richard, Robert and Henry had found the legendary herds of Africa that they'd read about, and not before time too. In the month that they'd been on the road, they'd seen only a few rhebok and by now they must have been wondering where on earth the game had gone. They'd been attracted to our continent by news that the grass plains of the central African plateau hosted herds of antelope that stretched – literally – as far as the eye could see. Reports from early white hunters told of wildebeest, springbok, quagga and blesbok roaming these parts in numbers so great that their migrations caused dust clouds that blotted out the sun for days on end. A man could shoot until his arm grew too tired to lift his rifle and not make a dent in their masses. Game beyond computation, sport beyond belief. At last, here were the herds.

First view of Tafelkop

Came on wildebeest and quagga in hundreds, blowing and barking at you all over the place... springbok, lovely antelopes, which bound along raising a kind of mane of white hair on their loins at every bound, in a most extraordinary manner. Of course we must mount and pursue, but we soon found that they could play with either horse or dog... We all blundered back one by one to the wagons long after dark with our tails between our legs, attracted by the firing of guns and cracking of whips. Saw two troops of ostriches, lots of other game also about, but the chestnut pony is not fond of galloping and I could not get near them. At last I saw an oribi lay down in some long grass; I walked up towards him, he jumped up at 30 yards [27.5 metres], and I rolled over my first African buck. Put him up behind the saddle and had a long 15 miles [24 kilometres] to find the wagons.

A flat-topped beacon

Tafelkop – as I learnt from Tim Couzens and his book *Battles of South Africa* (David Philip Publishers, Cape Town, 2004) – is a source of mystery and wonder to local people as well as those far away in the mountains of Lesotho. The mountain is known as Ntsoanatsatsi (the rising of the sun) to the Basotho people and, according to their myths, a swamp on its slopes is where humankind was born. To this day, local tribes turn the faces of their dead towards the mountain when they bury them, but Louis was sad to discover that most people no longer know why they follow this custom. Our legends are thus lost forever.

Many centuries ago, Chief Napo of the Bakwena moved to the area surrounding the mountain, where he married the daughter of a local chief. Generations later, his people moved south to Lesotho, but many of them still say that they come originally from Ntsoanatsatsi. Napo's descendant, Moshoeshoe, became one of the greatest of the 19th-century African leaders, renowned for his wise leadership and diplomacy.

One of the earliest descriptions of Tafelkop came from French missionary Thomas Arbousset in the 1830s. He and a colleague encountered the remarkable flat-topped beacon during an expedition from their mission base at Morija in Lesotho. The men were on a quest to locate the source of southern Africa's great rivers and Arbousset's writings about their journey include a chilling account of the depredations of Shaka. 'The fields of the dead', he called this area of the Free State, and described the remnants of cattle kraals as the only evidence left of the people who were slaughtered or driven from here in the Mfecane.

Tafelkop – much closer now

Safari's devastating legacy

Any study of the effect the early hunters had on the great herds of southern Africa is doomed to be anecdotal and conjectural. Simply put, we just don't know how much game was here before these men arrived with their horses and guns. African groups had, of course, hunted wildlife since time immemorial (see page 222), but it was the introduction of firearms into the southern African interior that took the most dramatic toll on its animals, leading to many species becoming locally extinct and at least two, the quagga and the blue buck, disappearing altogether.

The first whites to sally forth from the Cape Colony between 1700 and 1720 were seminomadic stock farmers in search of better grazing for their herds. They were known as *trekboers* and, like cattle-keepers everywhere, both they and precolonial Africans killed predators such as lion, leopard and hyena, which threatened their livestock. But in the hinterland, the *trekboers* also encountered abundant herds of everything from elephant to antelope, and they opened up a trade in wildlife products garnered from these animals – products such as ivory, hides, horn and meat, which they exported via the subcontinent's seaports. Before long, they were followed by commercial traders in these items – whose impact on the herds was more profound – and in the 1830s by the *Voortrekkers*, a large group of people intent on settling permanently in the interior.

But very few of the *trekboers*, early traders or *Voortrekkers* wrote about their hunting exploits. Even oral accounts of their lives are few and far between, so in order to track the demise of wildlife in the 19th century one has to resort to the published accounts of visiting British sportsmen, the hunter-publicists. And because these men describe experiences that span every decade between 1810 and 1880, one can deduce roughly what effect they had on game movements

Game beyond computation

A man could shoot until his arm grew
too tired to lift his rifle

and numbers throughout the century. Like Richard's, their journals tell a very sad tale, each of them a lamentation on the fast-disappearing bounty they had come to find and, with few exceptions, the hunters display a gross lack of understanding or sense of responsibility for what they were perpetrating. It seems that they simply could not conceive of a limit to the abundance they encountered.

On his arrival in the Cape Colony in 1811, William Burchell noted that white settlement under the Dutch had already resulted in the elimination of big game in the area. Indeed, hippo had been wiped out on the Cape peninsula as early as 1690, and by the time the British government introduced game laws in the late 1820s, elephant in the Colony had been reduced to two small herds in the inaccessible Knysna forest and Addo bush. Even bontebok and hartebeest had been badly affected by hunting and the spread of agriculture, and apparently only one herd of each still survived.

The most frequently quoted source on the munificence of the subcontinent's game is Captain William Cornwallis Harris who, as previously described, arrived in South Africa in 1836. He recorded the staggering sight of *trekbokken,* great herds of springbok literally covering the veld like locusts near the Orange River during their regular migrations. Further north, in the North West province, Cornwallis Harris came upon a hunter's paradise. Near the Mareetsane River he encountered wildebeest, zebra, tsessebe and hartebeest in numbers exceeding 15 000, making the countryside 'actually chequered black and white with their congregated masses'. He saw over 150 rhino in one day, buffalo were plentiful and at Olifantsnek near Rustenburg he witnessed a sight of 'intense, indescribable interest... The whole face of the landscape was actually covered with wild elephants. There could not have been fewer than 300 within the scope of our vision... a picture soul-stirring and sublime.'

Migrating herds that covered the landscape

By the end of his expedition, Cornwallis Harris had shot in the order of 400 large animals, but his effect on the subcontinent's wildlife became even more far-reaching when he returned home and publicised his adventures so widely through his books, thereby encouraging other sportsmen's interest in Africa's seemingly inexhaustible wildlife.

Gordon Roualeyn Cumming was the first of many sport-hunters to test its inexhaustibility after that. But by the time Cumming arrived in 1844, hardly a decade after Cornwallis Harris, the big game was already in retreat. Elephant had started moving northwards and a number of species had been virtually exterminated south of the Orange River – the last lion apparently being shot in 1842. Cumming spent five years hunting in Africa (see page 66), relentlessly pursuing everything that moved. What is now known as the North West province, he found still abundant with game, as was the area around the Limpopo River – game he did his best to decimate, killing crocodiles indiscriminately and leaving their carcasses in the water. He shot seven hippo and three rhino in one day alone and brought unparalleled destruction wherever he went.

The next renowned eye-witness account of Africa's bountiful wildlife – and its slaughter – comes from the pen of William Baldwin, who arrived here in 1851 and had good sport in northern KwaZulu-Natal before heading further inland late that decade. It is testimony to the animals' already diminishing numbers that it took him *six* years to find and shoot his first elephant, but having located the herds north of the Ngotwane River in what is now Botswana, he killed 61 of them on one expedition, along with 71 quagga and 23 rhino.

Indeed, by the 1850s and 1860s Africa's elephant were under enormous pressure as the huge demand for ivory in Europe encouraged near-rampant slaughter of our largest mammal. White settlement under the Boer republics was becoming entrenched north of the Vaal River and those economies were largely based on wildlife products – by far the most profitable being ivory. Boer elephant hunters now took to the field and brought home huge bags: Petrus Jacobs and Jan Viljoen, for instance, personally accounted for 500 elephant each during their careers. Missionary David Livingstone was alarmed by what he witnessed and, in 1865, estimated that elephant were being killed at a rate of 30 000 per year. He predicted their rapid disappearance and also foresaw that the trusting nature of the white rhino would be the cause of its extinction.

Close contact with dangerous game

Richard Glyn's diary of his 1863 expedition describes great paucity of game in areas like the latter-day North West province where his predecessors had had such good sport. By then Africans known as *swartzkuts* were armed and employed as hunting partners in areas that were inaccessible to horses and thus to whites and, by the 1870s the breech-loading rifle was in widespread use, allowing even mediocre hunters to secure large bags. Game was being routinely shot out to supply the *riem* trade (see page 109) – indeed one dealer in the Transvaal is reputed to have exported *two million skins* of springbok, wildebeest and blesbok between 1878 and 1880 alone.

The twin depredations of sport and trade sealed the fate of Africa's game. Elephant were by now extinct in the Transvaal area and could only be found deep within tsetse fly belts, which had been moving northwards and eastwards from the 1850s. Ironically, the continent's largest mammal was now conserved – if only partially and temporarily – by one of its smallest insects. In 'the fly', hunters were forced to go after elephant on foot, and their quarry became more wary and wily by the year. Mzilikazi settled in southern Zimbabwe and tried to regulate the ivory trade to his advantage, only granting permits to whites he felt he could trust. To this end, he appointed Johannes (John) Lee as an agent charged with selling hunting permits. Having 'bought' one, Martinus Swartz killed 165 elephant in the Ndebele kingdom in 1862. Jan Viljoen shot 200 there in 1865, and 210 in 1867. Henry Hartley killed 160 in 1868. William Finnaughty killed 500 in five years from 1864 to 1869, and he reports having found elephant in Mzilikazi's territory to be so ignorant of guns in the early years of his hunts that they literally stood around waiting to be shot. The killing was relentless and wildlife numbers declined rapidly.

By the time 'the greatest hunter of them all', Frederick Courtenay Selous, arrived in the 1870s, he had to work very hard indeed for his bags, doing most of his hunting on foot through hot, tsetse-ridden country. But by then opinion in Britain had shifted and people were beginning to question the conduct of these profligate and wasteful hunters. This was due to a growing sense of British imperialism, particularly with respect to southern Africa, and it brought with it the notion that these beautiful creatures were an imperial possession that should be preserved for the 'good of the empire'. Moreover, the Transvaal government had introduced stringent wildlife protection legislation in order to protect the trade in animal products. Reading the accounts of the later sport-hunters one senses an occasional defensiveness in their writings, possibly as a result of societal pressure. Killing could no longer be justified in terms of sport or entertainment and was now defended as a means of collecting scientific samples and data. Trophy hunting burgeoned and the records of Rowland Ward were carefully studied by armchair as well as active hunters. Even in the writing of mid-century hunters the rampant plunder often masquerades as the need to feed their camp staff or African people they met en route. William Baldwin, for instance, having killed three buffalo, one white rhino, one quagga, one lion and one elephant *in one night*, wrote to his clerical brother saying: 'This was not mere butchery, though it looks like it. The [blacks] are more than half starved, and it was only combining sport with charity.' Richard Glyn notes at the end of his diary that nothing his party shot during their trip was hunted at night or was left uneaten by his men – perhaps in self-conscious justification of his sport.

By the late 1800s, Selous was fully aware of what people like him were doing to the herds, but it seems he was quite unable to stop himself. 'Elephants are... now so scarce, that one cannot afford to leave even smallish ones alone,' he wrote in 1878. But the obsession of bloodsport and commercial interests kept him and others going – he, Viljoen and their cohorts slaughtered 100 elephant that season in the Gweru area of Zimbabwe. As Edward Tabler says in his book *The Far Interior*, 'Most of the animals, cows and young bulls should never have been shot and the record of his effort to recuperate his finances reduces the great Selous, and also his comrades of the chase, more to the status... of suburban butchers writing letters home filled with the bloody details of a day's outing to an abattoir.' The hunters had 'reduced an elephant paradise into a charnel house'.

Even the threat of being responsible for extinction did not deter them. In *African Nature Notes and Reminiscences* (Macmillan, London, 1908) Selous wrote – without apparent regret – that the two white rhinos he shot at a particular spot were probably the last of their kind he would ever see. Similarly, he dismissed the extinction of the quagga and blue buck as not being of great consequence due to their similarity with other species, describing the quagga as 'nothing but the dullest coloured and most southerly form of Burchell's zebra' and the blue buck as 'very much like a small roan antelope'. Selous sparked huge criticism in England from the nascent conservation movement and protective imperialists. He was even subjected to ridicule in *Vanity Fair* magazine in 1881. The struggle to repair the damage wrought on our continent had begun.

It is an oft-crowed truth that there is more wildlife in South Africa now than there has been for the past 150 years. That is true, but it can hardly be claimed as a conservation miracle, to my mind. With the reduction in agricultural subsidies, crop-farming and stock-farming of exotic animals like sheep and cattle is no longer profitable, so many farmers have switched to game ranching as a more economically sustainable manner in which to earn a living. Some farms are eco-tourist ventures, others attract trophy hunters and many are devoted to game-farming for the meat market. But there are people who are increasingly concerned about the detrimental effect these herds are having on the veld through their inability to migrate and the resultant overgrazing. Renowned Kenyan conservationist Richard Leakey has often made the point that, should the land these animals occupy be deemed in the future to be more profitably utilised for other 'produce', the game will once again be unprotected and threatened. Preservation driven by the philosophy of 'if it pays, it stays' is hardly a credit to a species such as ours, shouldering the custodianship of our planet by dint of our intelligence, if nothing else.

The killing had begun, and the many accounts of it in Richard's diary would make for some nauseating bedtime reading in the months to come. For Victorian hunters, the animals of Africa were 'brutes' and 'monsters', and shooting them was as innocuous as a game of cricket. In the 142 years between our journeys, however, behavioural scientists and others have given humankind ample evidence of animals' sentience, complex emotions and bonding rituals with family and group. Unfortunately, this knowledge hasn't stopped us from perpetrating all manner of cruelty towards the creatures that share our planet, and there are still those among us who derive pleasure from seeing them die under fire. Perhaps, then, ours are far greater crimes than those of our forebears who acted out of ignorance as much as blood lust and greed.

And Richard was now seeing evidence of the kind of greed that led to one of the first local extinctions of wildlife on our continent.

The country is covered with skulls of wildebeests.

What could have happened? Who could have perpetrated this slaughter? Well, therein lies a sad tale. The *trekkers* who arrived here in the 1830s saw in the great herds of their Republics an irresistible resource, which they plundered with abandon. Such was the demand for hides and *riems* (hide ropes) at the time that the Boers laid waste to hundreds of thousands of antelope within a couple of decades. The region through which I was now walking became

Riemlanders at work

A princely slaughter

Queen Victoria's younger son, Alfred, came on tour to South Africa in 1860, during which the Orange Republic (newly granted its sovereignty by Britain) laid on a hunt for the 16-year-old prince, no doubt in a gesture of gratitude for its independence. Over 1 000 Barolong tribesmen were sent onto the plains near Bloemfontein a few days in advance of his arrival on 24 April, where they slowly and methodically drove between 20 000 and 30 000 head of game towards a central point. No elephant, rhino or buffalo were among their number because these were already extinct in the region, but eventually a seething, confused mass of antelope, zebra and ostrich gathered for the prince's pleasure. About 600 oxen stood quietly nearby, ready to haul away the carcasses. The slaughter started, with the prince and his cohorts firing into the herd as fast as their guns could be reloaded – in the end, from a distance of a few metres as the panicked animals were driven towards the hunters. With increasing confusion, the herd stampeded in the swirling dust and several Barolongs were trampled to death in the animals' efforts to charge through the 'net'. Eventually, the Englishmen took to their hog-spears and set about driving their blades into the game in an uncontrolled orgy of killing. Alfred was described by his escort, Sir John Bisset, as resembling a butcher – covered from head to toe in blood. Sir George Grey (who had been shooting up to that point) was appalled, and directed the men to desist from such behaviour.

The plains finally went quiet that afternoon and although estimates vary greatly, up to 5 000 animals lay dead. Bisset's comment about the event is profoundly alarming, apart from anything else because it reveals a full understanding of the threat that southern Africa's game was already under at the time:

'It was a very exciting day, and were His Royal Highness to live for 100 years I do not believe he could ever see such a scene again, for the game in South Africa is fast disappearing.'

Baines' rendition of Prince Alfred's hunt

known as Riemland and tons of skins were exported to the British colonies and beyond. Buck carcasses lay rotting in the veld, lions and vultures gorged their fill until the massacre alarmed even the government. In the 1870s, the Legislature intervened to prohibit this wanton destruction of 'God's creatures'. But it was too late. The game was gone, and for a century or more 'Riemlander' became a name of shame. To this day, the title has connotations of 'backwoods boys' but, strangely, it is claimed with pride by some of the people of the region. Maybe they are ignorant of the destruction with which it is associated or the pejorative flavour it has for outsiders.

The game is slowly coming back to Riemland, however, and I walked past several private game farms. But it appeared to me that strains of white (or is it albino?) blesbok and springbok were being fostered, and that pointed to hunting trophies as being the ultimate fate of these animals. What an ironic case of *déjà vu* it would be, I thought, if the destruction of game that brought this province to the point of ruin in my ancestors' days now saved it from a similar fate with its reintroduction. And the Free State definitely appeared to be in need of saving. To a slow traveller like me, it was a ghost province. Day after day, I passed one forlorn farm house after another, either completely abandoned or left in the hands of

The Free State – a province in decline

factotums to prevent them from being ransacked. Big-bellied farmers in short shorts and long socks pulled up alongside me in their bakkies and bemoaned their fate. The plummeting price of maize, land claims and violent attacks were driving people into the towns, so they said, and the rest of South Africa was ignorant of their plight. John is finding it very difficult to find us camp sites. Said he tried seven or eight farms today but they all appeared to be deserted. Eventually pulled into Una and Eduard Bruwer's place and, despite the fact that they're clearly struggling to make a living, they're showering us with hospitality and gifts: home-made jam, milk, mielie pap and delicious kos in their warm kitchen. Our tents are next to their dam, in sight of that archetypal Free State symbol – a rusty old windmill. So overcome by their generosity. And I guess we should be thankful that the Boer/Brit hatchet has been (largely) buried.

The Bruwers' archetypal Free State farm

April 10ᵗʰ: Osborne lost his way, wandered about half the night, till he stumbled on a Dutchman's farm who put him supperless into an outhouse with a sack to lay on.

11ᵗʰ. Sharp frost. Went out to look for Osborne, who came back disconsolate about 8 o'clock.

14ᵗʰ. Osborne was absent all night.

15ᵗʰ. Osborne turned up about 10 o'clock; he had shot a quagga, quite lost himself, and passed a very cold night on the open veld without fire or food.

Our rainfall and weather conditions, I noticed, mimicked those described in Richard's diary and I thought often of the hapless Osborne on those freezing nights as Taps and I snuggled into our cosy little Oztent. But there was no mention in the journal of the hail and lightning we had to endure. Having moved on from the Bruwers, we had to settle for the municipal camp site outside the town of Heilbron, where we were awoken one night by what sounded like a train approaching our little camp nestled in a grove of gum trees. Closer and closer the storm came, gathering speed and fury until it hit us with a 120-kilometre-per-hour force that was truly Everestian. I felt my tent lift and tilt, like a parachute. Inside, Tapiwa and I spread ourselves around its edges to prevent lift-off. The canvas shook and shimmied as we huddled in awe at the power of the elements outside, feeling rather like Dorothy and Toto in *The Wizard of Oz*. Half an hour later, the train moved on as fast as it had arrived. Then I heard laughter. John stepped out of his tent and burst into peals of relieved giggles that we were all alive and in one piece. And he had much to giggle about. One of his 'veranda' poles had been hurled, javelin-like through the thick canvas of the Oztent and missed his head by inches. Both boys had seen their tent-stays snap like matchsticks and their homes collapse around them. Now they were sitting in what resembled children's plastic swimming pools with sopping gear strewn around them. Poor guys. What a stroke of luck that my tent was on the leeward side of the trees and had been protected from the full brunt of the storm. Until such time as Ashley Cooper of Oztent could fix or replace their little homes, they'd have to make do with somewhat mangled domes.

All in all, Heilbron's Municipal Caravan Park provided consistent interruptions to our sleep for the few days we were there. The park was pretty enough, with a large dam full of waterbirds and an affable gate guard who was permanently stoned on weed, but locals kept sneaking through the fence to poach buck in the middle of the night and it was ringed by roads frequented by kamikaze truck drivers trying to dodge the nearby toll gates. Inquisitive ostriches tempted Tapiwa into futile gallops after them and horses raided our camp after dark, trashing the crockery and stealing scraps from buckets and boxes.

My team was also far from the well-oiled machine I had hoped it would be by now. Moving camp was taking even longer than it had at the beginning of the trip and I was continually battling to get hold of John when I needed him on the road. His cellphone wasn't charged, it was turned off, he didn't hear it – I was getting exasperated with the excuses. Louis appeared to be deeply unhappy, and I was still losing my cool with uncharacteristic and humiliating regularity. Perhaps, I thought, we were getting progressively exhausted. I must try and fix that.

My tent, protected by the trees from the Everestian storm

To do so, I would have to renege on Richard's timetable and that saddened me. His party only rested on Sundays (as I presume everyone did in those devoutly religious times) but I had to write on those days and the guys had many chores to see to, so effectively we never took a break from the rigours of the expedition. I decided, therefore, to increase my daily distances and cover in five days what I had previously done in six so that the team could kick back and enjoy at least part of every weekend. I now walked 35, 36, 40 kilometres a day in dust and heat, keeping my pace moderate and steady so as to avoid pushing myself too hard. It seemed to work and I got steadily stronger and fitter on the back roads of the Free State. I still had my little stone – the one chosen for me by Louis at Howick Falls after the original one had been stolen – and I stubbornly continued to place it at the end of each day's walk and pick it up at the beginning of the next, despite Mrs Mthembu's advice that candles and coins should serve as my talismans. And I can only think that my defiance was the cause of a series of bizarre events that took place one day this week.

I was soldiering along when, out of nowhere, a raptor started to dive-bomb me over and over again, as if by command. Next, a snake slithered across my path, followed by a man who ran up and tried to kiss me. It was clear within seconds that he was deranged and that he had no intention of raping or molesting me, but the incident unnerved me considerably. I pushed him away and screamed, 'No! No! No!' repeatedly until he slunk away, giggling. And just when I was recovering from the fright I was hammered by yet another terrifying storm. It approached fast and caught me on top of an exposed hill with nowhere to hide from the hail and lightning. I dumped all the metal objects I had on me, ran a few metres and crouched in the long grass at the side of the road, my back pelted by thumbnail-sized ice and jagged electric strikes to my left and right.

All at once it was over. The sun came out, a friend made me laugh on my cellphone and I put all foolishness behind me. Half an hour later I reached the end of my day's walk to find that I had left the stone behind...

The Free State: dirt roads and big vistas

Extinction is forever – or is it?

The quagga was first described and illustrated for the 'outside' world in 1811 by the naturalist William Burchell, but had been given its popular name by the 'Hottentot' (known more appropriately today as the Khoikhoi) people in an onomatopoeic imitation of its bark-like call. It occurred predominantly in the Karoo and southern Free State and resembled the zebra in as much as it had black and white stripes on its head and neck. But, judging by contemporary sketches, its body was brown, it was stockier and it had a thicker mane and tail. In the 19th-century there was an

William Cornwallis Harris's painting of the quagga

indiscriminate use of the term 'quagga' for any zebra – particularly in the Afrikaans language – and this contributed to its demise not being recognised until it was too late to reverse. Indeed, the quagga was doomed to become one of the early victims of European extermination, hunted by sportsmen and shot by farmers who perceived it as a competitor to their grass-eating livestock. In 1878 this beautiful equine curiosity saw its last wild sunset and five years later the last specimen on earth died in cold and lonely captivity in an Amsterdam zoo, without anyone realising that she was the last of her kind.

But 23 specimens of the quagga had been left in museums around the world and about four decades ago they became the source of intense interest to Reinhold Rau, a taxidermist working in Cape Town's Iziko museum (who sadly died during the writing of this book). Rau committed himself to the ambitious goal of trying to revive the species. Slowly he gathered DNA material from dried blood and animal tissue left on the skins of the stuffed animals and sent it off for analysis by scientists interested in investigating its genetic links (or otherwise) to the plains zebra (*Equus burchellii*) that continue to roam our subcontinent. Those tests proved that the quagga's genetic code differed from that of the horse in 12 locations, from the mountain zebra in 10 – but from the plains zebra not in the slightest. Eureka! What Rau and his team had discovered was that the quagga was a subspecies of the zebra and not a separate species. Maybe, they thought, it could be brought back in a programme of selective breeding using zebra that exhibited remnants of its particular markings and colouration. The project was started in 1987 with Rau and his team using zebra from the Etosha National Park, which they brought to the Western Cape. Latterly SANParks has contributed more animals from different locations but the process is slow and will take decades, if ever, to reach fruition. Since 1987, 128 foals have been born, some of which have stripe reduction on their bodies and legs and others the lovely brown colour for which the quagga was famous. The latest youngster, Henry, was born in January 2005 and is described as being the most quagga-like product of the scheme so far. The Quagga Breeding Project is highly controversial among our country's scientists and conservationists. Its detractors claim that only a look-alike of the quagga is attainable because the original equine not only had different morphology (appearance or form) but unique genetic adaptations to factors such climate and habitat. They also have concerns that the programme creates the impression that extinctions can be reversed and that this will result in yet more disregard for the fragility of our planet's endangered species.

Heilbron to Potchefstroom

An important milestone in both of our journeys

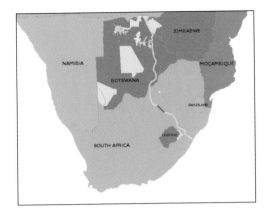

Heilbron to Potchefstroom
176 kilometres
Total: 729
Week 6
18–24 April

It was David Livingstone who said: 'Wagon travelling in Africa is a prolonged system of picnicking. Excellent for the health, and agreeable to those who are not over fastidious about trifles, and who delight in the open air.'

Following ghost wagon travellers was much the same, we had found thus far into our journey. The nooks and crannies of our vehicles were now filled with dust, and we'd got used to a bit of grime in the butter and the odd insect in our drinks. Our clothes were crumpled and our towels dank, but every night we went to bed deliciously wearied by sun and wind, lulled to sleep by nightjars and dikkops, then woken at dawn by doves and plovers. Having been on the road for nearly six weeks, our little habits were well known to each other. Franci was nauseated by mayonnaise and Karin abhorred meat. I liked my whiskies with soda and my tent pitched far away from the others. Louis hated doing laundry and never ate breakfast. John polished his boots and dressed up on Saturdays, in keeping with his Seventh Day Adventist faith. By now the team was a picture of health, if not cleanliness.

It occurs to me that some people chase stars, others dragons. Me, I chase wagons. And did lots of chasing this week in order to have Saturday and Sunday off. My distances have been: 30.69; 26.71; 40.00; 42.11 & 36.55. Found myself grunting with the effort at times. These are sore days, dig-in days, but I'm amazed how strong my body is – and how little I miss my stone!

Signs now that we're beginning to leave the grasslands behind. Acacias, bushwillows and sickle bushes in water courses and green mounds in the distance hint of the Vaal River ahead. I'll be glad to have the stimulation of new sights. The Free State turns you into a somnambulist with its gentle

Picnicking in a box on wheels

Early hunter/explorer journals provide some interesting and amusing insights into life on a 19th-century safari, and confirm just how tough adventure travel was at the time. Self-sufficiency was critical for the success of any expedition, and a traveller was called upon to be his own doctor, farrier, vet, carpenter, wagon mechanic, cobbler, whip-maker, blacksmith and gunsmith.

The Cape wagon most often used for expeditions to the African interior was little more than a rumbling box on wheels – its parts constructed strongly enough to withstand the strain of many years' rough travel, but suitably supple-jointed so as to give and bend for every unforgiving aspect of the terrain. For river crossings and high passes, the wagon could be taken apart, bit by bit, rather like a giant set of Lego. Brakes consisted of blocks of wood fashioned into crude brake shoes and lashed to the rear wheels – and descents of steep hills were sometimes managed by dragging a tree behind the wagon. Changing the extremely heavy, metal-rimmed wheels – let alone repairing them – could take the best part of a day. The wagon was hoisted by a 'lifter' (the early version of today's car jack) – a metal rod balanced on a block of ironwood that acted as a fulcrum, with the *trekboer's* wife often relegated the task of sitting on the other end of the pole while her husband changed the wheel. In the absence of today's oil for greasing, a mixture of animal fat and tar was used and this doubled as skin treatments and fly repellents for the livestock.

Richard Glyn's medicine chest and hunting horn

No AA on hand in the 19th century

Richard left us with a list of his food stores on his departure from Pietermaritzburg but neglected to describe the huge volumes of other necessary camping gear stored in his wagons' many trunks and side pockets – tools, goods for barter (particularly beads and tobacco), cooking utensils, water barrels, tar buckets, sewing and general repair kits, rolls of canvas, coarse-haired bedding, candles, writing material and navigation devices. His medical box is extant, much to my joy – a beautifully crafted mahogany chest filled with delicate glass bottles, hand scales, droppers, measures and a syringe. Its medicines comprise (among other things) laudanum, Epsom salts (almost empty), powdered rhubarb (untouched), sulphate of quinine, pure glycerine, essence of peppermint, cream of tartar and – most interestingly, given its current usage for sprains and contusions – Tincture of Arnica.

His contemporaries were known to also take leeches with them to induce bleeding, and used wet tobacco leaves for open wounds. Thomas Baines and WB Lord offer the following advice in their quite delightful campers' compendium, *Shifts and Expedients of Camp Life, Travel and Exploration* (Horace Cox, 1871). Noting that quinine is quite palatable in wine or rum, they deem it advisable 'if a man wants any peace while passing through most wild countries, or is doubtful of his own powers of self-denial... to convert all his wine into a strong solution of quinine before starting'.

Of course, when provisions or clothing were lost or damaged in the middle of nowhere, early travellers resorted to many an ingenious substitute. Ink could be made of a mixture of cow dung and milk, pipes constructed from a blesbok's leg bones and water carried in giraffe bladders. Crudely fashioned shoes or *veldschoen* were made out of recently slaughtered animals, with giraffe, eland or buffalo skins favoured for the soles and kudu for the uppers. Some of the African people made shoes by cutting the skin off the leg of an animal (as illustrated), sewing up one end and drawing it over their own feet, so that their heels rested where the hocks of the animal once were. (Readers wanting to try this must note, however, that zebra skin – despite being used in the illustration – is not recommended because it dries too hard.)

The culinary fare of my ancestors and other 19th-century travellers is not for fussy eaters, but the journals abound with advice for the unsqueamish facing a dead beast and an empty *potjie*. Antbear arms, so Richard tells us, are 'excellent scoff', but you'd be wise to avoid old

Zebra footwear

giraffe, which is 'rank and musty in the extreme and only the sausage machine enables you to get your teeth into it'. Elsewhere in the contemporary literature we are informed that Livingstone loved fresh crocodile eggs and that Frederick Courtenay Selous relished roasted elephant heart. Rhinoceros hump is, allegedly, delicious and tender as jelly after a whole night's baking in a hole covered with coals, and elephant foot, similarly prepared, is glutinous and not unlike brawn. Hippo head is best cooked with onions and cayenne pepper, pickled buffalo tongue goes down a storm and elephant-trunk steak or sliced roasted python make for ideal saddle-bag *padkos*. By far the most sought-after meat of the time was eland and (as many Africans will tell you to this day) flying ants are tasty both in their raw and roasted forms. After a good day's hunt, according to William Baldwin, everyone in camp was rewarded with an evening feast, the African staff sometimes 'chasing bites of roasted flesh with mouthfuls of raw innards and clotted blood'. Tea and coffee were precious commodities and alcohol was reserved for special occasions.

In these days before the invention of roll-up foam mattresses and camp beds, sleeping conditions were uncomfortable to say the least and in the summer months nights were passed in relentless bombardment by every insect the continent could provide. Baldwin experimented with using lighted cow dung as a means of repelling mosquitoes, but soon found himself smoked rather than bitten to death.

Should I have wanted to mimic exactly the rigours of an expedition of the 1800s, the aforementioned manual compiled by Thomas Baines and WB Lord provides 800 pages' worth of hints and recommendations that are humbling in their attention to detail. After many decades on expedition in Africa and elsewhere, these two seasoned campers compiled a book so comprehensive that it even recommends the number of pockets a traveller would find useful on his 'heavy serge frock'. Not only is a *Woman's Own*-type pattern provided for this shirt, but one for comfortable trousers too. Along with recommendations about larger and more obvious travel necessities (like boats, tents and wagons) are voluminous descriptions of the best stationery, cutlery, scientific instruments and fire-lighting equipment. Wooden bowls should

be used for tea because metal cups scald the lips; travellers should take extra tent pegs and, above all, not forget their frying pans. In a chapter entitled 'Demeanour towards Companions or Natives and White Servants', the reader learns of the benefits of military experience and discipline, along with the need for patience, justice, fairness and strength – and for knowing about local customs. The traveller is exhorted to remember that at heart all men are the same and that 'the difference between one and another is merely the overlay caused by etiquette, custom and education…'. Most importantly (in my case), the authors give the following advice:

'Everything during a journey beyond the limits of civilisation depends upon the good feeling and harmony among the party, and nothing short of unavoidable necessity should be suffered to interfere with this… forbearance is seldom repented of… [but] even an outspoken quarrel is better than the habit of "nursing the wrath to keep it warm".'

Life in the great outdoors

The Stalker!

monotony of cattle and mealies, more cattle and mealies, yet more cattle and mealies. So lulled by the landscape now that I hardly lift my head. Is listening to music a good or bad thing? It becomes a sedative, but I love time on my own on the road, letting random thoughts drift in and out of my mind.

Hilarious incident this morning. Louis was shadowing me in the truck, waiting to give me lunch, when three burly farmers, squeezed in the little cab of their bakkie, pulled up opposite me. They worried that I was being stalked by the 'white bearded man' in the Isuzu down the road. Did I want them to 'go and sort him out'?

The new sights I yearned for came in the form of a malachite necklace of hills that provided a spectacular end to the khaki universe we'd inhabited for the previous fortnight. The vegetation that covered this green chain of humps was an explosion of variety and form, and the quartzite rocks an explosion of chaos and colour. Explosion is an apposite word here, because what I walked into was the aftermath of the world's largest and oldest meteorite impact site – a geophysical treasure called the Vredefort Dome. Down into the crater I headed, the mighty Vaal River snaking around its edges like a piece of silver string.

Richard had given me no clues in The Diary as to which drift he'd used to cross the ancient waterway that is the Vaal – one of the oldest in the world – but Louis and I surmised that it could only have been at one of two places: Schoemansdrift or Scandinaviadrift. Using the latter would give me yet more legwork and I had, after all, paid my dues to the ancestors by slavishly following their Free State diversions, so I decided to take my 'wagons' over Schoemansdrift. Nowadays the crossing point is served by an ugly but functional concrete bridge and Tapiwa and I stopped on its midpoint to gaze at the rocky slab just visible beneath the fast-flowing waters where the old wagons would have crossed. How on earth, I wondered, had Richard's *voorlopers* and livestock got through that raging torrent? The diary was silent about their tribulations, but in the days before the Vaal was dammed upstream, the water must have been much higher than it is today, and fording the river must have taken huge bravery and effort, notwithstanding the fact that early travellers often had to wait days for floodwaters to subside before they could cross.

I sat down on the edge of the bridge with my little companion and paid silent tribute both to the old party and to my own at this important milestone in our journeys. With 700 kilometres behind me, I had covered one third of my walk

An earth-shattering moment

About two billion years ago (which is about half the age of our planet), this region was hit by an asteroid roughly the size of Table Mountain. It was travelling at a rate of 20 kilometres per second, exploded into our atmosphere and hit the earth with a force sufficient to excavate a hole about 50 kilometres deep and 150 kilometres wide. Soon afterwards the compressed earth started 'bouncing back' from the bottom of the pit, leaving Vredefort's famous pimple-like dome in the centre of the impact site.

The walls around the hole began to collapse, debris fell from the skies and the crater became shallower but wider, so that when seen from space it resembles ripples left by a stone in a pond. Concentric circles of hills were created around the meteorite's point of impact, the innermost of which is the one in which we were camped, the largest of which is as far away as Welkom and Johannesburg (about 150 kilometres). For the past century or so, the Dome has been the subject of controversy and debate among scientists anxious to establish why it is that our gold mines neatly follow the outer rim of this chain of disturbance. Did the explosion have the effect of driving what were once alluvial deposits deep underground? Or did the matter flung into the skies settle on our rich reefs and protect them from erosion? And what did the fireball do to life on Earth? At the time of this destructive visitor from space, only single-cell creatures – in the form of algae mats – were present on our little planet. Theories were bandied about (which have subsequently been discounted) that the asteroid drove matter within matter in some way so as to result in multicell life many eons later. Other hotly contended issues concerned whether it was a meteorite at all that caused all the damage, rather than volcanic activity or a gas 'shot' from the centre of the earth (dubbed a Verne shot after the science-fiction writer Jules Verne). But chemical traces of extraterrestrial matter have latterly been found buried in strange melt rocks in the area and they prove conclusively that the Vredefort Dome was created by a meteor in the greatest geological catastrophe yet discovered on Earth. The area's value has only recently been fully appreciated by those other than scientists. It has been declared a World Heritage Site and there are huge efforts underway to ensure that it is conserved and utilised responsibly.

Vredefort Dome – the inner 'ring' of the impact site

Crossing the Vaal – an emotional moment

without accident or injury and taken one million steps since leaving Durban, so the little Vitality pedometer on my belt told me. What a glowing endorsement this achievement was for bipedal locomotion, hard training, a moderate pace and good podiatry (thank you, Mark Karam, my podiatrist in Johannesburg who had made perfect-fit inserts for my takkies). Clearly, if ever there was an exercise perfectly designed for humankind, this was it. Here was a woman in her mid-forties who had covered one third of the width of this continent on foot and was feeling as good, in fact better, than she had on the day she started out. And to think that humankind got this marvellous, two-legged attribute (which freed our hands for all sort of mischief) in the mere wink of an evolutionary eye – long after the fireworks at the Vredefort Dome. Now I had crossed another of Africa's great rivers, and I would soon be on the last leg of the trip through South Africa before crossing into Botswana and eventually, Zimbabwe. I felt quietly elated.

April 17th: We came to Mooi-river-dorp [now called Potchefstroom], a town only a few years old but well watered, and with plenty of trees, each house is built on an allotment of 100 yards square, which of course makes the town cover a great deal of ground. This was the last town on our road so our supplies had to be replenished for the wilderness. Pavey, a store-keeper, entertained us in the most hospitable way, and his assistance, and our letters from Natal, particularly that from the governor, soon smoothed over all difficulties about passing our guns and gun powder through the

State. For the Boers are dreadfully afraid of these things being sold to Blacks, but look more after strangers than after their own people's smuggling. Our wagons were surrounded all day by Boers open-mouthed at our breechloaders, but they did not seem to believe in them, and could not understand where the cap should be. Field-Cornet Joubert and Pretorius, ex-president, also honoured us with a visit; a great heavy-looking Boer, with only a very small share of his father's talents.

I reached Potchefstroom late in the afternoon on Friday, as per Richard's schedule, but didn't fancy camping on its outskirts. Like many of South Africa's towns, it has an Ode to Americana on every corner and is a much less enchanting place than it was when the old party was here, so I asked Louis to find us a place to stay on the banks of the Vaal. He was the only member of our team who spoke Afrikaans and we thought it best for him to conduct negotiations on our behalf with the local farmers. Once again, he found us a magical home that fitted our most important requirements – beauty, privacy and simplicity. Not only was the camp site right on the river but it was at the end of a private road, far from unwanted disturbance. It had running water, a couple of loos and a thatched boma in which we could spread out our gear. Best of all, it was on land owned by GP Schoeman, the great-great-grandson of Martinus Gerhardus Schoeman, the man after whom the drift was named and whom I liked to think Richard, Robert and Henry would have met. Maybe they'd even stopped at the crumbling wagon house on the

Martinus Gerhardus Schoeman and his wife

corner of the farm. And maybe they'd guided us to this spot, I thought as I peeled off my shoes and socks after a long and trying week. The *sangoma* would certainly have believed so.

It rained intermittently that weekend (as it had for the Victorians) and we were treated to spectacular rainbows arching over the lazy Vaal River sliding past our camp. The crackle of rifle fire echoed in the *krantzes* on the opposite bank while I struggled once again to write my Web diary and John made good use of the boma's table tops to sort out problems and provisions. Louis went home to attend to some business, and my very dear uncle, Micky Bean, drove all the way from Johannesburg to deliver the maps

Generous host, GP Schoeman, Uncle Mick and me

we'd need for the journey through Botswana and Zimbabwe. Just looking at them made me nervous – I'd soon be walking through much harder terrain, sometimes without the vehicle back-up I'd had so far.

And my back-up was still of great concern to me. There is no doubt that John and Louis are trying hard, but cajoling, blasting, asking, moaning and praising don't seem to make a difference to the speed and efficiency with which these chaps work. Louis is an intellectual and I know he isn't enjoying the menial tasks of the expedition. John has a memory like a sieve and I'm getting so tired of reminding him to do things. I think we need help and I'm going to ask Sue Oxborrow to join the team.

Sue is an old friend who had been my second on The Blue Cross Challenge through Zimbabwe a few years before. During that race she'd proved herself to be efficient, intuitive and supportive, and I felt sure that her skills would dovetail nicely with those of the men. She's a seasoned camper, is knowledgeable about the African bush and has experience in driving a 4x4 through bad terrain. But could she leave her business in town?

'You'll have to give me a couple of weeks to sort out my life, Tricia, but I'd love to come. Really love to. Perhaps I could join you just before you leave for Botswana.'

I almost cried with relief.

The gorgeous Vaal

Potchefstroom to Coligny

Too many maize fields for my liking

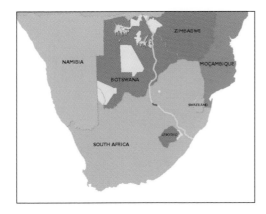

Potchefstroom to Coligny

67 kilometres

Total: 796

Week 7

25 April – 1 May

Richard's need to reprovision in Potchefstroom once again gave me a break from my walk. I yearned to spend this time lazing around camp, but there was filming and research to do, along with some pandering to my female vanity. *Local press want photos and I have folk coming to see me so went into town for a hair colour and blow dry. Really enjoyed the girlie day and having a break from the crew.*

In a welcome show of support, Rosemary and Ian Renton – friends from Johannesburg – drove down to take me out to dinner in one of Potchefstroom's restaurants, and their visit was followed by one from some members of the Glyn clan, headed by my 93-year-old uncle, Ronald. I was immensely flattered by his and his wife Mevagh's efforts to come all that way to see me, and decided I'd better clean myself up in preparation for 'civilised' company. So off I went for a hot shower in the local Virgin Active gym where the full-length mirrors of the ladies' locker room provided me with something of a shock. For the first time in my life, my pale skin had acquired a tan (albeit of the farmer variety with nut-brown lower limbs and lily-white uppers) and I had clearly lost weight, but my face was as dry as an old hide and I had a myriad new crinkles at the corners of my eyes. Sitting politely at dinner proved to be difficult – the ambient noise of hundreds of people was foreign to my ears after weeks in the great outdoors and I battled to make conversation over the din.

While John went shopping and Louis headed for the libraries, I paged through the books in my little travelling library for descriptions of life in early Potchefstroom. Professor Gert van den Berg, an acknowledged expert in the town's history, agreed to see me and, over tea in his home, this avuncular, intelligent man spun stories great and small about what Richard and Robert may have encountered here. At the time of their visit, the town was not only the capital of the Transvaal, but an inland trading Mecca, which was by far the largest in the region after the coastal towns of Cape Town, Durban and Port Elizabeth. The Voortrekkers' decision to settle here in the 1840s had been predicated on the fact that it was free from malaria, was close to hunting and trading destinations like Bechuanaland (now Botswana) and was largely unsettled – the local Batswana having fled in the face of raids by, among others, Mzilikazi and the Matabele.

Potchefstroom was originally laid out as a residential centre, designed to attract those Boers who had either been ruined by the trek or had failed at farming. Each was granted 10 acres of land on which it was hoped they would become self-supporting, and they soon developed their plots into cool oases that became legendary among travellers. Richard is not alone in having remarked on how beautiful the settlement was in the late 19th century, a garden town where everything grew in abundance – including dagga, which reached 15 feet according to early reports. Shady trees, sweet-scented orchards and

The Mooi River in the 1800s

colourful flowers covered the landscape, and the houses were so far apart that visitors could arrive at Market Square almost without realising that they'd entered an 'urban' area.

The crystal-clear Mooi River was led via furrows to the front of each plot and homeowners had a little sluice gate allowing them access to water according to a strict timetable. The town developed according to how fast these channels could be dug and it appears there were times when competition for water was energetic to say the least. Legend has it that one Boer woman became spoilt by her generous allocation of water before neighbours settled further downhill – and thus further down in the supply line – and found a novel way of preventing them from getting 'her' water by plonking her considerable behind in the furrow and wedging herself there to prevent the water from trickling downhill.

Tom and Day Coulter live at the source of the Mooi, on an old trekker farm called Gerhardminnebron, meaning 'Gerhard's beloved little fountain' and I visited them on one of my 'rest' days to learn more about this astounding river. Their house had been built in 1852, but despite the fact that it would have been there when my ancestors came through, it remains grand and sturdy. In a wooded glade at the bottom of the garden, the Mooi's water wells up out of the ground at a rate of 33 million gallons (150 million litres) a day, and this staggering amount of water neither diminishes nor increases year in and year out. The yield is seemingly independent of rainfall or seasonal influence, and regardless of summer sun or winter chill, the temperature of the water remains a constant 19° C.

Nachtmaal in Potchefstroom's Market Square

Community, commercial and religious life for the early citizens of Potchefstroom centred on the town's square, and it became the scene of brisk activity every three months when Boers from surrounding farms gathered for *Nachtmaal* or communion. Fernando do Costa Leal, a Portuguese diplomat who witnessed this gathering soon after the Glyns came through in 1870, left a colourful description of trekker society:

'All the products brought by the Boers, such as flour, corn, ostrich feathers, wool, cattle, butter, tobacco, hides and skins, even fruit and vegetables, everything is sold by public auction on the market. The principal square of Potchefstroom offers a picturesque sight to the stranger at the time of *Nachtmaal* (the same may be seen at Pretoria and other places). Everywhere are seen the heavy wagons of the Boers and square canvas tents, which look like small houses. The farmers, with their large felt hats adorned with ostrich feathers, and the women, with big headdresses with flaps, go from shop to shop, which are all of them full of people from morning till night. The bell rings for market and also for church. Weddings and christenings are numerous. At one of the doors is seen a long procession of mothers and their babies, whom they are anxious to have christened. At another door youths of 17 or 18 conduct to the altar, brides of 14. At night every tent on the square is lit with a lamp and all those happy families rest from the day's devotions and toil and lift up their voices singing psalms. Imagine the effect if you can: oxen tied in groups near every wagon, the white tents lit up inside contrasting with the dark of the night, and psalm-singing going on in 50 tents all singing different psalms at the same time. The Boers are very fond of talking about religious matters and know how to defend their opinions with quotations from the Bible. They strictly keep the Sabbath, which they spend, whether at home or in town, by going to church or singing psalms. They occupy themselves a great deal with politics but only as far as it concerns their own country. They take a great interest in the proceedings of the *Volksraad* (Legislative Assembly) and of the Executive Council and all the actions of the Government are strictly and severely criticised…. They are a race of strong men, who must however be considered ignorant and superstitious. The Boers are an active people, righteous, religious and unsurpassably hospitable, but suspicious of all strangers and particularly prejudiced against everything English.'

Indeed, it had been the Boers' original intention not to let Englishmen into the town at all. Having spent decades trying to assert their independence, the Voortrekkers were deeply suspicious of English traders and forbade them to settle or own property in Potchefstroom. With the normalisation of relations between Brit and Boer in the 1850s, however, the town soon expanded into a thriving, cosmopolitan hub where shopkeepers from as far afield as Sweden, Germany, France and England bartered with gusto. Everything from the latest Parisian fashions to giraffe-leg bones changed hands – the latter much prized as bed posts. Several of the Eastern Cape's 1820 settlers had 'branch offices' here and by the time Richard and Robert arrived, the storekeeper Pavey, mentioned in the diary, was one of about 30 doing business in the town.

The trekkers' social life, then, centred almost exclusively on the church. But it was the British who brought 'culture' to Potchefstroom, with both positive and negative consequences. The brothers Glyn would have been able to enjoy shows, cricket matches, horse races and parties in comfortable homes and hotels. The town had the largest number of 'public houses' in the Republic and a postal service that was both regular and efficient. When the mail coach arrived, it would tour the town, sounding a different tune on its horn according to the route it had just done, after which people would collect any post they were expecting. A less-than-admirable British import was a set of petty municipal by-laws copied exactly from those of Grahamstown. Boys were not allowed to fly kites in town lest they frighten the chickens, hoops could not be rolled above a certain speed, and men were forbidden from smoking pipes without caps outdoors (because the local tobacco was so inflammable).

They were rules for which former president Marthinus Wessel Pretorius must have had some sympathy, being the anglophile he was. His house is still meticulously maintained in the centre of Potchefstroom and I was struck by how beautifully it had been constructed. The rooms are cool and spacious and numerous photographs of the family adorn its white-washed walls. Mrs Pretorius looks strained and humourless and her husband fits Richard's description of him as being a 'great heavy-looking Boer'. But his expression is more resigned than dour and his blue eyes are sad. Poor man – he must have held more presidencies than anyone else in world history. First he was President of the Transvaal, next President of both the Transvaal and the Orange Free State, then back to only President of the Transvaal, and finally only President of the OFS. And despite his devoted (if lacklustre) leadership, he was never regarded – as Richard said – as having the talents of his father Andries (the trekker leader). To this day, Marthinus has never been forgiven by many Afrikaners for letting the diamond fields get into British hands.

Wild animals were common sights in the centre of Potchefstroom in the late 19th century, albeit mostly chained or domesticated ones. The German traveller Eduard Mohr, for instance, arrived in town with four ostriches, which he'd tamed to the point where they'd run after him like dogs when he went for walks in the veld. His journal *To the Victoria Falls of the Zambesi* (Books of Rhodesia facsimile edition, Bulawayo 1973) is a vivid account of his journey to the interior in 1870 and it contains several amusing anecdotes about his adventures with these birds. The ostriches 'must have travelled more than one thousand three hundred miles [2 080 kilometres] with me altogether; and as they grew bigger they became as accustomed to the noise of firing as old grenadiers. If I wanted to call them back when they were out with me, I had only to let off my gun, and they would come running up at once.' Mohr was summoned before a magistrate three times during his stay in Potchefstroom and heavily fined for the misadventures of his feathered friends, which trod on a small boy, panicked a span of oxen and indirectly caused the death of a foal. In answer to these charges, Mohr claimed that 'the appearance [of the birds] in the streets of a town was an ornithological event, which should be hailed by an intellectual and progressive community with joy and grateful admiration'. James Chapman, a famous young trader, had a habit of 'knocking up' (taming) quagga and bringing them into town, along with the rest of his menagerie of four young lions, two leopards, two meerkats, two springboks and one

What's in a name?

The origin of Potchefstroom's name is still the subject of some debate. Many believe the word to be a combination of the name of its founder, Voortrekker Hendrik Potgieter, *chef* the Dutch word for 'leader' and *stroom*, meaning 'stream' – a reference to the Mooi River. Others favour the theory that the name derives from pot shards or *scherf* found on the river banks, left there by the Tswana people who initially inhabited the area. The first foreign settlement on the banks of the river was upstream of the present town and was known as Oudedorp, resulting in many British travellers, like Richard Glyn, referring to the town as Mooi River Dorp even after it had been christened Potchefstroom. Some historians are of the opinion that they could also have done so because they were unable to pronounce the new name.

Marthinus the Misunderstood

Fernando do Costa Leal, the Portuguese diplomat, has left us with a far more sympathetic and comprehensive description of Pretorius than Richard's:

'The President of the Republic makes one think of the Roman Cincinnatus, as far as characters go, for he prefers the culture of his fields and the reins of his mule to the reigns of government. In a country such as this, in which every one of the inhabitants has lots of family relatives due to the many marriages between relatives, there reigns a spirit of familiarity and intimacy among all the people, and it is very difficult for a son of the people to enforce the law with strict justice. Pretorius is a tall and athletic man, with a tranquil and open face. Completely without pretentions, hospitable, incapable of doing the least bit of harm to anybody who does not obstinately molest him, full of placed indifference as regards his personal appearance, Pretorius is a good man in every respect, whether at home, in the *veldt* or negotiating some business of State. He likes foreigners very much and is greatly desirous to improve the social conditions of his people, and he is greatly in favour of education.'

Marthinus Wessel Pretorius

Zeederberg zebras

'weasel' (presumably a mongoose or otter). Teams of quagga and zebra were often used by commercial outfits like the Zeederberg Transport Company to pull their carts and carriages, owing to their stamina and their resistance to horse sickness.

And horse sickness must have been uppermost in the early Glyns' minds during their stay in Potchefstroom. This disease was known to be particularly rife here and contemporary accounts of the town make it sound like a charnel house, with large numbers of vultures hovering around to devour as many as five or six dead horses a day. Just three days before they arrived here, Robert had had to shoot one of his horses as it succumbed to frothing fluids and choking discharge and Moonlight had come close to taking a bullet in the brain for disobedience:

> *Moonlight was hard to pull up, and would run back and jerk your arm when you jumped off to fire, so I shot in vain, and after several attempts, the horse got away from me, and walked back all the way to the Cornelius River, which we had passed the day before, I following and feeling very much inclined to shoot him. I managed to catch him however at the water.*

Clearly the 'old butcher's hack' had a mind of his own – I liked him. The chances of acquiring more horses were slim for the Glyns after this point in their journey, and in order to allow for the possibility of losing more to the dreaded 'sickness', they bought two salted horses in town, one of which was a 'spirited chestnut' whom Richard named 'Nipper'. What trials those poor horses had ahead of them in the deep sand of the Kalahari periphery. The men picked up some more 'curs' at £1 each, bought mealies and yet more gunpowder and left Potchefstroom on 28 April, as I did.

> *Trecking by moonlight, our dogs bayed two porcupines, which were despatched with sticks, and another night we found them worrying an antbear, who did not try to defend himself, but only to dig himself underground; he had no teeth, but huge claws, and powerful arms, all these we found excellent scoff, and very fat.*

Pipped to the post

With the exception of David Livingstone, few 19th-century explorers of southern Africa's hinterland can rival James Chapman for his relentless wanderlust and insatiable curiosity. And, with the exception of Cecil John Rhodes, few entrepreneurs can rival this man's faith in the commercial potential of the African continent and his efforts to spearhead trade in its interior. Yet Chapman's exploits and discoveries remained largely unsung while he was alive and even today, while biographers acknowedge him as being one of the greatest pioneers of the period, they are slow to point out the precocity of his talents. James was born in Cape Town in 1831 and left home at the age of 13 to work for a trader in Durban. By the time he was 17 he had raised sufficient funds to purchase six wagon-loads of goods and set off for Potchefstroom where he opened the first store owned by an Englishman in the town. But a fall-out with a rival store keeper, Commandant Stephanus Schoeman, combined with the future he saw for himself as an ivory hunter, soon saw James closing up shop and heading north for the interior. He befriended Jan Viljoen and together they set off for the Zambezi in 1852. The party was turned back north of the Makgadikgadi Pans after threats by Sekgoma, who wanted to protect hunting in his domain, but the next year Chapman was back – this time heading for the Chobe River and Lake Ngami. Once there, he learned about an astounding waterfall on the Zambezi River and hired canoes and guides to go see the cascade. But his boatmen refused to take him the whole way for fear of being raided by the Matabele, and as a result Chapman narrowly missed becoming the first European to see what later became known as the Victoria Falls. He was only 22 years old at the time. The journey back was harrowing, with Chapman falling

James Chapman

victim to malaria and his oxen to *nagana*, but the following year – 1854 – he once again reached Lake Ngami and for a third time travelled to the area north of the Makgadikgadi Pans. Instead of pushing on for the Falls, however, Chapman struck out westwards for Walvis Bay, determined to assess the economic prospects of what is now Namibia and the viability of a trading route to and from the west coast of Africa. He sailed for Cape Town with a great dream in mind – to navigate the Zambezi River by boat – a dream that was to obsess him for the next 10 years. Marriage and children 'waylaid' him for a few years, but in 1859 he set off with Thomas Baines to try to fulfil this great plan (see page 261). Chapman ended his days in the diamond fields of Kimberley, dying at only 41 years of age. He is remembered for having pioneered the 'Salt Pan Route' on the eastern shore of the Makgadikgadi Pans (which the Glyns – among many others – were to use), for having 'discovered' the Gwaai River and for his many pioneering hunting/trading expeditions. But Chapman is also recognised now for the many specimens he collected for the South African Museum in Cape Town, the vocabulary of African languages he compiled for Sir George Grey, his pioneering efforts in photography (see page 20) and some of the most observant, frank and detailed journals ever written on the road. That they were compiled at such a young age makes them – and indeed all his efforts – truly remarkable.

Jack the Signalman

Stories of wild animals being put to work in the service of mankind don't come stranger than the one first published by Lawrence G Green and related to me by Tom and Day Coulter. Jack was a baboon who, believe it or not, plied his trade as a *voorloper* in the Eastern Cape. He was seen by James Erwin Wide, known as Jumper, leading a team of oxen into the market square of Uitenhage in the 1880s. Impressed by the baboon's ability, Jumper negotiated a good price for him, brought Jack home and taught him a whole lot of new skills. Jumper had recently lost both his lower legs in an accident and was battling to keep up with his duties as a signalman on the railways. So he trained Jack to operate his junction – and with impeccable results. When the Port Elizabeth train approached with its four hoots, Jack would get the keys, head to the signal box and dutifully pull the right lever to change tracks. When the East London locomotive, with, say, its three toots, came by, Jack was there on time, with the right combination. People being people, of course, local train users complained to the authorities about the dangers of having their fate placed in the hands of a baboon, so the railway management sent a commission of enquiry to Jack's Junction to see him in operation. And they too were impressed. So much so that they put Jack on a railway allowance and rations, which included his favourite treat – one tot of brandy per day. And lest you think this is the realm of fiction, there are photographs of Jack at work, there are no less than 25 written, eye-witness accounts of his abilities, and his skull can be seen today in The Albany Museum, Grahamstown.

'Jumper' Wide and his best friend Jack

Chatting to the locals

Only two days' walking this week, thanks to the ancestors' stop in Potch. Yet again I'm among too many maize fields for my liking. One farmer told me that the price of mealies has dropped from R1 600 to R300 per tonne in the last couple of years, so can't think why they continue planting the stuff. Weavers' nests like grass chandeliers; fiscal shrike looking for something to impale; blackened sunflowers hanging their heads in shame, burnt to a cinder by the force that they once turned to for life and sustenance. Taps killed a fieldmouse, its guts all red and throbbing against the brown veld. Blackjacks in my knickers after a road-side wee – not to be recommended! We're losing track of the days and world news now, and no one is happier about that than me.

L and J have developed good instincts for spotting which roads mirror the old wagon routes and invariably the local farmers know where we should be heading in order to mimic the 1863 route. The outspan points still thrill me – they're marked by large groves of old gum trees at the side of the road and spaced at a distance of roughly 30 to 35 kilometres from each other. By 1869 it was law that any farm on a wagon road had to offer outspan facilities to passing traffic – water, wood for fuel and fodder for the livestock. The government provided some of this (hence the quick-growing gums), but L tells me that the farmers were

No stopping at that outspan point

not compensated for the land they made available. He's having a battle finding us a new camp site. Loves these forays though – gets him away from 'teacher', I suspect.

Grothuis

Louis eventually settled on a position for our new camp, which he and John loved – and I simply hated. Once again, it had been offered to us by generous and hospitable locals and I didn't want to appear ungrateful, but to me the place was a monumental affront to nature and good taste. The house was called Grothuis, meaning 'cave house', and it had been built inside a wondrous, cathedral-like cavern that extended 200 metres into a dolomite hillside. Once upon a time, it would have been home to leopards, dassies and thousands of bats, but now it was still and sterile. In its cellars were some of the glorious formations that had originally been there before construction on the house began – ceiling-high shelves of rock, layered like chocolate pancakes in a tomb fit for kings and queens. A misguided amateur architect discovered the cave in the mid-1900s and decided he wanted to live within its mossy walls – with some improvements, though. So he set about constructing a four-storied monstrosity of concrete slabs, metal windows and doors, slasto flooring and bright pink bathrooms. Decades' worth of passion and pennies were spent on the ambitious eerie until he finally finished it in 1974. Triumphant and proud, the Sunday builder invited all his friends around for a housewarming, in the midst of which he suffered a massive stroke and dropped dead. Talk about Mother Nature's Revenge…

Fortunately, the new owner of Grothuis – or 'Grotty House', as I christened it – had renovations in mind, which the Earth Mum might like, but her cave would never be the same again. How difficult it is to tread lightly on the earth, and how indelible are the footprints we leave. We all build Grothuises of one kind or another, and our children have to live in them.

To me, the place had extremely bad karma and it affected the team extremely badly. I blasted Louis, he snapped back, John pouted and Tapiwa sulked. The boys want to sleep inside the house, and it may be hypocritical of me to use its facilities, but thank goodness my tent is on a slab outside so that I have my back to the monstrosity and can look out over the plains. Best we leave – and soon!

Coligny to Zeerust

Pumping head winds and clouds of fine red dust

Week 8
2–8 May

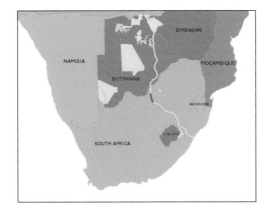

Coligny to Zeerust
147 kilometres
Total: 943
Week 8
2–8 May

My eighth week on the road started well, with a breathtaking dawn gliding past the Isuzu's windows as Louis drove me to my take-off point so far from our new camp at Grothuis. *Barbie-pink clouds against an impossibly turquoise sky.* I clocked up about 20 kilometres before joining three old friends for a picnic lunch at Coligny Dam. A few locals were celebrating the public holiday

Waking up to another spectacular African sky

on its banks and music blared from a marquee nearby. The dam's water was smelly and our thatched shelter tawdry, but Claude Goddard, Louise Ford, Gary Boswell and I giggled and reminisced until I took to the road once again, my legs somewhat wobbly after the wine we'd consumed. *Soon I'll be too far away to enjoy the support of dear folk like these and I will so miss it. They plied me with food, presents and love and sent me on my way, feeling confident about the task ahead. All three are cancer survivors – how much tougher than mine their roads have been.*

On the old wagon route north to Zeerust the next day, however, the God of Long-Distance Walking took swift action against the Boastful Betty who'd crowed so loudly at Schoemansdrift about feeling invincible. All at once I was visited with diarrhoea, bronchitis and a bad head cold. Pumping head winds slowed my progress and road-maintenance graders blew clouds of fine red dust in my face as I coughed, wheezed and sniffled my way through the hours. Walking 35 kilometres a day in these conditions was hardly the way to cure a respiratory tract infection, but the timetable was the timetable – it had to be kept. I even battled to raise a smile for wonderful Cora Bailey and her crew from CLAW (Community Led Animal Welfare). They had arrived with good news about our fund-raising efforts for township pets and plenty of collars for me to give out to the many chained dogs of the area. Animal cruelty issues had been much on my mind for several weeks now, as I passed these half-throttled creatures, cruelly restrained on short ropes, which they railed against in anger and frustration. I begged one woman to please release her dog, but she told me that farmers would shoot it on sight if it ran into their sheep paddocks. On the few tarred roads I walked, trucks had often overtaken me full of cattle, sheep and pigs being ferried to their slaughter. They craned their necks over the railings, not knowing that they were enjoying their last sights of the free world. I was beginning to find my carnivorous habits nauseating.

Eventually the God of Vegetative Variety arrived, with infinite rewards for my pain-wracked trudge through yet more of the region's grasslands. Little koppies began appearing, like leafy green islands in a lemon-and-gold sea. The hills are outcrops of dolomite and this beautiful, dark rock astounded early settlers with its capacity to retain water. Almost every road junction I came to carried a signposted reminder of the abundant springs and the wildlife the region once supported: Leeuwfontein (Lion Fountain), Wolvenfontein (Hyena Fountain), Duikerfontein. The game is long gone by now, of course, but I was alarmed to see in Richard's diary that it had even disappeared by 1863:

Verdant islands in a sea of grass

May 1ˢᵗ. Game scarce and very wild, but plenty of Koran [korhaan] of three kinds, which afford good sport, and are capital eating.

May 2ⁿᵈ. We trekked steadily on, the country pretty with wooded hills, but very bad roads for the wagons, deep watercourses and rocky ground, plenty of streams and a good many farm houses… This was the country where Gordon Cumming had some of his best shooting, but now such a thing as a buffalo or rhinoceros has not existed for years!

History gurus – Roger Webster and Izak Barnard

Dolomite country is also diamond country, of course, as I was reminded by two more friends who arrived for a quick visit. Izak Barnard is an elderly Afrikaner wilderness guide who is as close to a walking history encyclopaedia as anyone I've ever met, and Roger Webster has published several collections of our country's fascinating stories. Both men had given me invaluable help in finding the old wagon routes through South Africa and Botswana in the months before my walk started, and I was delighted to see them on the route we'd meticulously planned together. We munched on boiled eggs and tinned tuna next to a barn, while they told me more about the treasure-rich kimberlite pipes within the dolomite that lured fortune-seekers from the four corners of the globe. Nearby was the town of Bakerville, now comparatively quiet with some 20 diehard diggers left there, still clinging to the get-rich-quick dream. In 1926, though, it was the scene of a most frantic scramble as 25 000 men tore away from the starting line in a desperate bid to secure their claims on yet another corner of our mineral-rich country. Similarly frenetic but small-scale foraging was evident on many more of the area's hillsides – ugly gouges made by landowners hoping they'd strike it lucky.

Ironically, given how well watered the region is, an incident involving a severe shortage of water resulted in the birth of Lichtenburg, the largest town hereabouts. Louis found a wonderful story about one Hendrik Greeff who ran out of water for his family and oxen while trekking back to his farm after a hunting excursion in the 1850s. What his wife and children were doing with him on a hunt is not known, but things got so dire that he eventually knelt at the base of a white stinkwood and prayed for the good Lord to save his family. And a voice from on high was heard to say, 'Look in the tree.' So Hendrik got up off his knees and there, in a deep bowl formed between the two main trunks was water – lots and lots of water. So grateful was Greeff that he made a vow there and then (as trekkers were wont to do) that he and all his descendants would gather every year on that date and at that tree to give thanks for the family's deliverance from death. To this day, the Greeffs honour the tradition, we're told, but I doubt that it's the same stinkwood that they gather around. As a further gesture of gratitude for the saving of his family, Hendrik offered his farm to the government for the foundation of the town of Lichtenburg.

Now there is one man whom most South Africans associate with Lichtenburg and that is Ferdie Hartzenberg, one-time leader of the Conservative Party

The Mad Scot

Gordon Roualeyn Cumming undertook the longest of the 19th-century foreign hunting safaris when he travelled through the Cape Province, the Orange Free State, the (then) Transvaal and Bechuanaland (now Botswana) between 1844 and 1849. He was a flamboyant Scot and arguably one of the most bloodthirsty of the sport hunters to visit our shores. Cumming was an enormous man (6 feet 4 inches) with a long, bright-red beard, and he preferred hunting in veldschoens and his green-and-yellow Gordon kilt, which must give new meaning to the term 'saddle burn'. Described as quite mad by those who travelled with him, his appearance and conduct alarmed many whose paths he crossed – including the Boers, who could hardly be described as pictures of sartorial elegance at the time. But they loved the man, not only because he plied them with gin but because, being Scot, he too was anti-English. One shudders to think, however, what the gentle Livingstone thought of this extremely heavily armed, obsessive hunter for whom no bag was ever big enough. Legends which persist about Cumming centre on quite savage habits. He is reputed to have buried his head in the carcass of a kill to 'blood' himself, and to have strangled animals with his bare hands and eaten pieces of them while they were still alive. In lean times, he ate locusts with his dogs and was once spotted drinking warm milk from the teats of a dying oryx. But he was not altogether inured to the beauty of the animals he pursued, describing in his memoir *A Hunter's Life in South Africa* (John Murray, 1850) how he plucked a lock from the black mane of a magnificent lion he'd just shot and placed it carefully 'in my bosom'. Nor was he dismissive of the supreme tracking skills and bush knowledge of the Bushmen he came across and, unlike so many of his peers, developed a great friendship with one of them, Ruyter, who returned home with him at the end of his trip. Cumming was brave to the point of being reckless, resourceful, innovative and extremely tough (even by the gruelling standards of the day). He found elephant hunting 'overpoweringly exciting' and he excelled at very close pursuit of these and other big game. When he returned to England he took 30 tons of Africana with him, including his Cape wagon and a collection of specimens, which he made a living through exhibiting around the country – along with the loyal Ruyter. Despite his published journal being so popular that it briefly exceeded Dickens' novels in sales, when he died at the age of 47, Cumming was flat broke and, according to some, an alcoholic.

Gordon Cumming

– arch racist to some, tireless worker for Afrikaner unity to others, and friend since 'varsity to Louis. And who should I find myself sharing a pub table with one day that week but Mr Hartzenberg himself and his comely wife Judy. Never one to let a good opportunity for ribbing pass me by, I asked him how he felt about plans to change the street named after him to Mbeki Drive. 'It's worse than that,' he ribbed in reply, 'they're changing it to Beyers Naudé Drive. He was my *dominee* once upon a time – until he changed his views and I didn't change mine!' A little echo of the old diary, I thought, as I sat there with Ferdie. Richard too had met an Afrikaner 'hero' on his travels who could also be accused of having failed to feel the winds of change – Marthinus Wessel Pretorius.

Every day of my walk I was getting reminders of how grateful we South Africans should be that people like Beyers Naudé did change their views and help build our free nation. Take Elizabeth, for example, a 12-year-old Tswana girl who joined me with her two school friends. As we walked together they chatted about their ambitions to be doctors and teachers while I chatted about the dangers of teenage pregnancies (an old hobbyhorse of mine). Several kilometres later it emerged that they were staying with me in order to protect me against harm. 'There are many bad men around here,' said this tiny slip of a girl, 'and you should not be alone.' I was deeply touched by their concern. When they thought me to be past the danger point, they turned around for home, only to come running back after a few minutes, worried that I might not have eaten for a while. Not half an hour later, a man bolted through a barbed wire fence at the side of the road, wearing a grubby trench coat and looking every inch one of the 'bad men' about which Elizabeth had warned me. I shrunk back as he came towards me, grappling for the pepper spray in my bag. Then he took off his felt hat and asked if I was lost and needed help. 'Go left at the next road,' he said. 'There are some white people there who have a car. They will help you.'

Tapiwa and I had our first couple of cross-country romps during the week's walk on routes carefully mapped for us by Louis, who'd found some short cuts used by 19th-century travellers. What adventures they turned out to be for my little dog – guinea fowl and springbok to chase, squirrels to dig for and a stiff breeze to keep us cool on those undulating hills. We were having a ball when all of a sudden we came across a herd of about 80 cows, with their calves, in a fenced paddock we had to get through to continue our hike. I was worried about frightening the youngsters, so put Taps on his lead and started quietly moving through them. Closer and closer they came, crowding us on all sides with inquisitive stares. But their mood swiftly turned hostile. Very hostile. Suddenly it dawned on me that they really wanted to harm Tapiwa.

A large brown harridan with one crooked horn and an evil eye started bellowing and chasing us, at which point the rest of the herd followed suit. I picked up a stick and started trying to beat them off, screaming obscenities and getting increasingly alarmed that I wasn't deterring them at all. Fearing that we were doomed, I let Tapiwa off the lead, believing that he'd have a better chance of running away from them without me. But he immediately jumped to my defence and joined the fray. That only upped the 'anti' in the Mums. Eventually there was nothing for it but to run – and run fast – to a gate at the end of the enclosure and quickly sneak behind it.

'What on earth provoked that?' I wondered. 'These are bovine creatures, for goodness sake, known for their quiet and gentle dispositions!' Soon enough we came to the homestead of Hansie Snyman, a sixth-generation farmer in the area, who explained what had happened. The cows live, graze and calve in the bush and they have had to become very aggressive to cope with marauding jackals that attack their newborn calves. To them, Tapiwa was nothing more than a scavenging predator and therefore a threat to everything they hold dear.

On Hansie's farm we had well and truly arrived in the verdant wonder world of the Marico, great tunnels of olives, bushwillows, karees and acacias. I was approaching another important juncture in my journey and my excitement rose with every step.

> *May 2ⁿᵈ. Sent Gifford to ride in to Jan Viljoen's, the Commandant of Merico… to see what could be done about getting guides, drivers etc. for the far interior.*
>
> *May 6ᵗʰ. Gifford came back to meet us with Viljoen, a Boer of French extraction, very lively and spirited, very different from his neighbours, the Doppers, who are a kind of Quakers, and comprise most of the old original Boers. Viljoen was a great hunter, and killed no end of elephants, having been several years ago very near to the Zambezi Falls, much farther than any other Boer. He had once been dragged off his horse by a lion, and his shoulder dreadfully mauled; the saddle had been pulled round on the horse, who got frightened at it and kicked it off, the noise of its fall frightened the lion and he left Viljoen… We outspanned on the part of the road nearest Viljoen's house for 2 days.*

Finding Jan Viljoen's farm had obsessed me during my pre-walk research. For reasons I don't quite understand, I had been desperate to know exactly where

Richard, Robert and Henry had camped during their time in the Marico, and I would never have found the farm had it not been for the efforts of a local amateur historian with Sherlock Holmesian tenacity – Arto Toivonen. Arto is more than mildly eccentric and he lives in semi-seclusion on a remote farm in the district. He has made it his business to become knowledgeable in all aspects of local culture, particularly that of the Bahurutshe people, whose language he speaks with reasonable fluency. Over a crackling phone line, I had put him on the trail of finding Viljoen's farm and it took a fair bit of detective work to locate it. Not only has it changed hands often in the intervening years, but it carries the same name as several other old trekker farms in the area – Vergenoeg, meaning 'far enough' (as in 'far enough' from those pesky Brits with their acquisitive ways and liberal laws). After digging around in archival deeds in the town of Zeerust, Arto eventually e-mailed to say that he'd found the farm.

Although I had driven down to the area shortly afterwards to establish my route through it and had seen Viljoen's farm on that occasion, now I was about to see it on foot. It's such a different feeling from when we reccied by car. Simply can't credit that I've actually walked here from the sea!

I ended the week's journey at the quiet graveside of Jan Viljoen and once again breathed a sigh of relief for my safe arrival at yet another milestone in my walk. Jan lies in tangled grove of thorn trees next to his wife Maria, both of them honoured by large marble tombstones. Several of their 17 children, who didn't make it past toddlerhood in those disease-ridden times, surround their parents under tiny, unmarked mounds of earth that battle against invasive roots and weeds. Viljoen's massive farm, which was once truly Texan in extent, has been carved up into eight slivers of land, one of which is owned by an utterly charming man by the name of Derik Pelser. With the grace and hospitality we'd come to expect from Afrikaner people by now, Derik offered us a camp site next to a former school

Lekker locals – Derik Pelser and Arto Toivenen

on the property so that we'd have the use of running water and electricity. John set up my tent next to one of the classrooms and I collapsed into bed, knowing that the weekend ahead would be far from restful.

And sure enough, Oom Jan's *plek* was indeed the scene of frantic activity for the next couple of days as we set about doing a massive stocktake of our provisions. Within a week we'd be crossing the border into Botswana and would then be far from the luxurious shops that South Africa boasts, so it was important to buy as much as we could in advance of our departure. Sue Oxborrow drove up from Johannesburg and she and I slaved through piles of tins and boxes, and drew up lists of what she needed to buy in the city before coming back to join the expedition for good at our next camp. And the lists were very

Sue Oxborrow

long indeed, because I was determined that we would eat well throughout our journey, having experienced on previous expeditions what a negative effect poor nutrition has on both health and morale.

We tried out some of the camping equipment she'd kindly agreed to lend us because some of ours had already proved to be unsuitable for the rigours of a long trip, and I said goodbye at last to my (unused) hair dryer and other feminine indulgences. In a very rash moment, I even put my bulky soda-making machine into her car for transport back home, and regretted it the minute she left. I had developed a close relationship with another Walker on the trip, Johnny, and liked him best sparkling not still. It would not be long before I begged Karin for the machine to be returned to camp on her next filming visit. The most important aspect of our preparations for the wilderness ahead, however, was getting some training in GPS (Global Positioning System) navigation. Once we crossed the border, there would often be no roads and the vehicles would not always be able to shadow me. I would have to walk through the bush alone to prearranged rendezvous points where the team would wait for me. In order to get through Botswana and Zimbabwe safely, we'd have to be able to read maps well, isolate coordinates on them and become competent in all aspects of compass work. And as a woman who could hardly find her way around the city of Johannesburg armed with a street map, that was a daunting prospect.

Getting ready for Botswana

Mathys Thompson from Avnic Trading pulled into our little camp and we settled down dutifully for a morning's lessons. Avnic is the local agent for Garmin, whose astounding GPS navigation devices are used by adventurers around the world. These hand-held electronic mapping and compass instruments had the capability of guiding us through the terrain ahead with ease – if we knew how

Mathys Thompson and his bemused students

to use them. John, being the techno-fundi he is, cottoned on fast to Mathys's instructions, but Sue, Louis and I floundered around that little school yard like headless chickens, circling, backtracking and generally getting utterly confused by the data that confronted us on the Garmins' little screens. Our performance was simply abysmal and I became even more afraid of what lay ahead than I had been before.

It pleased me deeply to be camping on Old Man Jan's farm, but ever since I'd first seen it all those months before, I'd been consumed with curiosity as to where his homestead had been. Exactly where had my ancestors negotiated with him for the guides, oxen and advice he could provide for the wilderness ahead, I wondered. Where had they shared stories about the route, the game and the mighty Zambezi River? Neither Arto nor Derik could tell me, and the farm had nothing by way of old stone foundations to indicate where the 19th-century Viljoens had lived and loved. On Sunday, however, Arto and Louis managed to track down the last of Jan's descendants still living in the Marico district, and Willie Viljoen came around for tea and a chat. What he told me was nothing short of spooky. We sat outside my little tent while Karin filmed our conversation about his feisty forebear until I could contain myself no more.

'You know, Willie, no one can tell me where the old man lived. Would you perhaps know?'

'Ja,' he said quickly, 'right here. Your tent is pitched under the grand old belhambra tree the Viljoens used to plant at the front door of all their homes and you can just see a faint outline of the old house between the school rooms over there.'

I was gobsmacked. By pure fluke we were camped in exactly the right place on a tiny fragment of the old farm. Was it coincidence? Synchronicity? Or had the ancestors once again guided us to the right place?

Willie Viljoen

Feisty Jan Viljoen

Had he lived a century later, I have no doubt that Jan Viljoen – with his identity suitably disguised – would have featured in the tales of Herman Charles Bosman, the Marico storyteller who found such a rich source of larger-than-life characters in this region. There are indeed few personalities in the 19th-century hunting annals who provide such interesting anecdotes and contradictions as Viljoen.

Jan Viljoen, Elephant Hunter

authorities of the time. He was, apparently, the only Boer whom Sekgoma would tolerate – in fact, the Bamangwato *kgosi* once saved his life. After a group of *trekkers* sacked Livingstone's mission at Kolobeng (south of the modern town of Gaborone) in 1852 and abducted hundreds of Bakwena women and children – among them Sechele's son – Viljoen returned the child to the chief and secured a peace between the warring parties. Three years later he was with the first group to secure hunting rights in Matabeleland, and soon afterwards was sent by the President of the Transvaal to try to gain control of Mzilikazi's gold-bearing land for the Boers – albeit without success. Viljoen escorted James Chapman to Bechuanaland and taught him how to hunt elephant and he did the same for Frederick Courtenay Selous in Mashonaland 20 years later. He also accompanied Robert Moffat into the interior, gave advice and guides to countless other missionaries and adventurers heading northwards from his farm, and is described in the contemporary literature as being unfailingly courteous and hospitable towards travellers of all nationalities who passed through his hands.

Many contemporary accounts confirm Richard's impression of the man as being energetic, tough and vivacious. Viljoen commanded huge authority in the Marico (first as Field-Cornet, later Commandant of the area) and although small and wiry in stature, he was regarded by his peers as being the greatest elephant hunter of his age. After 30 years in the field, he was reputed to have shot more of these animals than anyone other than Petrus Jacobs, whose life-time tally was roughly 500. The quest for ivory lured Viljoen far into the 'Dark Continent' long before it was common to do so. He became an intrepid traveller through uncharted territory and was among the first foreigners to reach the Zambezi River. Some of his descendants claim that Viljoen saw the Victoria Falls before Livingstone, but his conversation with Richard Glyn confirms that, in fact, he never did set eyes upon that mighty cascade. Nonetheless, penetrating so far inland in the 1850s was a considerable feat and would not have been possible had Viljoen not been such a skilled negotiator with much-feared chiefs like Mzilikazi, Sekgoma and Sechele. Indeed, his well-fostered relationship with these men was much utilised by the Boer

That he even gave the time of day to the Englishmen who sought his help is remarkable, given that he had been captured by the British at the Battle of Boomplaats in 1848, had barely escaped hanging and had a price on his head for years. In fact, it was this threat that caused him to trek westwards and settle in the Marico, and resulted in his naming his farm as previously described.

But Jan Viljoen was also renowned for being obstinate, belligerent and arrogant. He was a dogmatic, religious fanatic who subscribed to the Dopper faith – the popular name for the Gereformeerde Kerk van Zuid-Afrika. The word *dopper* is believed to be a corruption of *domper*, meaning 'one who damps down', in reference to this church's strict Calvinist principles – principles that were far more conservative than those of the older Dutch Reformed Church (Nederduitse Gereformeerde Kerk or NGK). When Dominee Frans Lion-Cachet arrived in the Marico to establish an NGK community there, Viljoen and some of his cronies met the preacher on the outskirts of the district, told Lion-Cachet that he was not welcome and forcibly hauled his wagon off the road. Two days later when the Dominee returned, apparently undeterred by the threat, Viljoen took a *sjambok* and beat the living daylights out of him. But Lion-Cachet persisted and his efforts clearly paid off because his more liberal NGK now thrives in those parts, while a mere 800 Doppers remain in the Marico, still clinging to their somewhat quaint beliefs that it is sinful to dance or sing hymns other than the psalms.

Even more unsavoury are accusations that Viljoen betrayed Mzilikazi's trust by selling guns to some of the Mashona, as a result of which they were ravaged by their irate adversary. He led a revolt against the Transvaal Volksraad in 1863 when his choice of president (MW Pretorius) failed to be elected, was accused of instigating a war between the Matabele and the Bamangwato and is also reputed to have used every thug tactic he could think of to subvert the prosecution of his son, accused of murdering a Barolong woman and her child. Jan Viljoen lived to his eighties and was described as as energetic and feisty in his later years, as he had been when he first started roaming our continent.

A camp site chosen by the ancestors?

Here lies Oom Jan

Zeerust to Lekgophung

A turning point in my journey

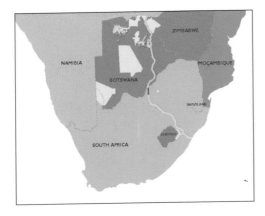

Zeerust to Lekgophung

106 kilometres

Total: 1 050

Week 9

9–15 May

'I'd rather have been on the 1863 trip,' I thought to myself as I steamed around Zeerust on Monday morning. For a start, this awful town wouldn't have been here at all, and I wouldn't have to be doing things like rushing to the bank for foreign currency, getting permission to take my dog across the border, organising payment for our satellite phones and waiting in a queue in the chemist for antibiotics for my bad chest. The crew had dinner at the Spur in town, where I learned by inference that they don't think I smell the roses enough. Hard to convey to these guys how much rests on my shoulders. Besides which, living with passion doesn't mean sitting around. It means burning yourself up long before you die!

While I sorted out a litany of bureaucratic nightmares, Richard and his crew were busy selecting staff who knew something of the road ahead, and oxen that could cope with the Kalahari's heavy sand better than the little Nguni cattle they'd used thus far. The recruitment drive for both men and oxen took place at the kraal of Chief Moilwa, so having had enough of town, I drove to his descendant's village with Karin and Arto (who had set up a meeting with the Bahurutshes' current paramount chief). What was a kraal in 1863 is now a sprawling settlement on each side of the main road to Botswana. It's called Dinokana, after the stream that feeds the village and that has never dried up in living memory.

Kgosi (Chief) Godfrey Moilwa greeted us looking like a former soccer star in a black-and-white tracksuit and matching cap. He has the easy charm of a man who's sufficiently comfortable with his authority not to be hung up on stuffy protocol. His home is modest and his manner affable, and we sat chatting in his lounge under an oil painting of the Bahurutshe people's totem animal, the baboon. I steered the conversation towards the hunting my ancestors had come here to do, and he told me of the long tradition his people had of supplying trackers and guides to wilderness expeditions.

'With the liberation of our country, though, I now have authority over what is shot on our land. There are lots of kudu and leopard in these mountains, but no one may kill them without a permit from me. People may not lay traps and they may not hunt with dogs. We manage our wildlife resources in collaboration with the National Parks Board.'

I asked whether the kgosi knew any stories from the very old days, which had been handed down from generation to generation, hoping that he might have heard something of the time in which his ancestor met mine. His great-great-grandfather was described in Richard's diary as a 'once-powerful man, now reduced to living on his own land by sufferance of the Boers'. My host slowly related the tale of that painful time, when the Bahurutshe collaborated with the Boers to chase Mzilikazi into Matabeleland (in what is now Zimbabwe). When Moilwa's people returned to their ancestral lands, they found them occupied by the trekkers and some historians are of the opinion that they were allowed to stay in the area on condition that they provided free (or virtually free) labour to white farmers. This view the kgosi could not confirm, nor had his oral tradition preserved any tales from the 1860s, but memories of his people's lengthy resistance to the apartheid regime were fresh and vivid. The evidence of a hand grenade thrown at his bedroom window was still there – the result of public dissent over the installation of another leader by the apartheid-backed Bophuthatswana regime of Lucas Mangope. At present, the African people around Zeerust are still battling to get their land back, but claims for its reinstatement are currently being analysed by the government and Kgosi Moilwa is confident of a successful outcome to their petitions.

By Saturday afternoon 9th, we had everything ready for the desert we were soon to enter, and by Viljoen's advice settled to take a road by the Ngotwane River, instead of that by Sechele's kraal, which tho' longer is much more used by traders... That afternoon we trecked only a short distance just to try our fresh hands and oxen, and stayed Sunday by the house of Martin Swartz, the greatest and in fact only regular elephant hunter remaining from this part of the country, for it no longer pays except when undertaken on a great scale, as the distance is now too great (far into Mzilikazi country) to obtain a load of ivory.

11th. Bush country, outspanned in a pass called Bassport... first taste of the fine loose sea sand we were soon to see so much of.

The Bahurutshe Baboon

Legends differ as to how the Bahurutshe came to adopt the baboon as their totem animal. Kgosi Moilwa has it that when Mzilikazi's impis rampaged through this area during the Mfecane, the Bahurutshe were chased to a cave near Rustenburg, which was home to a troupe of baboons. The primates left the cave but stayed at its entrance while Moilwa's clan hid inside and remained undetected by the Zulu warriors. In exchange for saving the lives of his people, the grateful Bahurutshe *kgosi* declared the baboon to be sacred and henceforth protected on all land owned by his people. Another version of the totem's origin asserts that an early female chief of the tribe, Mohurutse had a son who brought back a young *tshwenyane* (baboon) from one of his hunting expeditions and kept it as a pet. The primate became popular among his followers and reviled by his brother's — so much so that the group split over the issue, one branch retaining the kudu as their symbol and the other the baboon.

To this day, killing or harming a baboon is taboo for the Bahurutshe, and transgression is punishable by a jail sentence, so the *kgosi* told me. In fact, all Tswana groups have totem animals and the practice makes good sense to modern conservationists because it means that, with adequate control in their areas, species as diverse as leopard, crocodile and eland have havens in which they can live and breed with impunity.

Kgosi Godfrey Moilwa and the Bahurutshe Totem

The Dwarsberg – 'always in your way'

A lost city

When the missionary John Campbell travelled through the Marico in 1820 he came across an enormous, thriving settlement built on the crest of a flat-topped hill – and described it as being the most beautiful he'd seen in his travels. Its inhabitants lived in conical-shaped rondavels made of tightly packed stone, topped by neat thatching. The homesteads' walls were plastered in orange, brown and yellow clays and their entrances fronted with intricately woven mats. The kraal of the chief was festooned with drawings of elephant, leopards and birds; huge earthen pots of different shapes and colours lined its walls and the evidence of sophisticated smithery – in the form of hoes and assegais – was everywhere in evidence

Campbell described the people as 'jovial and cooperative', adorned in leopard-skin regalia and gorgeous beads. He watched their initiation and divining ceremonies, their medical procedures and animal husbandry – and he was astounded by this well-ordered, peaceful society.

What Campbell had come across was Kaditshwene – the largest Iron Age settlement ever built in South Africa, home to an estimated 20 000 people and the manufacturing, trading and cultural capital of the Bahurutshe. It is postulated that the name means 'what an incredible amount of baboons' and it was established in a range of hills called Tshwen-yane about 25 kilometres northeast of Zeerust. At the time, the city's population exceeded that of Cape Town and archaeologists now estimate that the site had been occupied since the late 15th century. But only a year after Campbell saw its wonders, Kaditshwene's hill-top defences crumbled in the face of an attack by Mantatisi, queen of the Batlokwa. Her ravaging hordes were followed by Sebetwane and the Bafokeng, the beautiful homesteads were razed to the ground and the villagers butchered in their hundreds. The rest fled westward for sanctuary among the Bakwena and other Tswana peoples. Some locals believe that Mzilikazi stormed through the town in the 1830s and finished off what little was left of this great city. Kaditshwene was ruined, and today all that can be seen as evidence of its heyday are crumbling stone walls extending for tens of kilometres across the hills. But there are efforts to make the site into a cultural and tourist destination and 'twitchers' will be interested to learn that two birds identified here by an early naturalist, Dr Andrew Smith, were named after the city in an English corruption of its name – the Kurrichane Thrush and Kurrichane Buttonquail.

Kaditshwene in its heyday

14ᵗʰ. Not much water about. Passed the last farm of all and came to a range of high hills now the northern boundary of Marico... outspanned by a rock spring amongst the hills coming from under a limestone rock.

Casual readers of Richard's diary cannot imagine, I suspect, the difficulty an old journal like this presents for researchers trying to identify a long-gone route. He talked of Martin Swartz's farm – well that was relatively easy for Detective Arto Toivenen to find in the archival deeds office, and any fool could tell that the 'range of high hills' Richard mentioned was clearly the Dwarsberg, but where *exactly* had the old party crossed the mountains, I wanted to know in my doggedly determined way. Where was the road to Sechele's kraal and the fine loose sea sand and the spring in the rock?

''Bassport' must be the neck called Buispoort,' said Arto, 'but there's a dam there now, so you'll have to walk on the tarred road nearby. And as for the 'rock spring' – there are several in the hills around here, so you're just going to have to be content with missing the exact one.'

Sensing my determination to get the route correct as best we could, Derik Pelser introduced me to a cattle trader by the name of Johann Coetzee, who knows these parts as intimately as any poacher would, so he and Arto pored over maps and drove the area with Louis and John to work out a way that was as close as was practically possible to that of the old Glyns' party. What they decided on was a mixture of tarred roads, dirt tracks and small paths and on the morning of Tuesday, 10 May, I set off along them.

The day started with my first little Garmin GPS test over the kopje at the back of Jan/Derik's farm towards what was once that of Martin Swartz. John did a great job of the coordinates, all went swimmingly and I lost a bit of my fear of this technology. Bad wasp sting on the back of my right knee – very painful even by my standards and over the course of the day it stiffened up and developed

Louis, Johann and Derik, trying to work out my route

into a great red weal. Asked a diminutive nyanga I passed how to deal with it, but the recipe was too complicated and I didn't have the time or knowledge to find the right herbs.

Rebellious scion of the volk

Buispoort is named after a controversial figure in Afrikaner history by the name of Coenraad de Buys who was the first white man to settle in these parts. For a nation in whom wanderlust and rebellion were deeply ingrained, Coenraad came to epitomise both, but he has long been vilified by the *volk* for his lifestyle and habits. De Buys (originally du Buis) was of Huguenot descent, grew up in the Cape Colony but soon grew restless – even lawless – under the restrictive regulations of both the Dutch and British governments, and equally intolerant of his countrymen's racist and religious ways. An independent, free thinker by nature, Coenraad was accused from an early age of stealing other men's wives, and was somewhat egalitarian in his choices. He wooed Boers' spouses, took Khoikhoi women as concubines, married the mother of the great Xhosa chief Ngcika (Gaika), then won the hand of Mzilikazi's sister. His political iconoclasm resulted in him living with a price on his head for years, travelling the country with his harem and a band of outlaws with similarly rebellious views to his own. Alternately befriended and berated by Boer, Brit, Xhosa, Zulu, Tswana, Sotho and missionary, Coenraad acted as both peacemaker and troublemaker in, among other conflicts, the Frontier Wars of the Eastern Cape where he was courted by both sides of the conflict for his interpretative and negotiations skills (he was fluent in English, Dutch and Xhosa).

De Buys' life story is one of increasingly remote exile as he constantly sought a place where he could live untrammelled by 'civilisation' and what he perceived to be injustice. After spending years among the Xhosa people, he tried conforming to the Cape's restrictive ways for a decade before heading north in 1814 at the age of 52. In the (then) violent, remote frontier of the Orange River he gathered a band of Griqua malcontents with whom he formed a commando and penetrated further and further north. Some chiefs he befriended, others he raided, gathering legendary status as he went, along with yet more wives and dozens of mixed-race children. He was a Herculean figure in every way – almost seven foot tall, imposing, dignified and good-looking – attributes that gained him the name *Khula* (The Big One) from the Xhosas. Eventually, his Western clothing was reduced to tatters and he ran out of ammunition, living the rest of his life in skins, and using bows and arrows for his conquests and hunts. In 1815 he arrived in the Marico (at least two decades before the first *trekkers* arrived there) and spent five years living in the legendary Kaditshwene city with the Bahurutshe before heading north yet again.

It is not known how Coenraad de Buys died, but his son Michael relates that the old man was travelling along the Limpopo River when one of his wives died of fever. So grief-stricken was he at her death that Coenraad walked out into the night and was never seen again. But, despite the fact that he'd been an embarrassing thorn in the side of the Afrikaner nation, Paul Kruger granted his descendants some land in the Zoutpansberg where they established the town of Buysdorp (near Makhado – formerly Louis Trichardt). Many of them live there to this day.

Not for nothing is the Dwarsberg so called – it is indeed a triple band of mountains that are 'always in your way' – but at least I had a tarred road on which to climb Buispoort Pass. I spared a thought for the new *voorlopers* whom Richard had just acquired, January, April and Swartboy. *How sad they must have been to leave their families, and how fearful that they might never see them again.* The road I was on didn't take me past any of the springs of the area, so having completed my first day's walk, John drove me to its most famous one, which Johann had showed him during their research foray. It's the site of David Livingstone's second mission station in southern Africa, a forlorn, bleak place called Chonuane, scattered with white limestone pebbles and still bearing the faintest evidence of his little oblong house. Livingstone spent only a couple of years here with his beloved Bakwena people before abandoning it in favour of Kolobeng, south of what is now Gaborone, where they hoped to find a more consistent source of water. Once there, the missionary made the one-and-only convert of his life – their chief Sechele – until the *kgosi* couldn't resist the temptation of taking a second wife and became one of the most famous back-slid Christians in history.

Crossing the Dwarsberg proved to be a turning point in my journey, but one I didn't fully recognise at the time. Sitting here on my veranda in Johannesburg, months later, I have the benefits of hindsight at my disposal and the chance to read my personal diary at leisure. Up to this point, it reflects the great joy I experienced at being alone on the road for hours on end, meeting people, looking at trees and singing songs to my Walkman. But from the time I descended the Marico's mountain range, my writing becomes positively euphoric:

An absolutely dreamy day – quite possibly the happiest of the trip so far – with the gentle Tswana people of the area. They show all the signs of being poor but content. Everyone greeted me with openness and they seem to have genuine interest in my trek and genuine good wishes when I move on. Their dogs are well looked after and I gave out several of Cora's collars to proud owners. Even the donkeys look happy! I feel the deep peace one gets from being in the landscape of one's birthplace – central African stuff with Dichrostachys, Acacia tortilis and Acacia nilotica predominantly. This is my treat after the physical toil and mental strain of the past two months. I feel excited all day at being in Africa proper.

Taps and I were now on red, hard-baked soil, weaving our way through head-height bushes designed to hook and snare. The warm, early winter air lay trapped in this thorny maze and at times the only sounds we heard were of far-

Johannes Tumane

off cowbells or raucous hornbills. This was an inhospitable, uncompromising environment and a little harbinger of the desert-like landscape that awaited us in Botswana. Johannes Tumane cycled alongside me for hours and pointed out his mother, a bent old woman walking up and down a sorghum field, beating a drum to keep the birds off her crop. *She probably does as much distance in a day as I do!* We came upon a wedding party in the middle of nowhere, the bride waiting in a darkened room for the time when she could be brought out to meet her groom. *She's a plump, pretty girl, but in no special finery at all – rather grubby green jersey and a blanket over her skirt. A cow bellowed mournfully in a thorn kraal nearby – it will be sacrificed before nightfall, poor thing. Taps played with three dogs identical to him. In fact, we're now in true Africanis country – many Tapiwas around with their gentle brown eyes.*

Kgosi Edwin Lentswe

In the second of three audiences with chiefs in the area, I met with Kgosi Edwin Lentswe, a refined, educated man with impeccable manners and an open face. I found him sitting in the shade of an old leadwood tree with his *kgotla*, or tribal council, a group of wizened old men who gave me permission to walk through their land and showered me with blessings for my journey through gap-toothed grins.

'Does your husband allow you to do this?' was their only question.

Celebrating 1 000 kilometres

And in the midst of all this pastoral euphoria, I enjoyed the triumph of clocking up my one thousandth kilometre. What a moment that was. What a never-forget moment of deep satisfaction and gratitude. Louis was with me but there was no sign of John as I got to within 100 metres of the end point. He's late as usual and I had a hissy because I so wanted us all to be together, but later realised why and felt such a heel – he'd been rushing around finding champagne, damask tablecloth, stylish ice bucket and tinned salmon for lunch. Dear John and his attention to detail – he even made a little poster to mark the occasion. We set ourselves up for a little party by the side of the road and were joined by my cyclist friend Johannes, Derik and Johann, who regaled us with astounding, amusing and downright unbelievable stories of the Marico. I looked up and realised that we were sitting underneath a withaak – the yellow-barked thorn tree that features so often in the tall tales of that most famous of the Marico's sons, Herman Charles Bosman.

Our last camp site in South Africa was, fittingly, the most beautiful we'd had to date, nestled in the bush on the outskirts of a village called Lekgophung.

Lekgopung camp

Karin had many friends there, having shot a TV documentary about its old folk a few years before, and the village headman gave us permission to camp among the ruins of an old hunting camp nearby. For the first time we were without running water and electricity so it was a good test of our self-sufficiency, and John and Louis set up our little bush shower under one of the tall jacket plums arching above our heads. We were happily going about our business when a bakkie drew up, its driver a very angry man with a very large rifle. 'I am Chief Suping and you are trespassing on my land,' he said. It turned out that we'd got the go-ahead to camp there from one

Karin and one of her *gogos*

of his sub-chiefs and in a method totally devoid of the required protocol. I apologised profusely and all was forgiven, but it was a tense moment and another reminder of how delicate and complicated these negotiations would be throughout our trek.

Struggling with the damned diary!

Sue and her friend Mandy Momberg arrived from Johannesburg with their 4x4 packed to the gunnels with our food and provisions for the next two legs of the journey. Box after box of goodies were laid out on what remained of a concrete slab under some collapsing thatch, and the girls sifted and sorted, labelled and packed what seemed to be an impossible amount of gear to fit into two vehicles. Mandy (who's the Pilanesberg Game Reserve's ecologist) gave me a quick refresher course on map reading, and with my customary large whiskey and soda in hand, I battled to finish my last website diary account of our travels through South Africa. Writing is proving to be the hardest but most satisfying thing I've ever done – how I dread the diary day, but how pleased I am when I have something on paper about this great adventure. I feel so glad that Sue's on board – it'll take the pressure off L, J and me in the much tougher times that surely lie ahead. Our Isuzus positively groan with food and we will enter Botswana tomorrow looking like we're emigrating there!

Sue sorting provisions

Lekgophung to Ngotwane River, Botswana

Within metres I was enveloped in dense thornveld

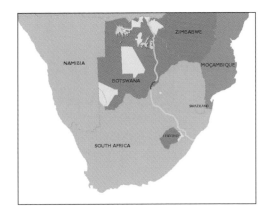

Lekgophung to Ngotwane
River, Botswana
99 kilometres
Total: 1 148
Week 10
16–22 May

May 15ᵗʰ: Trekked from the hills down to a plain level as far as could be seen, covered with thick thorn trees (mimosa), growing in a sandy soil sprinkled with tufts of coarse grass. This was real central Africa, and much the same country as we were to trek over day after day till we came to the Zambezi district. At midday we came to a kraal, which was near a vlei under some little hills composed of vast masses of split granite.

Cattle rustlers and diamond thieves ply their nefarious trade along a straight, dirt track to the Kopfontein/Tlokweng border post between South Africa and Botswana. Or at least that's what I imagined they did, as I jaunted along this sand ribbon, which runs through the bush, parallel to the tarred road on which thousands of vehicles haul their human and other cargo to and

Stretching for the last walk in SA

from our neighbouring states every day. The track saved me a couple of kilometres as well as the fumes and roars of long-distance behemoths, and Tapiwa and I were grateful for its solitude. Eventually I popped out of the bundu just behind the customs house and I don't know who was more surprised by my backdoor arrival – me or the off-duty official having a *dop* under a tree.

'What are you doing in there?' he asked suspiciously.

'Sorry, sir, I needed the loo rather badly,' I stuttered, an explanation that apparently satisfied him, much to my relief. The team was waiting for me in the Isuzus outside the border post, all of us tense at the prospect of trying to get our quite staggering amount of food and equipment through customs. But neither country's officials appeared to be in the least interested in our kit, nor the fact that I walked through their control gates. I cheerily strode past the boom guards saying, 'I'm so sick of sitting in the car that I just have to stretch my legs. My friends are right behind me with the vehicles.' Why I was worried they'd stop me trying to cross the border on foot I can't imagine – after all, thousands of African people do it every day.

With dusk approaching and time running out to find a camp site before nightfall, we stopped 500 metres into Botswana, where I marked the finish point of my day's walk. Only then did John sheepishly admit that he and Louis had forgotten to fill the Isuzus' fuel and water tanks. *Can you believe it?!* There was now no way we could head into the sticks for the night. A word much stronger than 'oops' came to mind, but I bit my tongue and we headed for Gaborone's city lights a few kilometres away, where Mike and Kirsten Main, very dear friends of mine, allowed us to put up our tents on their lawn. It was an inglorious start to this section of the trip.

Entering Botswana, packed to the gunnels

Mike has written several indispensable books on Botswana and he's something of an authority on the old hunters' routes through what was then known as 'The Far Interior'. He has an intimate knowledge of both local terrain and 19th-century explorer literature, and had managed to make sense of the antiquated references and long-abandoned place names in The Diary. Since I first mentioned my mad idea of walking to Victoria Falls, Mike and Kirsten had also done some impressive sleuthing to establish where the Glyn party might have travelled, and with their help I felt confident that I was going to get very close to treading the ground The Diary had outlined.

Bovine buccaneers – then and now

Subsequent research revealed that my instincts about the road I walked being the scene of illegal activities were right. During the decades after the Mfecane, tit-for-tat cattle raids between Boer, Tswana and Matabele in this region were rife, and in the early years of the 20th century the area was still the scene of many an illegal foray between the then Bechuanaland Protectorate and the Marico – so much so that in his first volume of *Voorkamer Stories*, Herman Charles Bosman included a composite of these wily local cattle rustlers in the character Gysbert van Tonder. To this day, the border between Botswana and South Africa is so porous, ill-defined and badly policed that cattle rustling and smuggling continues unabated. Indeed, some ranches in the area straddle the international boundary, making it as easy as opening a farm gate in order to drive livestock to South African markets, where it not only fetches a higher price but avoids months in quarantine facilities designed to prevent the transference of foot-and-mouth disease. And as they have always done, the smugglers using public land often burn the veld or tie branches to their cattle's tails to erase traces of their passage.

There are several cattle-drivers alive today who can tell of the great drama entailed in moving cattle between Ghanzi and Lobatse in Botswana prior to viable motorised transport. In these legendary treks, herdsmen on horseback drove their cattle a distance of about 600 kilometres from farms in the northwest of that country to the abattoir in the southeast. This was an entirely legal activity, of course, but it entailed a gruelling, month-long journey across the Kalahari's waterless terrain. As many as 1 200 cattle at a time would be slowly driven by farm workers towards Lobatse, grazing as they went and drinking at boreholes and wells along the way. In dry years, the trek was a nightmare, with one man reportedly losing 650 cattle out of a herd of 800 because the well on which he was depending turned up dry. During the early to mid-1900s Bedford trucks would struggle through the deep sand track parallel to the herds, carrying food and camping equipment for the horsemen and often transporting the cattle-owners' families to school and shopping in town. I imagine the trip must have been somewhat gypsy-like in atmosphere, notwithstanding the fact that marauding prides of lions stalked the herds by day and besieged their thorn kraals by night. About a decade ago the Trans-Kalahari Highway was built, making transporting the cows by truck viable, and sadly the great spectacle – and lifestyle – came to a rather abrupt end.

And it was by no means the ground that most visitors to Botswana traverse, like the game parks and the famous Okavango Delta. Once again, I'd be following the rivers and streams, pans and water holes that sustained the 1863 party, initially through tribal grazing land on the southeastern edges of the country. The area is now sadly devoid of the game that entertained Richard and Robert

but that suited me, frankly. I had my navigation skills to hone before having to face any angry 'whatsits' out there.

So, with Garmin in hand and heart in mouth, I returned the next day to the point at which I'd stopped near the border post and headed off into the bundu with a reassuring wave from Sue and a whine from Tapiwa, who I didn't feel should accompany me until I felt more confident in this new environment. With-

When in doubt, put on your lipstick!

in metres I was completely enveloped by dense thornveld and, for the first time on the trip, deprived of vehicle back-up. Facing me was a myriad cattle and goat tracks and the challenge of finding my rendezvous point with the team, roughly 10 kilometres away. Mike had assured me that the only threat to my wellbeing out there were a few sleepy snakes, but it was soon obvious that if I injured myself it would take a long time for the vehicles to find me. I felt utterly alone and vulnerable, and my mind dwelt on poor Bob and his terror at facing a night alone in this terrain when it was still crawling with things that were so much more lethal than what threatened me.

May 16th: Bob, I and Solomanink [one of the new staff recruited from Kgosi Moilwa] went out to hunt; finding some buck, I lost Bob and went back to the wagons; night came and he was still absent; we fired guns for a long time, and at last he walked in, in a sad plight. He had found some quagga he'd ridden up to, and killed one with his revolver, and then gone on after some tsessebes; his horse fell in a hole, and then ran off leaving Bob stunned and with a sprained shoulder on the ground. After coming to himself, he looked in vain for his horse, went back to the quagga and cut off a

Disappearing into the bundu

steak; then walked till dark but was quite lost, and set to work to make a kraal for himself for the night, but fortunately heard a gun and found the wagons in the dark.

A few kilometres later, my cellphone rang. 'Hello, Miss Glyn, this is Lancet Laboratories, Johannesburg. We're just wondering when you might be settling your outstanding account of R120?' Aah, not so remote after all, Patricia! I guffawed at my foolishness and headed on towards our meeting place. Having consulted our maps the night before, we had decided on an isolated hill in the area because, should my navigation skills fail me, it would provide an unmistakable hump to aim for in an otherwise flat landscape. Little did we know that when you get into that bush you're unable to see 50 metres ahead of you, let alone 10 kilometres. I had no choice but to trust the little red compass line on my Garmin, and stared at it neurotically as I weaved my way through the narrow tracks among the trees. An hour later I stumbled into camp to whoops of congratulations from the crew. I had done it – my first solo navigation of the walk – and I was elated. The magnificent dolomite koppie the boys had chosen for our camp consisted of a great tumble of boulders with yellow, split-rooted figs clinging to its sides and hidden corners where leopards must surely have lived in the old days. That night, I snuggled into my sleeping bag and opened Richard's diary to read: *'We came to a kraal under some little hills composed of vast masses of split granite.'* Had we, once again, unwittingly shadowed the ancestors?

Richard and Robert had been advised by Jan Viljoen to head for the Ngotwane River after they left the Marico because it would provide the only water they'd find before the Limpopo river system further north, and so it was that the next day I found myself heading towards the very same stream on another 'Boy's Own' solo romp across the peripheries of the Kalahari. This time I faced a harder task – or at least a longer one – because our new camp on the banks of the river was a whole 33 kilometres away, and I'd have to walk through more of the 'fine loose sand' Richard had warned me about in The Diary. The pale red silt sucked at my shoes and tested my ankles with its unevenness. *This is no joke – especially if you're worrying about your coordinates at the same time.* Suddenly I understood why my ancestors had started travelling slower. Not only were they now hunting regularly, but they too were facing this awful, deep silt. My pace slowed considerably and I gulped water greedily in the dry heat of the thornveld.

As I walked, it felt as if my progress was being monitored by old biblical characters in the guise of twisted and gnarled shepherd trees (*Boscia albitrunca*) and stink bushes (*Boscia foetida*). But, by and large, the trees around me appeared to be different in their proportional occupation of the area from the ones my ancestor described. The ravages of overpopulation and overgrazing here have resulted in a preponderance of resilient 'pioneer' invaders like black thorn (*Acacia mellifera*) and sickle bush (*Dichrostachys cinerea*). For a walker, they provided greater headaches than the most complex of man-made mazes

Boscia guardians

and the air around me was often blue with my cussing as I prised myself from their clutches. The 'great undergrowth of tangled grass' that Richard described was no more and I continually wondered what sustained the few Batlokwa people and their livestock remaining in the area. It was thoroughly depleted. Dead. Even the birds and beetles had flown. I came across the odd turtle dove and sparrow weaver, and got inordinately excited at the rare sight of a bird that should have been common there – the crimsonbreasted shrike. As little as 50 years ago, this area was renowned for its rhino, but I wasn't seeing as much as a hare.

Alec Campbell and Mike Main's book *Guide to Greater Gaborone* (published by the authors, 2003) tells of the widespread poisoning of vultures and jackals in these parts, and a high percentage of people living below the breadline whose bush clearing and firewood collection have impacted on the environment virtually to the point of no repair. I searched in vain for the tracks of wildlife but the sand whispered of nothing but livestock, and the trees talked no longer about the long-necked browsers that once nibbled at their highest shoots. It was here that Richard shot his first giraffe – an old bull that was dispatched, by his own admission, with 'bungling work' in a slow, messy process that made for difficult reading in his diary. But if I found his description of that kill difficult to stomach, I found the conduct of his friend quite nauseating. Richard reports having met a 'clerical gentleman of my after acquaintance' who joined them in a giraffe hunt but it is unclear from his writing when and where this took place. Nonetheless, the incident is highly representative of the kind of cruelty 19th-century hunting involved and is worth quoting in full:

'...he fired twice at an old bull and brought him to a standstill; loading again, he found he had but one bullet left, and in his excitement got the ramrod stuck on the top of that; nothing could get it out, so he fired ramrod and all into the brute's shoulder, still he did not fall, and parson was at his wits end, he tried a button but it did not go through the skin, a pebble no better, still the camel stood looking quietly at him,

The ravages of overgrazing

thinking he must die; parson lit his pipe, and sat under a tree for a long time, but the camel showed no signs of death; at last he could stand it no longer, so cramming his gun with gravel he fired several times at the brute's eyes in hopes of blinding him, but could not do even that, so he rode off to an African station and got another gun and bullets, but when he returned the camel was not there and though he spoored him some way he never was seen again.'

Today was dominated by a little dog called Sand who was in such a bad way – suppurating sores on her neck and ears, great black ticks hanging from the edges of her wounds and a long gash under her 'armpit', which looked deliberately inflicted. Tried to buy her from the old man who was clearly struggling to look after her, but he wouldn't sell. He had an adult son who was as mad as a march hare, dribbling and slack-jawed, pawing his way through a watermelon with the juice running down his chest and arms. Pathetic sight and it broke my heart having to leave the little dog to her inevitably sad end in a couple of weeks, and the son to his equally sad life, so far from specialised care.

Slowly I approached my goal, wobbling through the thick sand and amazed by how quickly my senses were becoming attuned to the demands of navigation.

Already I was instinctively using my own shadow to check my general direction and was keeping a constant mental note of interesting features I passed should I find myself lost. During times of insecurity I disciplined myself to trust my instrument, rather like an airline pilot does in thick cloud. If I didn't defy my Garmin's directional recommendations, it would get me safely to the Ngotwane.

And so it dutifully did. Just when I was beginning to seriously doubt myself I found our little camp, camouflaged on the banks of a slimy green channel. Tapiwa rushed out to greet me and John thrust a welcome cup of tea into my hands. The crew had found a perfect spot, in sight of an enormous leadwood tree (*Combretum imberbe*) that was so old it most surely would have been there when the old party came through. Maybe they'd seen it too. Perhaps they'd even camped under it like we had. I allowed myself such fantasies as I leaned back against the bank of the river and relaxed after a long, hard day's walk. But as for the river… *'Such a river. Two little duck ponds such as you may see at the bottom of a farm yard, a few inches deep, black and moving with water beetles,'* wrote Richard. His disappointment is palpable, no doubt due to the fact that he was relying on those 'two little duck ponds' to water his thirsty staff

Sweet success – finding the camp

and livestock. But there is every reason to believe from earlier references in his diary that he had read Gordon Cumming's book *A Hunter's Life in South Africa* (John Murray, London, 1850) and was once again alarmed by the changes he was seeing. Cumming had visited the more southerly reaches of the Ngotwane (near modern Ramotswa) only 20 years before and had written that the river was '….a little crystal river, whose margin was trampled down with the spoor of a great variety of heavy game… an open tract of country adorned with a carpet of the most luxuriant herbage. The vlei was beautiful with a dense crop of waving green reeds, forming a favourite resort of buffaloes and their invariable attendants the lions.' All rivers, of course, are subject to seasonal fluctuations but maybe Richard too was seeing the ravages of environmental exploitation, way back in 1863.

My disappointment in the Ngotwane was for similar reasons. The river that had been the object of my solo trek and the subject of my dreams for so many kilo-metres was frog-less and beetle-less, stagnant and murky. Its water was clearly undrinkable, so although its banks would be our home for another week as we headed eastwards towards the Tuli Block, John would have to drive many kilometres to find other sources of water. But at least the river was proving to be a rich source of amusement for Tapiwa. Herds of cows came down to drink morning and evening, vervet monkeys teased him from the trees and there were even a few feral pigs snuffling around the tents at night. He found a long-dead cow, whose bones he methodically picked up and buried in secret larders. We watched with amusement as he struggled to move the larger body parts to his burial sites, and battled to dig sufficiently big holes in the hard-baked soil.

The next day Tapiwa was allowed to accompany me because I had a short walk of only nine kilometres. Well, nine kilometres as the crow flies turned into 14 kilometres as we hit fields of impenetrable thorn trees that forced us to wind and weave, advance and retreat. We came across a few hunting dogs but they were strangely reluctant to play, as were the dogs guarding herds of goats. The Batswana raise their Africanis hounds among their goat kids so that by the time the dogs reach adulthood they regard themselves as more ruminant than canine, and no amount of beguiling invitations from Tapiwa would get them to budge from the herds they protected. After a couple of hours we finished our walk near a road that was accessible to the vehicles and I phoned Sue with our coordinates on the satellite phone (for at last I was out of cellphone range and the reach of my Johannesburg creditors). Lay down in sight of an old turquoise wagon (how appropriate!) and had a snooze with Taps. Perfectly at peace doing what I like best – lying on my back under an old African tree. Three and a half hours later we were still waiting – Sue had

The waiting game

just got her first taste of getting lost among the myriad tracks of southeastern Botswana. It would not be her last.

The night treated us to a full moon and touchable stars, and we dined around a roaring fire. It was Louis' farewell meal with the team. Over the previous weeks it had become clear that he was not enjoying the expedition at all and, as a result, things had become a little sticky around camp. In the morning we drove him to Gaborone from where he caught a flight home. We were all sad to see him go, particularly John, and I will always be grateful for the contribution Louis made to my quest.

Where once there were buffaloes, now there are cattle

Signs of the old times

What, though, was I to make of the fact that in another spooky echo from the diary, Richard too was encountering difficulties with his staff at the very same time and in the very same place? It would be grossly unfair of me to suggest that Louis and John were guilty of insubordination like the 1863 staff but there did seem to be unnerving parallels in the two expeditions. When Richard had restaffed in the Marico, he had employed a man called Solomanink as an after-rider, along with two 'tottie boys' Harry and Peat (sic). The duties of the after-riders were to follow the huntsmen on horseback, help track or drive game towards the guns, then butcher the animal and bring the meat home to the wagons. Solomanink soon showed that while he knew nothing about hunting, he was certainly adept at looking after himself:

18th May. Solomanink with the pack horses, did not come back from the camel (giraffe) till 11pm, bringing very little meat, saying they had been frightened away by wild beasts, so in the morning the sjambok was administered, for these blacks have a way of staying by dead game, eating the fat and all the tit bits till it is dark, and then hurrying home with very little meat, in fear of lions.

Two days later, Solomanink pushed his luck too far:

As usual they did not return till next morning, though the giraffe was not very far from the wagons. As I had threatened, we proceeded to tie Solomanink to the wagon wheel, preparatory to sjamboking. The other totties said they would run away if he was licked, however, we did not believe they were in earnest, except Gifford who said they would do as they threatened. Solomanink managed to slip away and escape into the woods. The other two drivers and two after-riders then packed up their things, but still I believed they were only making a demonstration; hours passed and it became a most unpleasant certainty that we were at least seven days' journey from Viljoen's and as much from Sekomies, with no one who knew the road, and only one driver for three wagons.

Defining duties and refining techniques

As his descendant living in an egalitarian age, these lines were not easy for me to read, and while it is always unwise to judge a man out of the context of his life and times, I felt ashamed of Richard's conduct. This kind of corporal punishment would often have been administered to the soldiers under his command so one must not necessarily regard it as having been motivated by racism. Nonetheless, it was not going to be tolerated by the people of Africa. How very unwise of him not to take the advice of James Gifford who knew so much more about dealing with those of different traditions and cultures.

But there was another reason why I found this diary entry difficult to deal with – it shone a light on my own conduct. I am an extremely driven woman, with huge physical and mental energy and high standards, which I expect those in my employ to meet. Several times, John and Louis had complained that I was driving them too hard and that I never relaxed. Were they right? Certainly Sue didn't seem to have problems with my leadership style or work pace and I was relieved to have someone in camp who shared my attitude to life and living. Was this a gender issue? Were the men battling because their 'leader' was a woman? Were they unable to cope with the work load because they were men? I couldn't decide, but after Louis' departure I spent many a kilometre of my walk thinking about where I might have failed my team. After all, good managers are able to motivate and inspire those who do not necessarily share their ambitions or personalities.

What was sure, though, was that Sue and John were more than capable of managing their back-up duties for what was left of the expedition. Their skills were complementary and I felt sure that their routines would improve by the day. Sue was cooking imaginative and nutritious meals, keeping the camp as neat and clean as humanly possible in the Kalahari dust that now surrounded us, and giving me the kind of moral support I'd so valued on The Blue Cross Challenge. John was pulling off communication and electronic miracles, maintaining the vehicles and doing some sterling map reading and navigation. By the end of our first week in Botswana he and I were quite comfortable with our Garmins and able to isolate GPS co-ordinates from our maps. We'd call each other on our 'sat' phones if rendezvous points changed but because satellite time is so expensive we also started a quaint little system of bush telegraph to help us find each other in the maze of thorn trees – little notes nailed on trees like clues in a treasure hunt that provided much amusement when we came across them.

We, it seemed, would be just fine – unlike my ancestors who now faced mutiny and abandonment in this most unforgiving environment.

Ngotwane River to Mookane

Walking along the beach *above* the high-tide mark

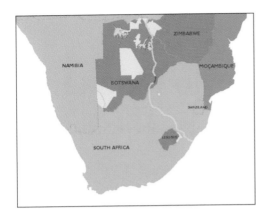

Ngotwane River to Mookane
102 kilometres
Total: 1 251
Week 11
23–29 May

Did I say we'd be fine? Well, not for a while yet, it seemed…

Papery harbinger

Tuesday, 24 May. A complete bugger-up with me and Taps in the boiling sun with no resupply of water or food for five hours while Sue packed up for move-out and John recced ahead for a new camp. Lots of snake tracks and swarms of irritating flies that head straight for your nostrils and mouth. J then went to Mochudi to collect Franci. Disappeared there, as is his habit every time we're near a village or town, so now we're setting up camp by moonlight. Very tired, no shower, no supper. The sat phone isn't charged, so the e-mails won't go. Etc., etc., damn it, etc.

Walking in Kalahari sand is rather like walking along the beach *above* the high-tide mark, and during the eleventh week of my walk I covered a further 102 kilometres of this character-testing terrain. Although I had reconciled myself to the fact that I would have only one short stretch of tar between now and Victoria Falls and that the Botswana 'beach' would be underfoot for six weeks yet, there were times when the effort of slaving through it had me grunting like Martina Hingis on Wimbledon's Centre Court. My thighs were beginning to look like a body-builder's and my calves resembled inverted milk bottles but at least I was beginning to lose some of my adipose addendums. And the fitter I became, the more I derived a kind of perverse pleasure from stomping and crashing through the bush tracks that run parallel to the Ngotwane River.

Calves like inverted milk bottles

We're experiencing the extremes so typical of semidesert weather – boiling at midday, freezing at midnight, still as a church nave or blowing with gusto. Nothing by half measures on the edges of the Kalahari, it seems. The bush improves with every passing kilometre as we get further and further from human settlements. More birds, squirrels, variety of trees. Came across some hyena spoor; Taps chased a klipspringer.

Waiting for the walker

He has this sweet habit of running ahead to wait for me in the shade of the next tree till I catch him up. The sand is hot, but Africanis dogs have very thick pads to cope with this. The joy at being out here comes in shafts. It lifts you, bathes you in light, then leaves.

Richard's poor oxen, dogs and horses must have viewed this terrain with considerably less glee. Take the fearless Nipper, for instance. He had to gallop at full tilt across this sandpit, chasing everything that moved and often having to make do with little more than melons to quench his thirst between water holes. Early accounts of the hunting life in Africa abound with reports on the staggering stamina and bravery of these horses, many of them small Basuto ponies. They were unafraid of big game and were trained to come from full speed to a complete stop within metres when their riders gripped their manes. They'd stand as still as statues while the hunter fired over their heads and faithfully remain in the place they'd been left, should the hunter have to stalk his prey. Amazing creatures they were indeed, and they died in their droves out here – of everything from snake bites to exhaustion.

Not that Nipper et al were dashing around much at this point in my ancestors' trip because their sport was all but over – at least for now.

> *May 25th: The want of after-riders prevented us now from spooring big game, and to hunt at all without them was almost more pain than pleasure, for in that endless bush without anything in the way of a landmark, the fear of being lost was considerably on your mind… we could now no longer afford to give our horses mielies, and therefore never rode them out of a walk except when in pursuit of a beast. The dogs also had to feed when a beast was killed and had to go without until the next came to hand.*

I could well appreciate Richard's fear at getting lost out here – the bush was so thick and the terrain so featureless that without my Garmin I would have been lost within 200 metres. How he must have regretted his mishandling of the Solomanink rebellion. His great African adventure had suddenly turned nasty and his diary is much more serious in tone. The possibility of getting drivers at the next Tswana kraal (a week hence) were slim, and going back to Jan Viljoen's farm would make them too late to get to the Falls and back before the rains started. They were now in an arid, uncharted place where – as I'd witnessed – plants and animals cling to life by the proverbial tips of their hooks and claws. And with so many animals to feed and water every day, that must have been a terrifying prospect.

Even our tiny team was learning water-wise ways by now, knowing that we'd have to drive so far to replenish our tanks. Apart from the river water, which looked lethal, there was absolutely no surface water for hundreds of square kilometres and we soon became reliant on the boreholes of herdsmen and villagers for our survival. Botswana is beef country and cattle owners tend to live in town, while employing people to look after their herds out in the sticks.

Most of the caretakers appeared to be lonely bachelors enduring a stiflingly boring life and their stupefied reaction to a white woman striding past their cattle posts provided me with many a laugh. 'Footing?' they'd ask, aghast. 'You are footing to the Victoria Falls?' Once they'd recovered from their shock, they invariably had one of only two follow-on questions for me: either 'Where is your car?' or 'Where is your husband?' At times the shock was mine, such as the occasion

Replenishing water tanks from a village pump

when a well-modulated voice came floating through the bush and enquired in perfect English:

'Good morning, ma'am. Are you lost by any chance?' The voice belonged to Cole Tshipana, a businessman from the nearby town of Mookane.

'No, thanks, I think I know where I'm going. I have a compass,' I replied.

To which he said: 'Ah, so you are an explorer, like David Livingstone!'

A home in the sticks

There is an easier way of getting through Botswana

Eating up the earth

Most visitors to Botswana head for its magnificent game parks and Okavango Delta, but during my walk in the country's southeastern region I encountered terrain tourists hardly ever see. Botswana is beef country and there are an estimated two cows for every person living there. Cattle husbandry forms an important and age-old part of Batswana culture – both as a source and measurement of wealth – but what the (apparently untrammelled) herds have done to the countryside is devastating. And given that water is such a precious commodity here on the peripheries of the Kalahari, one has to question whether meat production constitutes a responsible use of the country's natural resources. Indeed, extrapolating from the situation in Botswana, one must ask whether excessive meat production is an appropriate way of meeting our planet's food needs at all. David Pimentel, a water resource specialist at Cornell University, estimates that it takes roughly 2 000 litres of water to produce a kilo of soya beans, 500 litres to produce a kilo of potatoes and 100 000 litres to produce a kilo of beef (*Bioscience*, Volume 42, 1997). Yet much of the earth is critically short of water – in fact, lack of water is now recognised as the greatest single threat to food security in the world. Not only is it required for growing crops, but also for the processing of meat in abattoirs – roughly 14 litres being required in the cleaning of a single chicken. And the enormous volume of waste produced by farm animals is also a major concern, causing high levels of ammonia and nitrate pollution of land, water and air. According to a report by the Compassion in World Farming (CIWF) Trust (*The Global Benefits of Eating Less Meat*, CIWF, 2004) the world has to deal with something like 13 billion tonnes of effluent every year and in the Netherlands, for instance, pig slurry has resulted in nitrate levels in the groundwater that are more than double the maximum allowable level. Excessive use of fertilisers and pesticides creates further environmental damage and although the effect livestock has on global warming is also largely ignored, it is responsible for a dramatic increase in the carbon content of our soils and an estimated 10 per cent of all greenhouse gases, including approximately 25 per cent of methane emissions.

As far as land usage is concerned, it is sobering to note that 19 people can be sustained for a year on a hectare planted with rice, and only two people by a hectare supporting beef or lamb. Historically, the big meat-eating cultures of the world were predominantly those of the West and demand for beef, chicken, pork, lamb and dairy products in these rich countries has resulted in producers having to resort to intensive farming methods in order to keep up with consumers' eating habits. Instead of being grass- and pasture-fed, cows (and other meat-producing animals) are now raised on grain and concentrated in small areas. Animals kept in these conditions are denied the opportunity to socialise, forage or roam according to their natural inclinations and they endure abominable cruelty and neglect in the course of being 'grown', transported and slaughtered. But leaving aside the tragic animal welfare issues inherent in this system (which could fill an entire book on their own, as could the disease epidemics to which these conditions are well suited), it is becoming quite clear that the planet is simply unable to produce sufficient wheat, maize and soya to keep up with demand. As Jonathan Porritt, Chairman of the UK Sustainable Development Commission, says:

'Although there's some controversy about the different ways in which the calculations are done, the basic rule of thumb is that it takes two kilograms of feed to produce every kilogram of chicken, four for pork, and at least seven for beef.' And we simply don't have enough land on earth to grow these crops – certainly not in the developed countries, which consume the most meat and therefore scour the globe in search of cereals for their animals and land to produce it. Thus poor farmers in Africa grow crops to feed European pigs and not their own children – and Brazilian forests burn so that Parisian diners can eat steak. The aforementioned CIWF Trust report cites the following bizarre situation: 'At the height of the same 1984 famine that inspired the historic Band Aid concert, Ethiopia exported feed crops to the UK.'

In the second half of the 20th century, worldwide meat production increased roughly fivefold and demand is expected to grow from 209 million tons in 1997 to around 327 million tons in 2020. Put another way, it has been estimated that by the middle of this century we will need *four* planets the size of Earth to grow the grain to feed the livestock to feed ourselves. This is not only an inefficient but a completely untenable means of producing food for humankind. Colin Trudge, a zoologist and author of *So Shall We Reap* (Penguin 2003) writes in his book: 'If present trends on meat-eating continue, then by 2050 the world's livestock will be consuming as much as 4 billion people do: an increase equivalent to the total world population of around 1970, when many were doubting whether such human numbers could be fed at all.'

The exponential increase in demand for meat is largely due to new eating habits in poorer parts of the world – areas such China, India and Africa, which now seek to imitate the tastes of Western nations. Consumption of broiler chickens in India, for instance, has shot up from 31 million birds per annum in 1981 to 800 million in 2000. China's consumption of meat products rose by 85 per cent between 1995 and 2001 and is forecast to be responsible for 40 per cent of the total world increase up until 2020.

The livestock population of the world is having a devastating environmental impact. Science and technology are not showing any signs of coming to our rescue through genetically modified grains and animals, more efficient fertilisers and effluent processing devices. For the sake of our own health and that of the planet, we simply *have* to eat less meat.

Meat at what cost?

Some of the cattle-post minders were poorly paid Zimbabweans living in exile and, in the words of one, they were finding it 'hard to resist becoming cowboys' (criminals). The men were almost pathetically grateful for company or food and never once did they refuse us help or water.

The old brothers Glyn were also, no doubt, pathetically grateful to come across

a lone black man called Jansi who happened to be travelling north 'on his own account' and who 'thought he knew part of the road'. Better still, Jansi undertook to try to handle one of the two wagons that had been left driverless after the mutiny. With Gifford now at the reins of the other one, the party rumbled off in search of water. Twenty kilometres later they found a small pool, thanks to some well-used game paths that led them there. It provided just enough water to keep the party going till the next 'very bad' one, 'the water only standing in the old elephant footprints, green and stinking'. The hunters continued their pool-to-pool limp along the river, their hopes of staying alive continually dashed by locals who reported that they'd not find a drop of water for five days hence. Full moon came and with it the opportunity of trekking at night so as to relieve the animals of at least some of their terrible thirst. And in that ghostly blue-shadowed landscape, Richard heard his first African lion.

A white chick strolling past

> *May 25th: At night I first heard a lion roar, not the fine thundering sound I always imagined the king of beasts produced, but a low moaning noise very like a cow, and not nearly so loud as a wolf. After this the road turned much more to the north and we passed a fine pool (the last on the river).*

It was time, then, so The Diary hinted, for me to leave the banks of the Ngotwane River and veer towards the north. And quite fortuitously there was a dirt road that I could use to do so. It runs along the back of the massive private farms of the Tuli Block whose owners would not have welcomed a trespasser and whose high game fences were insurmountable anyway. During the next month, however, I would have several other barricades to hop over – albeit less-daunting ones – and the first was now in front of me. Botswana is crisscrossed by veterinary fences designed to stop the spread of foot-and-mouth disease. They divide the country into huge blocks or paddocks and all passage through these areas by man, beast or vehicle is controlled. The fence was easy enough to cope with – I just climbed over and continued my romp on the other side – but we had to get the vehicles through it too, and that entailed a long drive along the fence to the control gate many kilometres away. I marked my stop point with my GPS, jumped back over the fence and climbed into the Isuzu with Sue for the drive to the Dibete Veterinary Gate. We were heading, little did we know, for one of the greatest gifts of the trip.

The paparazzi!

The guards at the gate were friendly and helpful and we lingered at their post, filling our water tanks and chatting to folk back home on our cellphones, having found that we had reception for the first time in ages. In the midst of a call, Sue shouted to me that there was a puppy crossing the road. Well, describing it as a puppy was flattery in the extreme. Out of the bush had emerged a truly pathetic canine skinbag. It slunk away from us, picking its way through the thorny scrub on emaciated, wobbly legs. John and I quickly ran down either side of the fence to head it off, with Franci and her camera in hot pursuit. Crouching down among the bushes, John caught it with ease and handed it to me over the wire. It was a little female, and she collapsed in my arms, semi-comatose from shock and terror at all the people crowding around her. It soon became clear to all of us that we had found the dog during her last 24 hours on earth. Gently Sue tried to wet the puppy's lips, but she was too weak to take either food or water and lay on the sand as if awaiting some dreadful fate. One of her eyes was blue and cloudy – no doubt as a result of a snake bite or poisoned thorn bush. Her spine protruded like marbles from beneath her mangy skin and fleas made merry across her emaciated belly.

I stared down at her, my mind in a quandary. Should we take her with us? After all, we were heading for Big Five territory where Tapiwa, let alone a sick puppy, would be tasty leopard bait. We were far from a vet, and what if she had some awful disease that would infect Taps? My team was stretched to the limit – should I ask yet more of them? I struggled with my thoughts and eventually said 'Sorry, guys, she's coming with us.' I put her on my lap and we drove away.

The whole incident resounded with *déjà vu*. Three years before, I had found Tapiwa in exactly the same pitiful state, at exactly the same age and with exactly the same colouring and looks. When his sister Ningi died, friends had encouraged me to find him a companion, but somehow I knew I'd find a dog on my walk that I couldn't leave. This was she.

Describing it as a puppy was flattery in the extreme

And she was very sick. With the day drawing to a close, we headed for the nearest village (Mookane) in the hope of finding her some help, but that turned out to be naïve – the few vets that Botswana has are all in its big towns and cities. So we made camp outside the village under another stunning granite kopje while the newest member of our travelling band slept like the dead in the front seat of the car. I phoned my sister Shirley in Johannesburg because she's nursed many a sick animal in her time.

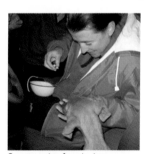

'Hydration is critical,' she said. 'You must squirt a solution of sugar and warm water into her mouth every few hours and hope that you can stimulate her appetite. Keep her warm and, most importantly, give her a cuddle from me.'

I decided that night to name her Mpho, that being the Setswana word for 'gift', just as Tapiwa means 'gift' in Shona. Lucky little princess – she soon had a day nurse,

Sugar water for starters

a night nurse and a babysitter pandering to her every need as if she were the new arrival in a royal household. Tapiwa, however, was not at all enamoured. Mindful of the necessity of reinforcing his position as top dog in camp, I gave him extra attention and affection, but he growled menacingly at the emaciated form at the farthest corner of our tent.

Leaving John on dog duty the next day, Sue, Franci and I drove out to try to find my start point near the vet fence. Two hours later we were back with our tails between our legs, having once again been flummoxed by dead-end cattle tracks. After a quick cup of tea and a check on the nursery, we headed out again – for further floundering around the bush. At times it felt as if we were on the Paris-to-Dakar Rally, me with maps and GPS on lap, screaming instructions like 'Go left, mind the tree, deep sand ahead', Sue clinging to the wheel with her eyes on stalks as we skied through the good sections and ploughed through the bad. We pushed and retreated, pushed and retreated down those tortuous paths until we eventually found ourselves at the fence. It was 2pm by the time I took my first step and once again we got back to camp in the dark. Felt rather proud of what we girls pulled off today, and the fact that our senses of humour remained intact throughout. The vehicle is a mess, though. Its paintwork is a mass of scratches and the tyres are full of thorns – rather like my legs and takkies I guess!

Mpho's first home with her new travelling troupe

Sunday, 29 May. It's four days since the rescue and Mpho is bouncing back in fine style. Gave her half a worm tablet and she's taking solids now. Lying in the sun at my feet as I write this, her tummy a round ball and her bones already receding from view. Hasn't uttered a sound yet, but her tail goes constantly and her one good eye shines with enthusiasm. I bought her a grey blanket and a large plastic wash basin where she sleeps between feasts. Have to keep a constant lookout for her because there are jackals on the hill above us. Taps still being perfectly horrible to her but I do believe she's getting slightly less of a wigging every time she creeps out of the tent for a wee, so this story might just have a happy ending...

Enough is never enough

Mookane to Shoshong

A city of stone and silence

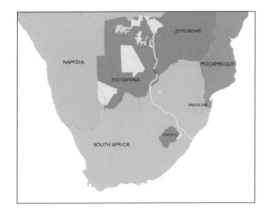

Mookane to Shoshong
117 kilometres
Total: 1 368
Week 12
30 May – 5 June

May 30ᵗʰ: Though we sometimes got off the road for a time, we managed to find our way and water enough also for two days more, when after sighting the blue hills of Bamgamvato, we jolted down a rocky gorge and found ourselves amongst the corn gardens of Sekomie's people, some of them guided us to his kraal, a great assemblage of earthen huts, built up a narrow gorge between steep hills very bare and stony.

'Where on earth are the blue hills of the Bamgamvato?' I thought to myself when I first read Richard's diary. 'And who was Sekomie?' As someone who is not familiar with the yellow-papered world of Africana literature, there were many references to places and people in the journal I couldn't understand but these two worried me more than most. Even a novice like me could tell that they would be critical in establishing my route through Botswana and that it was therefore imperative to find out more about them.

So where are those hills?

I phoned my Botswana guru, Mike Main. 'Ah, that's Sekgoma you're after,' he said without hesitation, 'Chief of the Bamangwato, and his kraal at Shoshong was protected by a stunning granite ridge. The Glyn party would probably have followed the Bonwapitse River towards his settlement so you need to head northwest from the Ngotwani until you hit that river.'

For the next week, therefore, I walked as directed along the utterly dry Bonwapitse banks and on paths nearby to it. And the further north I travelled, the hotter it got. Hell hath no oven like this one, I reckon. By 11am I'm flaked, despite really early starts, but must soldier on until late afternoon because I'm so far behind the wagons. Going to be four days late getting to Shoshong despite my best efforts, so bang goes my rest there as per R's diary. Picking up Mpho set our timetable back a bit, I know, but I can't understand how the lads got there so quickly. Bad blisters now but must press on.

Once again I was walking (and working) towards a prominent landmark, but this one seemed to be particularly hard fought for. Day after day I scanned the horizon for sight of those 'blue hills', only to be greeted by flat-topped thorn trees on a table-top landscape. Sweat formed an oval stain on my shirt, and ran down my legs in dusty rivulets. Sunscreen lay in greasy streaks on my cheeks and my lips became dry and scaly. But late in the morning on 1 June I finally saw the hills I'd struggled for – huge formations that rose with imposing grandeur out of an otherwise flat plain. And they were indeed very blue. I felt a gust of wind from the ancestors. Here I was, seeing on foot and with my own

... and they were indeed blue, those hills

two eyes something I'd only read about in an old family diary months before, written by a man I'd never meet from a world I'd never inhabit. With the right help and a little gumption, I had transformed a dusty old journal reference into a vibrant adventure. Experiences rarely come so all-at-once humbling and triumphant. I felt a flush of chest-swelling joy, a gasp of purpose and peace and a tearful echo from my past.

Shimmering sentinels

A rocky bed on which to lie

Biblical wells

John found us a glorious camp site just outside modern Shoshong, nestled in the mouth of a rocky gorge. Our tents were perched on the edge of an ancient riverbed, surrounded by high walls of tumbling granite blocks that resembled the product of a gargantuan, chaotic chocolate factory. From the cliffs above, baboons huffed at us and tittle-tattle birds announced our comings and goings. The rocks were dotted with fairytale, silver-barked trees (*Commiphora marlothii*) that shimmered in the setting sun like Inca sentinels, and further up the gorge was a series of deep wells used by the Bamangwato people to water their livestock. It felt as if we were living in the midst of a biblical parable, with incessant tinkling of bells and clacking of hooves on rock as herds of cattle, goats and donkeys made their way up and down the mountain to drink.

And, as we'd come to expect by now, we had the odd coincidence to remind us that perhaps the ancestors were ever-present. We weren't as lucky as we had been at Jan Viljoen's farm, where we found ourselves camped in exactly the right place by sheer serendipity, but without knowing it John had set us up in a gorge adjacent to the mighty one in which Sekgoma settled his people and where the Glyns had visited him. Sitting around over the weekend and congratulating John for his brilliant choice of home, Mike Main (who was visiting with his wife Kirsten) remarked with great casualness. 'Well, he's not the first to have seen its merits, that's for sure.' And there, under our feet and completely missed by our untrained eyes, were some Bushman ostrich-egg beads, stone implements, shards of Iron-Age pottery and dagga remnants from long-gone huts – indicators of wave upon wave of human settlement in these hills.

But greater gifts from the dead were to come from this spectacular place the next day. Mike took us to find the site of Sekgoma's kraal – the place where Richard and Robert spent five days trying to get permission to travel and hunt in the *kgosi's* territory. I was most anxious to see it because the settlement had impressed Richard so deeply that his description of it is by far the most expansive of The Diary.

May 30ᵗʰ: A very small stream flows down the gorge, but is expended before it reaches halfway through the kraal. This is their only water, though they are said to number 40 000. Long lines of women carrying calabashes, and earthen pots may be seen fetching water from the stream all day. Outside the town we found the wagons of traders going to Lake Ngami and to Mzilikazi, a chief originally a fugitive from the Zulu country, but now very powerful and much dreaded by Sekomies. At the far end of the town was the house of the English Missionary J Mackenzie, to whom we had letters of introduction, and who kindly gave us most reasonable assistance in combating the wily and avaricious Sekomies. Mackenzie took us to his kgotla, or the place of assembly, a circle palisade in the middle of the town, but we found the chief asleep and not to be known from his subjects except by the superior dirt of his karros. Afterwards he came down to our wagons, asked for everything he saw, drank coffee, brandy or anything he could get, bothered us for wine, which we had not got, and said he must have a horse and a gun to let us go through his country.

After several days of talk, Mackenzie induced him to give us two guides for the promise of a horse on our return, but he would not believe we had no guns to sell, and kept saying, 'Are you sure you have not got one at the bottom of your wagons?' For the Boers and English traders are by law not allowed to sell guns to the blacks, who, however, in spite of that, have hundreds, such as they are. Drivers were out of the question, as they were very scarce in the place, so we had to make up our minds to leave Osborne's wagon behind, and to take the two others and the pick of the oxen, for many of them already were very lean and several lame.

Meantime we laid in a store of mabela (sorghum), buying it by the basketful, about a pint at a time for beads and handkerchiefs; we got about eight sacks altogether. The mabela is a small brown seed very nutritious for men and horses, makes very good porridge but will not bind enough to make bread.

A Circumcision festival was held during our stay, long processions of boys and girls every evening, with drums and music, and kinds of howls in chorus afterwards, all through the night. The girls were draped in all their finery, their heads plastered with fat and grains of mica, their hair cut very short indeed, and their necks, arms and legs loaded with pounds of beads (their jewellery), some had bits of hard wood on their legs, which they clicked together as they walked. A grand assembly, or senate, also took place; the headman in the kgotla made speeches on the affairs of the nation and the boys painted their faces and legs with yellow and red earth in honour of the occasion.

A grand hunt was also held, Sekomie mounted on an old horse, in an English-made moleskin suit, with a high felt helmet and double gun; his sons also were mounted and got up in perfect English style. Every man had to turn out, and a large space of country was surrounded; they enclosed two ostriches and other game but did not manage to kill anything.

What an astounding place the Bamangwato people's home must have been in its heyday. Thirty thousand people living in one gorge. And what a city of stone and silence it is today. Slowly we penetrated the fortress that protected Sekgoma's people from Mzilikazi's raids, winding our way ever upwards through the stifling ravine. On either side of our Lilliputian figures were more of the split granite formations that guarded our camp site. But these were cathedral-like in their size and beauty. Some of the rocks were layered with the precision of medieval stonemasons. Others tumbled over the edges of the gorge as if after an almighty explosion. It seemed like the Valley of Death, and I could almost hear the banjos of *Deliverance* echoing in my head. 'What kind of madman would even *try* to sack these ramparts?' I thought as I cowered beneath them. One of the Matabele king's attacks had been repelled by the Bamangwato only a couple of months prior to the Glyns' visit in 1863, so the atmosphere in the town must have been extra tense and Sekgoma extra mean, even by his standards (and there's hardly a kind word written about him in all the 19th century missionary/explorer literature).

A regimental display

Richard and his party were fortunate to witness a *bogwera*, a Bamangwato circumcision ceremony, not only because they took place infrequently but because they were discontinued within a couple of years of the Glyns' visit. These coming-of-age rituals took place only when a child or near relative of the *kgosi* was ready for the initiation and were thus not annual events. They were also timed to coincide with the sorghum harvest (in about May) and would last two to three months. As is often the case in southern African 'tribal' custom, many of the circumcision rites of the men were protected with utmost secrecy – not only from outsiders but from the group's womenfolk as well, so many of the practices are still unknown. The rituals were also subject to numerous taboos, with initiates being denied certain foods (such as salt), activities and associations. Defying these laws resulted in severe opprobrium or even the penalty of death. Teenage boys were kept secluded in special camps (*mephato*) for about three months by teachers or elders known as *dinare* (buffaloes), during which time the initiates were circumcised (without anaesthetic or antiseptic), pierced with sharpened sticks, subjected to starvation, forced to sleep without clothes or covering, and expected to endure many other trials designed to 'toughen' them in readiness for manhood. The young men learnt songs (of a very ribald nature about sex and women, according to some sources), were taught about loyalty to their *kgosi* and family group, as well as how to hunt and fight. And until young men passed these tests they were not regarded as adults and therefore not permitted to marry or have sex.

At the graduation ceremony, the *kgosi* gave the group a regimental name, which became an indicator of a man's age, home and royal affiliations and by which he would be known for ever afterwards. The name of the regiment was usually derived from an incident that had taken place during the time of trial, for instance *maYakapula* ('Those who go with rain' – after weather conditions) or *maLwelamotse* ('Those who fight for the town' – after some conflict). Members of the regiment were known as *balekane* or *bankane*, loosely translated as 'mates'. The regiment not only gave the group lifelong solidarity but demanded lifelong loyalty. A disgrace to one was a disgrace to all, just as an honour to one was an honour to all. And because

Brothers in arms – Bamangwato soldiers

Bamangwato girls dressed for the *boyale*

birth dates were not recorded at that time, it was not customary to ask someone's age, but rather to what regiment they belonged.

The female initiation rites were known as *boyale* and did not involve genital mutilation but rather some form of physical operation such as branding on the inner thigh. The young girls also underwent schooling in marital duties, respect for elders and other traditional laws and customs, and on graduating, the young women were also made part of the same regiment as their male counterparts.

Owing to pressure from missionaries such as John Mackenzie and converts to Christianity such as Sekgoma's elder sons (see page 201), circumcision practices were discontinued among the Bamangwato people and are rarely practised in any Batswana groups today.

A home to thirty thousand people – Sekgoma's kraal site

God's Army too had seen potentially rich pickings among Bamangwato souls, and the missionaries who lived in the village at the time were a couple of Livingstone's colleagues from the London Missionary Society, John Mackenzie and Roger Price. They were both remarkable men, and Mackenzie was clearly indispensable as the Glyns' negotiator with 'the wily and avaricious' Sekgoma. His diaries about his time with the Bamangwato contain some vivid descriptions of 19th-century missionary life in the settlement, and while they show the author to have had great affection for these people, they also show him to have a well-developed sense of humour. He describes the Sunday morning church service thus: 'We had the usual members of the congregation, most of them neatly dressed. But sticklers for "the proprieties" would have been shocked to see a man moving in the crowd who considered himself well dressed, altho' wearing a shirt only; another with trousers only…'

In the absence of being able to witness those somewhat individualistic interpretations of London fashion, I thought the next best thing would be to see where John Mackenzie had his mission. And after some trouble, Mike and Kirsten managed to find the rectangular outline of their schoolroom-cum-church and their little house next door. They were sad, like all abandoned places, but they spoke of great effort and commitment in a most inhospitable environment. For 12 years Mackenzie looked out of his front door onto nothing but rock and cliff while battling for the souls of a few hundred converts.

But some of them were, if nothing else, the *right* converts in that they became men of great influence in the affairs of the Bamangwato. Richard went on in his diary to describe Sekgoma's son Khama as 'a very great improvement on his father, thanks to the missionary's teaching'. Now there are those who would put Khama's attributes down to anything *but* Christian conversion, but the fact remains that with Khama III, the Bamangwato entered an unbroken period of enlightened, compassionate leadership. Their current Paramount Chief, Ian Khama, is deputy president of Botswana, on whom many hopes are pinned for the prosperous future of the country's people, wildlife and resources. I had pinned my hopes on meeting him in Shoshong, but he was abroad at the time, so I spent an interesting afternoon with his regent, Kgosi Sediegeng Kgamane and a couple of historians, learning more about their long and remarkable lineage.

Kgosi Kgamane

The sad remains of Mackenzie's church

On 5 June, the Glyns and Osborne – now minus his wagon – left Shoshong, 'much rejoiced at escaping from the old tyrant Sekomies on any terms.' They had had to leave many of their stores behind, along with 27 oxen, gifts of saddles and coats for the chief and his sons, and letters that Mackenzie promised to forward to England. (Interestingly, there is no mention at this stage in Richard's diary of the very important letter he was now carrying. It was addressed to Sekeletu, Chief of the Makololo people, who lived near the Zambezi River, and contained Mackenzie's apology that although the London Missionary Society would not be able to set up a mission station there in the foreseeable future, Sekeletu would one day have the word of God spread among his people. Mackenzie's letter – according to his book *Day-Dawn in Dark Places* – also contained a cautionary that the presence of the missionaries

Lion of God

The Bamangwato people called John Mackenzie *Tau*, meaning 'Lion', in recognition of his large stature, strength and determination. And certainly his numerous letters and autobiography (*Ten Years North of the Orange River: A story of everyday life and work among the South African tribes from 1859 to 1869*, Edmonston & Douglas, London, 1871) reveal him to be not only a compassionate, wise and moderate man, but one who was not averse to getting his hands dirty in the pursuit of his very varied duties. Like Livingstone and Moffat, Mackenzie came from humble Scottish origins and rose above his poor education and background to become one of the greatest missionaries ever to serve in Africa. And while it is common now to judge harshly the religious imperialism that inspired these men, they cannot be faulted for the passion with which they undertook their missions, the earnestness of their belief that they had divine sanction for their work and the hard labour demanded of them in the name of the Gospel. During his time at Shoshong, Mackenzie not only preached the Gospel and trained student ministers, but designed and built a church, three schools and a home, making and firing his own bricks. With his great medical knowledge, he treated the peoples' illnesses, inoculated them against smallpox, cleared the town of marauding hyenas, washed and ground his own corn and wrote books in Sechuana – all in an environment rife with malaria and dysentery. He and his family were caught up in a Matabele raid on the town, as well as the chaos and infighting that characterised Sekgoma's reign (see page 201), often hiding in their house or having to flee for the protection of the neighbouring hills, where they dodged bullets and hid under bushes. Indeed, with wry understatement, he wrote of these politically uncertain times: 'A native town is an awkward place for warfare; an enemy may be within some hut or behind some fence, and take dead aim at you before you are aware.' It is testament to Mackenzie's powers of diplomacy and negotiation that throughout the years of Shoshong's dynastic turmoil, he maintained the trust of all the leaders fighting against each other in the town.

As his career and his affection for the Bechuana people developed, Mackenzie became increasingly active politically – largely because he was anxious to prevent their land and gold reserves from falling into Boer hands. He therefore campaigned in Britain for the extension of Imperial control to Bechuanaland and was appointed Deputy Commissioner for the Protectorate in 1884, although he was soon replaced by Cecil John Rhodes. With his lifelong friend Khama III (see page 202), he helped eradicate what they both regarded as unacceptable cultural practices such as polygamy and circumcision, and on a broad scale, the missionary had great influence on the early political and social development of what is now Botswana. To this day, he appears to be most fondly regarded by the people of that country.

John Mackenzie

could not guarantee the Makololo people protection from Mzilikazi's raids, as Sekeletu had hoped would be the case.) But the party had acquired all-important guides who could take them through the wild and dangerous country ahead. And on the day they left town, I did too.

Covered an impressive 3.29 kilometres today – an ignominious walk record! Was bombing along the main tarred road parallel to the mountain range when I realised that it was stupid not to investigate whether there was a cutting through it that would save me having to walk all the way around. R said in The Diary that he used 'Unicorn Pass', but not even Mike knew where that was so marked my stop, jumped in the vehicle with Sue and drove towards the range to try and find it. Complete waste of time – notwithstanding the fact that we came across a beautiful hidden valley. Aborted the walk and headed back to camp for roast chicken in the Cobb with Mike and Kirsten. Fine time with fine people.

Shoshong – 2005

Botswana's First Family

Sekgoma's endorsement was crucial to the success of any expedition through Bechuanaland in the 19th century because travellers had to cross his land on their way to Lake Ngami, the Zambezi River and Matabeleland. But negotiations with the *kgosi* proved to be harrowing for most of the early explorers and missionaries. John Mackenzie described Sekgoma as the 'man with the sinister face who was the greatest sorcerer in Bechuanaland', Robert Moffat as 'a rather insignificant man with one eye... well known for his forbidding countenance', and James Chapman as 'a very hard bargainer [and] a great beggar'. Over the years, according to Edward Tabler's *The Far Interior*, (AA Balkema, Cape Town, 1955), Sekgoma developed a 'bad reputation with whites for personal unpleasantness, thievishness, begging, stinginess, and duplicity'. But he was also reported as being receptive to Livingstone's missionary overtures, kind and civil to Moffat and tremendously loyal to Jan Viljoen, whose life he saved when he'd been ordered by Sechele to murder the Boer hunter. And one must bear in mind that Sekgoma had good reasons for driving a hard bargain with travellers through his land – not only was it in his interests to control trade in the north (as far as possible), but he needed weapons to protect himself against Mzilikazi's frequent expansionist raids and for ivory hunting.

But if Sekgoma was unpopular with foreigners, he was equally so with his own people, and his rule was characterised by vicious power struggles and disputes for the chieftaincy – both with his half-brother Macheng and later with his elder sons Khama and Kgamane. For a couple of decades, the Bamangwato seat was subjected to a violent succession of deposals and reinstatements that are too complex to explore here, but the final and most

Sekgoma and his council

profound division within the people of Shoshong happened when Khama and Kgamane adopted Christianity in about 1865. After several years of tension and divided loyalties, the people threw their weight behind Khama, who seized control and started a long period of reform and peace. Khama III became known for his political and economic acumen, 'gentlemanly' ways and wise, inclusive leadership. John Mackenzie's son and biographer, William Douglas Mackenzie, is swift to attribute this to religious conversion: '... Throughout his career [he] refused to dip his hands in the blood of any relative to secure himself in the chieftainship, [and] yet when occasion arose manifested in the most trying circumstances true physical courage and noble moral heroism, [and he] must stand out as one of the most striking trophies ever won by the Christian religion upon the battleground with heathenism.' (*John Mackenzie – South African Missionary and Statesman*, Hodder & Stoughton, London, 1902). Khama helped establish British authority in the Protectorate, outlawed the drinking of alcohol at Shoshong and abolished certain traditional practices, which he regarded as unChristian. In his twilight years, he grew disenchanted with British rule, but nonetheless died a legend both at home and abroad, having become known as 'Khama the Great'.

Leadership of the Bamangwato people then passed to Sekgoma II, who had a brief reign of only two years (1923-1925) and one that was, again, characterised by conflict between various factions. But his son, Sir Seretse Khama, became, like his grandfather, one of Africa's greatest leaders. Seretse acceded to the chieftainship when he was only four years old, so while his uncle Tshekedi administered on his behalf, the young man studied law in England. As is well known and voluminously described in many books and articles, Seretse fell in love with a white woman named Ruth Williams while he was in England, and their decision to marry incurred the wrath not only of Tshekedi but also of the British and South African governments. For six years, between 1950 and 1956, the Khamas were forced to live in exile from their people and became international celebrities on account of their struggle for justice and acceptance. Throughout this time, the Bamangwato continued to regard Seretse as their leader and when he was eventually allowed to return to the Protectorate, he formed a political party, the Bechuanaland Democratic Party (BDP), which won an overwhelming mandate to lead Botswana to independence in 1965. Under Seretse's leadership, the country developed into a stable democracy with a thriving economy and on his death, in 1980, the world's leaders paid tribute to his outstanding contribution to this continent. Tanzanian President, Julius Nyerere's eulogy at the funeral included the following lines: 'Seretse Khama was a democrat – by inheritance, by nature and by intellectual conviction. The Equality of Man was so deeply engrained in him that he noticed neither race, colour, religion nor creed – only character and actions.'

Sir Seretse Khama's eldest son, Ian, presently maintains custodianship of this family's great legacy and continues to realise both his and his father's dreams for Botswana.

And over dinner Mike and I suddenly realised why I had battled to keep up with the wagons before Shoshong – I had approached the mountains from the wrong side. From Richard's description of the position of Mackenzie's house in the gorge, we worked out that he'd camped on the northern side of the Bamangwato Hills, and that he had probably found a quicker (if not shorter) route to them than mine. And because 'Unicorn Pass' was probably in that part of the range, I would have their shorter route out of the area also denied to me. My poor pins.

Mpho, meanwhile, was coming along in literal leaps and bounds and had easily adapted to the little gypsy caravan she'd joined. Hills puppy food (brought in by Franci from Johannesburg), love and a worm tablet had already changed her from a cringing, characterless lump into a playful, affectionate motormouth. Tapiwa was beginning to play with '*that* woman' when he thought we weren't looking and had even allowed her to share his cushion at night. But having her with us was already proving to be a logistical challenge. Dogs are not allowed through Botswana's vet fences without a rabies inoculation but a visit to the government vet in Shoshong revealed that they didn't keep these vaccines in their clinic. We'd have to

Building up Buttercup

go to Mahalapye, 40 kilometres away. But a phone call to that vet revealed that they too didn't have the drugs. We'd have to go to Serowe, some 100 kilometres away. Well, that was on my path, so Mpho would just have to wait for her vaccination 'passport', and until such time as she got it I would just have to break the law by smuggling her through the fences. I cannot admit to having had a crisis of conscience about this decision, because we'd seen so many (patently uninoculated) dogs crawling through the fences at will, but I did worry about the implications for my sponsors if I (or any member of my team) was caught doing something illegal in a foreign country. Mpho was clearly free of any communicable diseases and we'd just have to be careful. And so, the canine contraband smugglers moved out of Shoshong.

Sekgoma's view – and ours

Shoshong to Paje

A hostile sun and a hot, dry wind

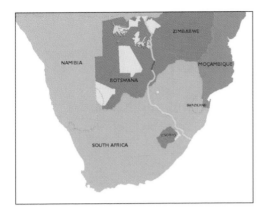

Shoshong to Paje
123 kilometres
Total: 1 491
Week 13
6–12 June

Hallelujah, praise the ancestors – camp strike was at last slick and quick! J and S worked hard for a pain-free move. Team dynamics have clearly changed. J is now much more efficient and enthusiastic. S battles to get up in the mornings, which I'll have to work on because I rely on the 'coolth' to make good progress, but the duo have a new modus operandi and it's working – Yay! Yay! Haven't the heart to tell them, but R says in The Diary that by this stage they needed only half an hour to get up, pack up the tents, yoke the oxen and get a cup of coffee and a rusk!

'The longer I'm on this trip, Patricia, the more I realise how tough your ancestors were,' said John as we arrived at our second camp of the week, deep in the bush north of Paje. It's something I too continued to marvel at, as we moved further and further into the thirst lands of Botswana. Richard and Robert were English gentlemen, after all, born not so much with the proverbial silver spoon in their mouths as the whole family dinner service, and prior to their arrival in Africa they wouldn't have encountered anything more menacing than a Dorset fox. Having seen active service in the Crimean War, Richard must have been somewhat inured to carnage and suffering, but how did he and his party cope with this pitiless place? And how did they *feel* about what they endured out here? It was one of my great frustrations with Richard's journal that, like all men of his time and class, he considered it inappropriate to express fear, elation, passion or pain. Each night as I read his journal before sleep, I found myself trying to join the dots of his narrative with emotional subtext, knowing full well that I would never get close to reading the manly Victorian heart and mind.

Understatement is common to most of the 19th-century explorer travelogues, and it can result in the modern reader underestimating what these early adventurers and missionaries endured. My friend Michael Callender (a respected hunter himself, with an excellent Africana collection) wrote a mini-thesis on Richard's journal for me, comparing the Glyns' experiences with those of other hunters of the time. As he continually reinforces in this fine piece of work, life in the interior of Africa was about thirst and dust and discomfort. 'They survived on sparse rations (apart from what they shot), exposing themselves to constant perils from hostile tribes, searing heat, their mercurial weaponry and the savagery of wild beasts.'

And the 1863 party's thirst was quite horrendous in the region through which I was now walking. Indeed the battle for water was to become a constant lament in this section of the journal, and because I had the unique opportunity of traversing the same semidesert on foot, I was beginning to appreciate as I never had before how essential water is to strength and (ultimately) survival. Soon after leaving Sekgoma's kraal, the expedition's guides found a beautiful spring called Lotlocke, where they spent a whole day enjoying the bounty of this 'striking fountain', but after that things simply went from bad to worse.

8th June. Outspanned by the Loghaganing pits but they were dry; five hours more and we only got enough for the horses at a rock spring Loak.

9th. The guides talked of more water nearby, but could not find it; I shot an impala however, which was almost as much wanted as water, as we had got nothing since Sekomie's camp. Trekked at 10 o'clock, finding about one bucket full at Metse Mashu, and kept on, only just resting the oxen for a couple of hours till dark, for they were too thirsty to feed.

10th. Trekked from earliest dawn over the most hopeless-looking sand flat, the guides giving most contradictory and vague reports about the next water, and the oxen looking most wretched. About 2 o'clock we saw hills to the south east, and soon after spotted a native who eventually took us to two springs filling small rock basins... The oxen had not drunk for three hot days and fought and struggled for the water till they worked it up into such a mud paste that, thirsty as they were, they would not drink half enough. We tried filters, muslin etc. on it, but in vain; it was quite undrinkable.

This was life on the edge, a dreadful struggle for survival under (as I was now finding) a hostile sun and a hot, dry wind that sandpapers the skin, scalds the lips and saps every drop of energy from the body. And, unlike my two dogs who were in an air-conditioned Isuzu when the going got tough, my ancestors' horses were beginning to pay the ultimate price for being out here:

6th June: At 8.30 when the moon got up we inspanned again and were just about to trek when the screech of a horse startled us, and about a hundred yards from the wagons we found Bob's chestnut lying on the ground; fierce growls close by told us who had done the deed. We loosed the dogs but most of them attacked the wounded horse, the rest barked at a safe distance from the lion, who dodged us about the bushes and kept coming back towards the horse... Finding the dogs would not bring him to bay, we went back to the horse who did not look much wounded; we put a bandage on his neck, but it was no use – he died in half an hour; his vertebrae must have been touched.

And poor old Moonlight, the 'butcher's hack' from Durban, was about to breathe his last in similar circumstances. Kiwi, an after-rider hired at Shoshong (who turned out not to be able to ride at all), was swept from Moonlight's back during a giraffe hunt, after which the horse bolted. Thinking (quite rightly) that it would head back towards the nearest water, Richard sent Kean there the next day, but there was no sign of Moonlight.

I heard nothing of him till I returned to Sekomies months afterwards, when a blood stained saddle was brought to me, and the tale told that it and a few horse bones had been found not far from Lettoche.

Lettoche, Lotlocke, Loghanganing, Metse Mashu – I rolled the words around my tongue, trying to work out to what places these Victorian corruptions might refer. They'd intrigued Mike Main and Izak Barnard, too, along with the third man in Botswana's trinity of history pundits, Alec Campbell. All three thought that the last name referred to the Metsemasweu River, whose headwaters are close to the modern day town of Serowe, but the rest of the places remained an intriguing mystery. Mike and Kirsten had done some impressive research on the Glyns' route through the area in advance of my arrival there, but had run out of time in finding old villagers who might have known where these springs were. My casual conversations with Shoshong residents had yielded nothing either, so I was going to have to settle for following the general direction of the old party. Looking at the maps, I had no doubt they'd travelled through the maze of rocky outcrops called the Mokgware Hills, but I would use what

A hunter's best friend

Early European visitors to Africa's shores would have encountered a long tradition of hunting with dogs already well entrenched here – a tradition that was (and is) as highly developed as beagling in England or coursing in Scotland, though not nearly as well regarded. And the packs of hounds that ventured forth into our hinterland with the early explorers and their staff were a mixture of both continents' tried-and-tested canines – among them local pariahs, greyhounds and pointers. After years of colonial rule and 'expeditioning', new breeds were developed, drawing on the best of both worlds, until dogs like the Rhodesian ridgeback and boerbull came into being and were soon much sought-after as protectors and hunters.

The practice of hunting with dogs is, however, very cruel – both to prey and pursuer – and it is outlawed in South Africa today. There are common misconceptions that dogs were used in 19th-century hunts to kill game, but while the pack was certainly free to bring down (and eat) smaller species like hares and duiker, dogs were employed to keep big game at bay before the hunter could despatch his quarry. The hounds would distract the animal's attention by barking furiously, and wear it down to a state of exhaustion by darting back and forth just beyond the reach of claw or tusk. And they suffered appalling wounds and terrible deaths during these activities – indeed, the vast majority of them never made it home alive. William Baldwin, for instance, brought seven deerhounds with him from England – and not one survived. Gordon Cumming lost 70 dogs on his five-year safari. Richard's diary is sobering in its description of the attrition among his English pointers and by the time he reached Durban only four of the 20 dogs he'd bought in Natal had made it back to the Colony:

Cruel to both prey and pursuer

One of my dogs, Venture, had died of a fit, several others had before this departed this life, run over by wagons or strayed ox. Of the three [pointers] we took to the Zambezi, one died of distemper, one was given to Mosotani, and the third seemed quite well till after we left [the Falls], when he suddenly lost all flesh and strength, and though he fed well and lived for some time, Osborne shot him, as he was a living skeleton, a victim to the tsetse fly.

Because the hounds were viewed as useful adjuncts to the sporting life and were largely not the object of affection or emotional attachment, they were often given away for favours, ivory, food or water. Apart from being mauled by leopards or taken by crocodiles, they were sometimes accidentally shot or strangled by the tackle of the wagons. When game was scarce, the dogs went hungry, but the reverse applied too – they could gorge themselves on entrails and unprized bits of a carcass until they could hardly move. Sometimes a large hole was cut in a piece of meat and slipped over a dog's head so that it became its own food porter on the long trek back to the wagons.

There are, however, cases in which canine companionship is lauded in the hunting literature of the 1800s, particularly among those adventurers who chose to travel without the company of their compatriots. Burchell loved his Wantrouw (from the Afrikaans *wantrou*, meaning 'distrust' or, more appropriately, 'take care, this dog is suspicious of you'), describing him as a 'keen expert in comparative anatomy [and] the greatest canine traveller in memory'. Baldwin much admired his Ragman – 'a faithful and plucky young dog of my own breeding' – and owed his life to his greyhound Hopeful. On one desperately cold night in the wilderness, far from the wagons, Baldwin tied the legs of the dog together with stirrup leathers so that it would lie still, then placed it on his chest like a blanket, 'the warmth of his body saving my life'. In his famous book *African Hunting and Adventure from Natal to the Zambesi*, Baldwin also relates this story about a hunter falling into a pitfall:

'He had a dog with him, but it was chasing spring-buck, so he went head first into the hole himself, and succeeded in reaching the buck, but, in his endeavours, had got so far that he could not make an effort to get back; his arms were right before him, and his back wedged fast. He struggled so hard that he became insensible, and must have been all but suffocated, when his dog (bull and pointer – I have often seen it) saved his life by going back to the wagon, and attracting the notice of his [staff], who followed the dog to his master's assistance, and dug him out more dead than alive, having been about five hours in this situation.'

Canine companionship

became a busy wagon transport route between Shoshong and Serowe in the decades following the 1863 trip.

The old wagon road is now tarred – or at least that's what I thought, until I got another welcome visit from Izak Barnard who pointed out a dirt track running parallel to the highway. *Stupid klutz – I hadn't even noticed the original road!* Izak, Roger Webster and a coterie of womenfolk were returning from their investigation of an archaeology site further north and pulled up next to me in two cars. *Seeing Debbie (Roger's wife) and the girls all pretty and made-up and smelling nice made me feel like a sweaty old prune. Was I like that once upon a time?*

Had they come across me later that day, or the day after that, they would have found me in tears. *Digging deep now – really, really deep for the first time on the whole trip. The tar is like a bitumen hot-plate, the soles of my feet*

The wagon route from Shoshong to Serowe – now tarred and well populated

are scalded and bruised, thigh bones feel like they're shunting through my hips, my voice sounds like a cartoon character's I'm so exhausted. I had hit what runners call 'The Wall' and I continued to bang my head against it for three long days. Doubt began to niggle away at my self-confidence and fear gnawed at my strength. It felt as if I would do myself great injury if I carried on and I was at a loss as to how to solve the problem. By now I was superbly fit, I was eating and sleeping well and loving every minute of being out on the road. So why was this happening? And what must I do?

I needed to speak to someone who has encountered The Wall and knows how to scale it – Bruce Fordyce, South Africa's premier marathon champion. 'Just keep walking, Tricia,' he bellowed down our bad line. 'You're not going to do yourself any damage. Whatever happens, *you must not stop*, regardless of the pain. Because if you stop you'll never get going again. Keep walking.' So I did. Hour after hour, I used the rhyming mantras I'd learned from Karen Davies and Sue Oxborrow on The Blue Cross Challenge:

Calling the running guru, Bruce Fordyce

If it's to be
It's up to me
If it's to be
It's up to me

I had a good job
For twenty-five bob
And I left
I left, right, left
I had a good job
For twenty-five bob
And I left
I left, right, left…

And sure enough, three days later I blasted through the bricks of The Wall, feeling suddenly – miraculously – like it had never been there in the first place. A Batswana man pulled up in his bakkie and, having heard me tell my story of the walk, says to me: 'I want to marry you, strong woman.' To which I replied: 'You have no idea how much trouble you'd be taking on!'

What I also blasted into was the first vet fence we had to get Mpho through undetected. Sue and I hatched a plan. I would stride up to the guards as the advance decoy, regale them with the tale about my walk and forewarn them that my back-up vehicle was right behind me, during which time Sue would drive through with a cheery wave and her foot on the pedal. We waited until the dogs were asleep on the back seat and swung into action. A big Batswana woman sat splay-legged and sullen in a rickety chair next to the boom. She stared up at me, clearly not believing a word I told her, but I babbled on until I saw Sue safely over the grid and speeding down the road. It had worked. But we'd both had near heart attacks in its execution. The sooner we got that rabies jab the better.

Smugglers waiting for the signal

And the inoculations were available, thank goodness, in the next town – Serowe. So while Sue headed for the vet, I spent time learning more about this eye-catching place, built among hills shaped like Basotho hats. It is one of several seats of the Bamangwato people who used to move every couple of decades once they'd exhausted local grazing or water supplies. There is a commendable museum in the town, which is dedicated to the story of the Khama dynasty, and I was shown around it by curator Scobie Lekhutile. He's a gentle Rastafarian guy with a slow, loping gait and peaceful demeanour. His hair is tucked under a conical tube that resembles the one worn by The Cat in the Hat in Dr Seuss's children's books. Scobie is distantly related to the redoubtable Sekgoma who gave my forebears such a hard time at Shoshong, but he was quite candid (and humorous) about the

Scobie – the only Rasta Man in Serowe

old man, describing him as reactionary, fearsome and very quick to order summary executions of his captives. Together we walked to the top of one of Serowe's fabulous rock formations and the place where Sir Seretse Khama, his wife Ruth and many of the family's leaders have been laid to rest. This has to be one of the most impressive burial sites in the world, overlooking the plains below and protected by rocks of pyramidical proportions. Even Cecil John Rhodes must be green with envy. Wonderful to see Lady Ruth Khama up there with the family she sacrificed so much for. One comes away deeply impressed by the civility and natural gentility of this family.

I asked where that old devil Sekgoma was seeing out eternity. 'Oh, I wouldn't know that,' said Scobie. 'In his day, only a few trusted members of the tribe would bury the chief, and always in an unmarked site in the cattle kraal – that way his grave would be trampled to obscurity within days, and not vulnerable to other tribes who might desecrate the site and make *muti* out of his body. Only when the Khama family adopted Christianity did they build grand tombs up the hill.' Pity that. I find the notion of taking my rest under bovine mastication and methane farts strangely comforting!

North of Serowe I left the tar, thankfully, and started another section of the journey that had been meticulously 'recced' by Mike Main to mirror that of my ancestors as closely as possible. And the potential dangers of the 'hopeless-looking sand flat' that Richard described were not lost on my mentor. Mike had left us with a comprehensive series of GPS coordinates, detailed notes and (knowing me to be the wilful girl I am) a set of very strict instructions aimed at encouraging me to adopt a conservative approach to the territory ahead:

'Think caution,' he wrote. 'Do not read this casually. Plot the following positions carefully. Once you leave Paje, I forbid you (this is Uncle Michael speaking!) to attempt fancy "you go on now and I'll meet you this evening at the foot of that hill" short cuts when you are in very thick bush. In some places it is way beyond the capacity of any normal vehicle – except perhaps a Sherman tank – to get through. Any rescue will have to be effected on foot.' I'd gulped when I read this, and gulped again when I saw what he was talking about. Now we were truly in the middle of nowhere and after filling our tanks outside Paje, our 300 litres of water will have to be used sagaciously.

Last water re-fill and last download of e-mails before the 'hopeless looking sand flat'

I guess having no water could be used as a fine excuse for doing less washing. We've got our auto-laundry down to a fine art by now. Clothes are put into a bucket of water and suds, then placed in the Isuzu for a day's worth of shakin', rattlin' and rollin'. By the time you come to rinse out your gear at the end of the day, it's guaranteed Cleaner Than Clean – depending on whether or not you've chosen the right wash cycle, of course.

Water-wise washing

Selecting the correct programme is critical: 'delicates/minimum iron' do well on tarred roads, 'lightly soiled coloureds' prefer a sand track, but 'stubborn stains' require corrugated gravel!

Our new camp – brilliantly located and set up by John – is in the only clearing in the bush for kilometres. It must have been the site of an old kraal. We're on the side of a hill, so at least we're seeing the horizon for the first time in ages and I'm looking at a crescent moon and brilliant stars as I write this. Once again, Taps has named our new home – this is 'Crow Camp' because he spends his time ensuring that those 'beastly birds' don't steal from our kitchen. A previous one, 'Squirrel Camp', got its name from his furious digging in their many burrows beneath our feet – all to no avail. Like him, Mpho has worked out how far she can wander from camp without being in danger and she never goes further than those self-imposed limits. She has no fixed abode, but all the confidence of a dog whose home is where her heart is. They're good chums now, and I cannot describe the sense of peace and privilege you get after a long day in the hot sun, followed by a hot shower, then a whiskey by the fire with your two dogs curled up at your feet. Nothing comes close to beating the feeling and I'm so lucky to be here that I'm sometimes quite overcome.

Nothing beats the feeling

Paje to Tlalamabele

The smallest mistake can lead to death

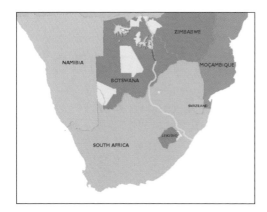

Paje to Tlalamabele
164 kilometres
Total: 1 655
Week 14
13–19 June

Over a cup of tea and a rusk on Monday morning I read more of Mike Main's meticulous notes: 'I am quite an experienced underwater diver. Being in the Kalahari is, to me, much like underwater diving. It is beguilingly simple to do. But the smallest mistake can lead to death. The idiots think they know it all, think they can handle anything and ignore Big Mamma Nature. Regrettably, in this harsh and marginal environment, she does not tolerate fools lightly.'

It was a sobering start to the week. Mike and Kirsten had plotted a route from Paje to the Tlalamabele Veterinary Fence whereby the vehicles would always

Whither?

be able to get to me, should I make one of the 'smallest mistake(s)' he warned me about. They'd had only three days in which to find a way through this broken terrain and due to lack of time it was, by their own admission, not necessarily the shortest one. The area is dotted with flat-topped hills that are fragments of the north-south escarpment that separates the true Kalahari to the west and the start of the Limpopo Valley to the east, and following the Mains' plan would mean weaving along the valleys between them through a mixture of (yet more) very deep sand and some rough rock, until I reached a belt of flat grasslands.

Looking at their zigzagged lines on the maps, I realised that I would have to do a lot more mileage than I would if I did a cross-country bush bash and met the vehicles at prearranged points. Should I risk it? I wrestled with my thoughts while Sue drove me to my starting point outside Paje and by the time we got there I had decided that I should err on the side of caution. It was the dogs, principally, that made up my mind. If I went off without vehicle support I would not be able to have Tapiwa with me in case I got into trouble, and if I did meet with some accident I was worried about my team having to cope with the responsibility and drama of a rescue effort while looking after the animals as well. I would be a good girl and stick to Mike's plan, even though it entailed covering over 160 kilometres in five days – a longer weekly distance than I'd done thus far in Botswana. And I knew that, with his great navigational nous, John would find short cuts for me on his searches for camp sites.

I set off from Paje, leaving Sue behind to send e-mails as the town had cellphone reception, and sallied forth into some of the deepest sand I'd encountered to date. But 20 kilometres of the harrowing silt did little to dampen my enthusiasm, for this was another momentous day on the walk and I was buoyed with anticipation at reaching an important marker. At lunchtime I clocked up my two millionth step on the Vitality pedometer and, fortuitously, I did so just outside our little Crow Camp. I ducked into camp and there lay a great surprise. John had done a whole 'two million steps' fandango, including a silver ice bucket (silver foil over a cut-off water bottle!), a nice piece of old wood in which he'd put my special bottle of whiskey, full table decorations, freshly baked bread etc. I was so touched, and we had a great time. After several cold beers, found it difficult to move out again and get another 10 kilometres under my belt, but there are big treats around every corner here, such as the Manketti tree (*Schinziophyton rautanenii*) – wondrous thing, which looks very like a baobab with palmate leaves and bark like a Venetian marbled

Going Big this week

A five-star party – bush style

column. Came upon my first belt of mopane, which means we're entering a new phase of the journey. Gratified to see that Richard saw his first here too.

In fact, the area was splendidly varied in its topography after the sand flats of the past few weeks and it had some truly amazing trees. During my long hours in their company, they came to resemble friends and confidants – silent witnesses to my trials, my terrors and my deepest secrets. By now I had become an inveterate chatterer both to trees and to myself, my imagination fuelled by the non-stop movie I was walking through. One minute Richard Attenborough was escorting me through clouds of golden and lime-green butterflies as the wind rustled the folded mopane leaves and they took to fluttering flight. The next I was trapped in the fleshy fingers of the Transvaal sesame bush (*Sesamothamnus lugardii*) like some twisted arboreal captor straight out of a scary scene from *Lord of the Rings*. Unlike us, Richard's expedition was making good use of the local flora to supplement their boring diet of meat and grain:

> The natives here eat two kinds of quadruple berry, one tasting like a dried currant (Moquana), on a bush of that shape, and the other red and oily tasting, on a smaller shrub; but their chief food is a grass root, like a crocus bulb, which the women root up all day; they also find a large long root, and roast the bean of a trefoil shrub, and the seeds of the bitter melon; they never grow anything, and rarely have a few goats.

Clearly, in 1863 the region still supported small communities – now there are none. We came across about three cattle posts and as many vehicles in the entire week, one of them owned by a rotund, bespectacled ex-policeman who was visiting his herds from town. Kaiser confirmed that the old wagon route is over the hill I'm walking next to, but am not going to do a big detour – this is close enough for me! For the rest, the area was utterly deserted. But

So exactly whose would these be?

there was plenty of evidence that it had been home to many people thousands of years ago. The ridges and hills of the escarpment were rimmed by rough stone walls and other remnants of Iron Age life and their summits littered with ancient globs of smelted iron and grain-bin outlines. From their table-top heights we gazed out onto blue-grey plains on which belts

Africa's Amazing Arbors

Living off the land

Walking through this arid terrain, it was hard to believe that it contained within its soil anything worth eating at all, but to the expert and trained eyes of Batswana groups and the Bushmen who used to live here, the trees, shrubs and tubers of the area have provided adequate (and, in some cases, tasty) nutrition for centuries. But it is food that often entails very hard work to harvest and prepare. The 'berries' to which Richard refers in the diary are more than likely those of the *Grewia* and *Ochna* families, and on ripening with the rains they bring rich pickings for local people. *Grewia flava* (Velvet raisin) has bi-lobed fruits that form the summertime staple diet of Bushmen living in the Kalahari, not only because the shrub is so abundant there but because the berries can be stored for a long time. When freshly picked, they taste like raisins, but they are also dried and ground to make porridge, and brewed into a beer with a powerful kick. The Bushmen also use young *Grewia* branches for arrows and drinking straws as the pith can be loosened by tapping the bark and then easily extracted. *Grewia retinervis* also occurs in this area but, while its seeds are very sour and vinegar-like, they are nevertheless eaten in extreme circumstances of hunger or thirst, particularly as they prevent perspiration. The 'oily tasting' berry of The Diary is probably that of *Ochna pulchra* (peeling bark *Ochna*, or *lekkerbreek* in Afrikaans), which yields an unpleasant-smelling greenish brown oil that can be used as a soap or skin treatment. As for the 'roasted beans of a trefoil shrub', perhaps Richard is referring here to *Tylosema esculentum*, whose roasted seeds taste very like peanuts. And further north Richard would have encountered *Bauhinia petersiana* (coffee Bauhinia), which was well known among early explorers for supplying them with 'Zambezi coffee'. Thomas Baines was the first foreign explorer to describe collecting the seeds, roasting and grinding them as a coffee substitute during his 1863 boat-building expedition (see page 261).

Izak Barnard (see page 251) has often witnessed the keen eye Bushmen have for signs of tubers buried deep within the Kalahari's sands – and their even keener memory for exactly where they saw this telltale evidence. Often the stems are mere sticks, just a few centimetres long, but their location will be remembered with GPS-like accuracy for months afterwards and relocated with astounding precision. The tubers, melons and bulbs of the region provide its people with both food and water in the dry winter months and they are gathered largely by women during highly sociable, gossipy outings to the veld. No food source is over-exploited to the detriment of the environment and young plants are invariably left or replanted for the next season's harvest. *Raphionacme burkei* is a round tuber weighing up to 2.5 kilograms which is a precious source of hydration for the Bushmen but its juices are milky and bitter, so the women grate the tuber and mix the pulp with briefly chewed *Grewia flava*, *Aloe transvaalensis* or *Terminalea sericea* leaves whose tannins neutralise the sour taste of the tuber. It is a painstaking process that yields what we would regard as very little moisture for the efforts expended. Even more work is entailed in harvesting *Cucumis kalahariensis* – a long, thin tuber that is buried at a full arm's length beneath the sands and takes hours of digging to bring to the surface. It can be eaten raw but, when roasted on hot coals, tastes like potato. Its 'cousin' *C. metuliferus* has spines that belie its fresh, sweet taste, rather like that of a watermelon or cucumber – a taste that is also found in the so-called 'wild cucumber', *Coccinia sessissifolia*. Richard talks of 'seeds of the bitter melon' – this is more than likely the tsamma melon (*Citrullus lanatus*), which at times litters the veld in great abundance, and whose seeds are ground and cooked into a porridge. The melons vary considerably as to their bitterness – the most stringent of them likened by Izak to chewing on 10 quinine pills without water. So the Bushmen cut a small square out of the melon and place it on the tip of the tongue to test for bitterness before consuming the flesh further.

In the absence of guns, African people at the time of Richard's visit had many ingenious methods of hunting game. These included poisoned arrows (the use of which was perfected by the Bushmen people), spears, harpoons, packs of dogs, nets and traps such as this one described by my ancestor:

Coming down to the water we narrowly escaped some spear traps which were set round the springs. A heavy log of wood with a spear head in it is fixed high up in a tree, by a string, which is brought down

The deadly spear trap

and passed across the game path below; some natives had just killed a quagga with one

The use of pitfalls - known by some explorers as *fanghuts*, an Anglicisation of the Afrikaans *vang gat*, meaning 'catch hole' – was also common, and although they resulted in cruel and agonising deaths for the animals trapped within them (often impaled on sharpened sticks buried at the bottom of the pit), they were an extremely effective method of capturing many head of game in a short time. Thomas Baines, for instance, describes a driven hunt with the Barolong people in which they killed 2 000 head of game in one day. Andrew Anderson, a traveller through these parts at much the same time as the Glyns, describes such a hunt in his book *Twenty Five Years in a Wagon* (Chapman and Hall, London 1888):

'In those extensive plains, where tens of thousands of antelope species roam, a favourable spot would be selected,

A slow but sure death

and from eight to 12 large pits dug, ranged in a row 15 feet apart, the earth taken out to the depth of five feet... These would occupy a considerable space; at the extreme ends a thick bush hedge would prevent the game leaping over, and several hundred men placed in addition to prevent the animals going round, When all was prepared, men would drive the game by thousands towards the pits... until the pits were full. Then the grand slaughter commenced; as many as 1 200 have been caught at one time. All the men, women, and children set to work; fires made, cooking begins, the skins taken off, and the meat cut up into lengths and hung up to dry in the sun for future use; not a marrow bone is wasted, and it takes days to complete the work.'

Baines also described (in *Shifts and Expedients of Camp Life, Travel and Exploration*, Horace Cox, 1871) the use of *scherms* – pits in which hunters waited for game to pass, and the equally surreptitious use of holes dug along known game paths and covered over with grass and sticks to await unsuspecting animals. These pits were deeper and tapered towards the bottom, with the intention that any animal that fell into them would be wedged between their sides without being able to touch the bottom with its legs and so lever or launch itself out. Both types of pits, however, were often left in the veld for years afterwards, resulting in many a man, ox and dog falling into them, sometimes remaining there undiscovered and slowly perishing over many days.

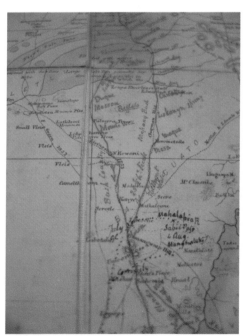
Richard's map of this section of the journey

Maps on paper... and on sand

of tall mopane trees alternated with bands of crisp grasses and groves of fantastical trees – *360 degrees of Hollywood Africa, Meryl-Streep-and-Robert-Redford Africa!*

Panoramic views to equal any movie

The plains, I thought, must once have been home to massive herds of practically every African mammal imaginable, but – barring a few red hartebeest, duiker and jackal – they were certainly not there for us. And nor were they there for Richard, Robert and Henry. Although their animals were no longer battling with water shortages, they and their staff were now going hungry – very hungry. It was time to throw the bones in the time-honoured African tradition:

> *15th June. The natives had a cast with their dice, i.e. bits of bone wood and little bucks hooves and foretold that we should kill game, which came to pass by my shooting a wildebeest.*

But the dogs, it seems, saw little of the wildebeest's bounty:

> *17th June. Having no meat for my dogs, I shot and cooked a vulture for them, but though very hungry only one would touch it; it certainly did not taste inviting.*

Well, I should think not. A few days later Richard at last shot a giraffe and there was a veritable orgy of eating in their camp:

> *19th June. Loaded the back of the two wagons with great joints of giraffe meat; the servants had cooked and eaten, eaten and cooked the whole night long. I don't believe any of them had stopped once, and they now each started with four or five pounds on a stick to eat as they went along.*

By contrast, I wanted for nothing, having the luxury of Suzi's Snack Bar following me in the Isuzu. We lunched on crisp lettuce-and-tuna sandwiches, fruit sticks and orange juice. *Yes, it's tough out here and, yes, I'm very proud of the self-discipline required to walk 35 kilometres per day in these conditions, but without mounting an expedition in which resupply from Johannesburg and the use of borehole water is disallowed, we cannot know what it's like to truly suffer in this beautiful, cruel land.*

The very, very old days

Mike Main's book *Kalahari* (Southern Book Publishers, Johannesburg, 1987) provides a useful synopsis not only about the intensive research taking place on Iron Age sites in the Kalahari but also about the debates raging about when these hills were first occupied – and by whom. Those debates are too lengthy to reproduce here, but Mike graciously pays tribute to the work of an American archaeologist called Dr Jim Denbow and his outstanding successes in this area, among them an ingenious method of locating non-walled Iron Age sites by means of aerial photography. Jim, so Mike tells us, 'was aware that most of these sites had had cattle kept in or near them. It is a phenomenon of this part of the world that a particular grass, *Cenchrus ciliaris*, grows rankly on old cattle middens. It has a bold, white flowering head and, if it occurs in sufficient quantity, appears clearly on good aerial photographs.' Using this method, Denbow discovered at least 10 sites here and on the edges of the Makgadikgadi Pans dating from the first millennium [ad] – making the settlement of agricultural-

pastoral people in this area over 1 000 years older than was previously estimated. And the reason for these people's choice of home is well described in Mike's notes on one of the sites, written for his fellow archaeology fundis and forwarded to me prior to my walk: 'It seems to me that, in Botswana, escarpments are important places. Behind them lies the hinterland of waterless Kalahari. On their slopes and at the foot will be springs and seeps where the Ntane Sandstone 'weeps' from the vast quantity of groundwater it holds. Escarpment lands are seen from experience to be riven with stream beds, gullies, rock pools and small waterfalls where water might easily be found and valleys on the sides of which will be deeper, better agricultural soils. Isolated outlier formations give access to these benefits in addition to providing a measure of protection from wildlife and other threats, a good view (for security) and the relative coolness of elevated positions.'

So, in short, this was a peach of a place for early inhabitants of the region – and a place that they occupied from roughly AD700 to AD1700, according to an e-mail I received from Jim Denbow. Extrapolating from one well-investigated site, called Bosutswe, Jim writes that the earliest settlers here would have lived in small, Iron Age villages, made pottery decorated with simple neck bands and tended goats, whose kraals they moved every 20 years or so after the dung had built up to such a height within them that the livestock could jump over the barricade. Hunting

A tell-tale circle of stones

Gargantuan tables on endless plains

of zebra and wildebeest supplemented their diets and their farmlands would have produced crops such as sorghum and millet.

After about AD900 the sites became more important politically, as their people started trading with 'Iron Agers' to the west in Ngamiland, made ochre-burnished bowls, did less hunting and began raising cattle and sheep as well as their traditional goats. Then trade with the East, via the east coast of Africa, began, with ivory and hides being exchanged for glass beads, marine shells and other status items attendant on the newly emergent hierarchical society. Interestingly, chickens would now have been kept at the sites – brought all the way from Indonesia – and European rats (no doubt from ships) also found their way onto what was now becoming a luxury trade route. Around CE1200, it is thought that drier conditions in the Kalahari affected the agropastoral lifestyle negatively and so trading took on a more important place in the area's economy. More direct connections were forged with the powerful chiefdom at

Mapungubwe in South Africa and a select group of families who aligned themselves with this trading 'Mecca' built more substantial, double-walled dwellings, while moving lower-status households off the hill entirely. Now, ceramic utensils were used and bronze items began to be produced, supplementing those of iron and copper. Soon the sites' inhabitants were in competition with Zimbabwean settlements or they may perhaps have been under the control of locally based Zimbabwe chiefs – whose influence can be seen in the Great-Zimbabwe-type chevron patterns in ruins near Sowa Pan. Between CE1300 and CE1500 Zimbabwean settlements came to dominate the regional political economy but it seems as if the people near Paje maintained some kind of cultural independence. Jim indicates that there is still much work to be done in finding out what happened here between CE1500 and CE1700, but that the final occupation of some sites was by people who built low, semicircular, stone-walled enclosures that may have been precedents for the *kgotlas* we see in Batswana culture today.

Peeing with the paparazzi

We had now perfected a system whereby John would do a recce of the following few days' walk (to confirm or alter Mike's recommendations), en route to finding our next camp site. He would then set up the tents, shower and 'kitchen', phone us on the sat phone with route changes and GPS coordinates, and stay behind in camp while Sue shadowed me on the 'road'. Seconding a runner or walker can be dull and boring work and I felt for her, sitting in the car hour upon hour, waiting for me to catch up. Driving around here is hectic – really bad roads, sometimes none at all, deep river gullies – and so, so easy to get lost as we've found to our cost. Sometimes I think it's a miracle we find each other at all! Profound exhaustion before lunch each day – is it lack of nutrition or water or electrolytes? The sand is abominable and I often get ratty with Sue. She takes it on the chin, brave girl, and we usually end the day with a huge laugh.

Saturday, 18 June. Mpho is sick. How sick I can't tell but she's refusing food, her gums are pale and she's listless. No vet for 150 kilometres, so called Mark Verseput, my dog doc in Jo'burg. He reckons her temperature isn't high enough for her to be suffering from biliary, which is such a quick killer. Although I have the necessary drugs to cope with such an emergency, sometimes I feel burdened by the responsibility of getting my two little dogs through this trip alive and in one piece. At least S and J are here by choice, but T and M don't have a say in whether they want to take these risks.

While I watched my little puppy languishing in the corner of my tent, I couldn't help but think of missionaries like David Livingstone and Holloway Helmore who subjected their children to these desperately harsh conditions in the name of God and 'civilisation'. Of course, having their families with them inspired confidence in the local peoples they wanted to convert, but were they (was I) foolish, grossly irresponsible or deluded to travel with dependants? Did seeking these hazards in the name of the Gospel dispel such doubts, or were they too kept awake by their fears, listening to the mournful pearl-spotted owl practise his descending scales in the dead of night?

I opened up Stella Kilby's account of the desperate Helmore expedition (*No Cross Marks the Spot*, Galamena Press, Southend on Sea, 2001). What must a mother feel, witnessing this?

'The poor children continually asked for water. I put them off as long as I could and when they could be denied no longer doled the precious fluid out a spoonful at a time to each of them. Poor Selina [aged 8] and little Henry [3] cried bitterly. Willie [6] bore up manfully, but his sunken eyes showed how much he suffered. Occasionally I observed a convulsive twitching of his features showing what an effort he was making to restrain his feelings. As for dear Lizzie [12], not a word of complaint, she did not even ask for water but lay on the ground all day perfectly quiet, her lips quite parched and blanched.'

Those are the words of Anne Helmore, written in these very parts during a seven-month trek from Kuruman in 1859. She was one of four London Missionary Society (LMS) representatives on their way to the Linyanti area to start a new mission among Chief Sekeletu and his Makololo people. It was a trip from hell, and remains one of the darkest stains on the reputation of David Livingstone. He had motivated for the founding of a mission there, despite knowing that the area's marshes were riddled with 'the fever' (malaria) and that Sekeletu was an ambitious tyrant capable of summary executions and selling his people into slavery. He also knew that Sekeletu was specifically awaiting him and his wife, Mary, because as the daughter of Mzilikazi's great friend Robert Moffat, Mary's presence in his kraal might prevent the Matabele from attacking him. Without the Livingstones' influence it was also extremely unlikely that Sekeletu could be persuaded to move the Makololo out of their swampy, sick home at Linyanti and settle in Barotseland, further north. Despite knowing these things and having undertaken to establish the mission, Livingstone promptly resigned from the LMS to pursue a career as an explorer and 'government emissary' for the Royal Geographical Society. The Directors of the LMS nonetheless assumed that he would meet the Helmore party at Linyanti and smooth its dealings with the leprosy-riddled Sekeletu. But Livingstone never pitched up, having been prevented by the Cahora Bassa Falls from navigating by boat up the Zambezi River to the Victoria Falls – and the chief's wrath at his non-arrival was to be taken out on Helmore's hapless group.

Holloway Helmore, his wife Anne, their four children, 24-year-old Roger Price, his wife Isabella, two Christian Bechuana teachers and some servants (making a total of 21) sallied forth from Serowe and soon struck the first of a litany of disasters in the baking mopaneveld I had zigzagged through over the previous few days. Like all travellers (including the Glyns, old and new), they were restricted to this route because it was bounded on the left by the Kalahari and on the right by the escarpment. It was tsetse free, but was renowned for its dryness. The missionaries'

Holloway Helmore

circumstances became increasingly dire and their oxen increasingly thirsty and recalcitrant until it was decided to outspan and drive the livestock northwards in the hope of finding water, which could then be sent back to the 'marooned' wagons, spaced several miles apart. Helmore and one of the servants stayed behind in the first wagon, after sending his wife Anne and their children ahead in the family's second wagon, with the Prices moving yet further along the 'road'. But the pools turned out to be muddy and yielded virtually nothing – prompting Anne's moving account of her children's suffering. Many of the oxen now bolted back to the last water hole they'd come across, so Price and some of the men walked about 56 miles (90 kilometres) and returned with enough water to keep the party alive for another few days. Two of the other men went in search of the oxen and returned many days later, having neither eaten nor drunk in the interim.

Anne Helmore

Anne Helmore was sitting in her wagon late one night, her children expiring around her, when she saw 'some persons appearing. They proved to be two Bakalahari bringing a tin canteen half full of water,' sent by Isabella Price who felt she could spare it. 'The Bakalahari passed on after having deposited the precious treasure, saying that though they had brought me water they had none for themselves. They were merely passing travellers. I almost thought them angels sent from heaven.' Later that night Anne 'saw in the bright moonlight a figure at a distance coming along the road. At first I could not make it out, it looked so tall but on coming nearer who should it prove to be but my servant Kionecoe, 18 years of age, carrying on her head an immense calabash holding about a pailful of water. On learning of our distress she volunteered to assist us. She had walked four hours… alone in the dead of night, in a strange country infested with lions, bearing her precious burden.'

How do you comment adequately on that kind of self-sacrifice? To my mind, it's the kind you often find among people who inhabit the most inhospitable regions of the earth. It is based on the philosophy that you do for others what you might need of them one day. I saw it on Everest, and not to put too dramatic a spin on things, we see it every day here in Botswana. We're moving among people who have nothing, but who expect nothing of us in return for water, advice or directions. In all the weeks I've been alone on the road in this country, I've never once felt unsafe or unwelcome.

To conclude the sad missionary saga, the families limped northward, across the Mababe Depression (where they suffered yet further thirst) and reached Linyanti seven months after they'd left Kuruman. Within two weeks of their arrival at Sekeletu's kraal, they started dying. First to go was their driver Molatsi, then little Henry, even 'littler' Eliza Price (born on the road a few months before), Selina, her mother Anne, Setloki (one of the Bechuana preachers) and finally Holloway Helmore himself. They assumed the killer was 'the fever', but in fact Sekeletu had poisoned an ox and some beer and sent it to the missionaries as his 'welcome' present – a fact that Stella Kilby had corroborated by Sekeletu's descendants when she visited the area 140 years after the disaster. Ironically, because Roger and Isabella Price did indeed have malaria on their arrival;

Roger and Isabella Price

they were too sick to partake of the meat and survived – little did they know that David Livingstone had left supplies of quinine and other medications not more than a few hundred metres from their camp but neglected to tell his fellow missionaries about them.

Not surprisingly, the young couple, now left in charge of the Helmores' two orphans, decided they should pack up and go. But Sekeletu wasn't going to make that easy, either. He robbed them of virtually everything they had, save one wagon and the clothes they stood up in. Then he sent them off with some guides whom he'd instructed to lead the Prices into tsetse country and abandon them there. A few days after their departure, Isabella finally succumbed and died, so Roger buried her under 'the only tree on the whole of the immense plain of the Mababe'. The tsetse claimed all but three of his 44 oxen before he staggered to the safety of Chief Lechulatebe at Lake Ngami and eventual rescue by his good friend John Mackenzie. But one last blow remained for poor Price. When he was on his way back to Kuruman, he met a man who had just come from the Mababe where he had buried his wife. 'I thought when I had put her poor body in the ground it would be allowed to mingle with the dust, but no! The horrid cruelty of the Makololo had not yet been satiated. When they left me they went and disinterred the body of my dear wife, cut off her face and took it home with them to be exhibited in the town… The agony of soul I have suffered you can more easily imagine than I can express.' Months later, Arthur Tidman, foreign secretary of the London

Missionary Society, wrote a scathing letter to Livingstone, charging him with at least some responsibility for the whole ghastly affair, but the 'great' man not only refused to accept any culpability for what had transpired but forever afterwards publicised a version of the incident given to him by Sekeletu. He didn't even bother to 'interview' the only survivor of the trip, Roger Price, to establish what the missionaries had experienced in that terrible place.

Sunday, 19 June. Mpho seems much better and I couldn't be more relieved. In fact, her recovery is nothing short of dramatic, so it seems I panicked for nothing. Hardly slept last night, but we had a good laugh around the fire this evening, coming up with names for our tents, inspired by the way the Helmore party named their wagons. Being Victorian, of course, they chose

A Walt Disney Incredible Journey

sober titles like 'Contentment Hall', 'Experience Tower' and 'The Nursery' (on account of the four little children it was home to.) In similar vein, we have christened our abodes 'Milton Manor', on account of Sue's prodigious use of Milton's germicide around the camp, and 'Navigation House', in honour of John's mapping skills. Mine is called 'The Kennel' for obvious reasons, but despite it being by far the dirtiest, it is definitely the most fun place to be at early-morning tea when Mpho is in top form. I wake up to a half-hour romp, during which buckets of sand are brought in from the Kalahari via eight flying feet. The big game is to charge out, do a couple of circuits around Mum's tent, then bundle back in and land on top of her prone form. Next there's a great time to be had with the broom while she tries to get rid of the muck before packing up her tent! Viva Africanis and onward Christian soldiers!

Tlalamabele to Sowa Pan

A magical desert of trompe l'oeils and mirages

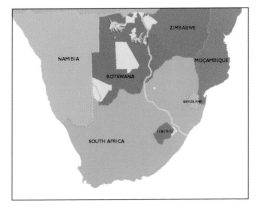

Tlalamabele to Sowa Pan
139 kilometres
Total: 1 794
Week 15
20–26 June

The hills are behind me now, and I'm walking in grassland predominantly, with bands of what looks like limestone every now and then – harbingers, no doubt, of the salt pans ahead. No palm trees in sight, though, as they were for Richard and none of the 'great white shells like whelks' to which he refers – maybe they're still ahead. Getting sad now that we're moving into the last month of our trip. What will my life be like when I get home? And how will I get used to not having these spectacular views every day?

John's reconnoitre of the Tlalamabele Veterinary Control Gate revealed that it was much busier than the last one we'd been through and that we'd have to get cleverer (and, sadly, more duplicitous) in getting Mpho safely through the fence. He drove along the far side of the wire barrier and phoned us with GPS coordinates of a point where we could meet him for the 'handover' about 1.5 kilometres from prying eyes. So while Sue did the dirty deed, I jovially walked past the pleasant policemen at the boom. Done. Whew! *I really don't like behaving like this among a law-abiding, hospitable nation but we have no option. Can't send M home because she won't be allowed through the border and don't have the time or the heart to find her a temporary home with some complete stranger in the area.*

I crossed the busy tarred road and set off along yet another vet fence, this one running parallel to the eastern shore of Sowa Pan. Within a few kilometres, I would reach the goal that had fired my imagination as none other on this trip, barring the Victoria Falls. My excitement mounted as the sand under my feet changed colour and texture from coarse yellow to fine white. I climbed a rocky ridge, surrounded by elegant seringas (*Kirkia acuminata*) and stately tick trees (*Sterculia africana*) and at its crest stopped dead in my tracks at the perfection of the view before me. Extending from one horizon to the other was the bleached shoreline of the spellbinding Makgadikgadi Pans. It was a sight so moving and beautiful that it had even melted the contained, Victorian heart of my ancestor – and teased out of him as close to an emotive description as I'd seen in his diary:

19ᵗʰ June. We saw a salt pan glistening like a distant sea in the sun. As we got nearer, the bush disappeared, the grass got more scanty and a white saline crust very like the top of a well-made apple pie cracked under our feet.

20ᵗʰ. Journeyed along the edge of the salt pan reaching to the western horizon, flat and glistening and whiter than water, the edge covered with belts of mopane trees, short grass, shingle of quartz pebbles, fine grey dust, or white lime crust, through which the wagon wheels sometimes broke into a moist marshy earth; some low hills were to the east and a gigantic baobab tree or two, but not a living thing, a wild dismal strange country; all distant objects inverted or doubled by the mirage. The wind gathered up the fine dust into tall pillars, which stalked each other over the plain and reminded one of the genii of Arabian Tales who used to travel in that form.

Makgadikgadi – 'what is above is below'. So the Tswana people named this tranquil place with its sky mirror. Once upon a time it was home to Jurassic mammals and science-fiction fish. Then the earth grunted and moved in its crusty old bed, tilting the blankets and diverting several of the rivers that fed this 120 000-square-kilometre inland lake. Slowly it shrank, leaving a stepped shoreline as evidence of its slow demise, and bands of pebbles to show where waves once pounded its periphery. Its waters evaporated, leaving concentrated, salty water in two comparatively tiny pans, the smaller and more easterly of them called Sowa, meaning 'salt'.

I descended the ridge towards the pan, and an hour later I was in tears: MY FIRST BAOBABS! And I have walked all this way to see them! They're the trees of my childhood, the symbols of my African-ness, of my dreaming. And to think that Richard and Robert would probably have seen these very ones too. What a feeling – I must keep it in a corner of my heart for ever.

To my ancestors, these strange forms were equally remarkable, but for different reasons. I imagined Bob reaching for his sketchbook while Richard sought words to describe their totally foreign attributes:

> ... [the] first baobab, a stunted giant, the trunk the colour of red granite and larger than English ideas can conceive, but the limbs quite out of proportion, which makes it a very ugly tree; they are fine landmarks, however, generally standing singly, far above everything else... [The] Dutch call it the cream-of-tartar tree as it is covered with nuts, which contain a powder round the seeds, which tastes like tartaric acid and makes a good drink with water.

Symbols of childhood, signs of 'home'

A moment to savour

One of the reasons for my great excitement at reaching Sowa Pan was that I would now have my first opportunity of doing a night walk. Since leaving Durban, I had wanted to mirror the old party's habit of trekking by full moon, but up to this point it had either been logistically tricky or downright dangerous for me to do so. At last I would have my chance – and in the most magical place of all. We set up camp on the highest point of Kokonje Island, one of the many vegetated spits that protrude onto the flat white clay of the pan like peninsulas on a sea, and watched a red orb drop out of the sky.

21 June. Dad's birthday and I paid tribute at sundown to his kind and gentle influence on my life. So regret that he's not here to witness this, but if he were around he would probably have tried to prevent me from doing such crazy things! Little did I know that Richard's genii (and perhaps my father's disapproval!) were to conspire against my moonlight amble, along with many more of our best-laid plans for the week ahead.

Arboreal landmarks

When the Great Spirit made the earth, so the Bushmen believe, he gave each animal its own tree. But the hyena was last in the receiving line, and when it saw that it had been given a baobab, it was so disgusted that it planted the Creator's gift upside down – so that the tree had its branches in the earth and its roots in the sky.

Judging from this charming legend, it seems that the first peoples of Africa were as deeply impressed by the bizarre appearance of the African baobab (*Adansonia digitata*), as later wagon travellers like Richard would be. Livingstone likened the trees to giant carrots or parsnips due to their upside-down appearance, and many writers have remarked on the fact that the trees' fat, contorted trunks seem so disproportionate to their (relatively) modest heights. But even if the baobab's beauty is lost on some, one thing is sure – the tree is impossible to ignore, particularly if one is travelling through the flat, arid landscape of northern Botswana. Here, baobabs are landmarks that dominate the horizon, often visible from a great distance. For many centuries they have been seen as desert 'lighthouses' by which travellers could navigate, places where passing 'wagon-ships' could leave post or provisions for each other, the trees' copious boles sometimes a source of life-saving water after a thirsty trek. Under their fleshy branches many a

Robert Glyn's sketch of a young baobab

camp was established by 19th-century hunters and traders – and several of these men were unable to resist the temptation of carving their initials into the trees' smooth and copiously folded bark. Despite being avowedly anti this practice, Livingstone hid his trademark *inside* a large baobab on the south bank of the Zambezi River near Chiramba – as if he knew how such desecration would be viewed by following generations. Near our route up the eastern shore of Sowa Pan, John was thrilled to find a different spelling of his surname, Ker, carved into one of these sentinels by an early (unknown) traveller. Further east, near Ntwetwe Pan, is Chapman's Baobab – a giant, six-stemmed specimen bearing the signature of the famous hunter/ explorer, along with those of Holloway Helmore's benighted expedition members (see page 229). Frederick Joseph Green gave his name to a tree not far away after he left his mark in its trunk while on his way to Matabeleland with his brother in 1858/9. The painter Thomas Baines, on encountering a stunning group of baobabs to the south of Nxai Pan, turned to his paint brush rather than his knife and left the world with a renowned painting of what have become known as the 'Seven Sisters'.

As one would expect, given their size, baobabs are home to many birds and mammals – among them fruit bats, galagos (bushbabies) and swallows. Hyena and leopard have been known to take shelter in large holes that sometimes form in the trees' trunks and many a *Homo sapiens sapiens* has found a use for their generous caverns and broad branches. Chapman describes having seen the Bushmen people making their huts high up in a baobab near Kaungara Pan in order to avoid troublesome lion in the area, making a ladder up to their 'home' by driving ascending pegs into its bark. More recently, the trees have been variously used as storage barns, a prison, a pub and – at Birchenough Bridge – a bus stop that could accommodate 30 to 40 people.

And apart from providing shelter, baobabs have many uses. Richard describes the refreshing drink that can be made from its seeds, and Africans make ropes, mats and even beds from the tree's bark. The people also cure all manner of afflictions and curses from its leaves, flowers and fruits. Baobabs are the object of superstition and legend to many groups on the African continent, for reasons that must include the fact that they are known to spontaneously combust. Elephant love the water-laden bark and can do immense damage to the trees' trunks – trunks that have been known to shrink and expand in response to the annual rainfall of the area in which they grow.

Above all, perhaps, it is the baobab's longevity that is its most impressive – and intriguing – quality. The trees grow extremely slowly and while botanists have yet to pinpoint precisely how old the largest specimens are, they estimate that those with trunks exceeding 10 metres in circumference are between 1 500 and 4 000 years old. So the baobab I came across that had me in tears at the thought that my ancestors too had seen it was in fact growing at the time of the Buddha.

What the dinosaurs saw

Roughly 70 million years ago, when what is now Africa was still home to dinosaurs, one of the world's mightiest rivers flowed through the southern African subcontinent. This huge river, which scientists call the paleo- or proto-Limpopo, rose in the Angolan Highlands and travelled thousands of kilometres in a southeasterly direction until it emptied into the sea roughly where the modern Limpopo does in Mozambique today. Well it flowed, that is, until shifts in the earth's crust placed a huge obstacle in its way about two million years ago. This ridge, called the Zimbabwe-Kalahari axis, ran from the heart of modern Zimbabwe in a southwesterly direction towards Gaborone in Botswana and caused the river to dam up. Slowly a superlake formed behind the barrier, its lowest and deepest points being where the Makgadikgadi Pans lie today. Astronauts can plainly see the evidence of this lake from space and their photographs show it to have been so large that it covered much of what is now Botswana – an area of between 60 000 and 80 000 km². And were you to drive around the lake's periphery (and no doubt some have in the course of their paleo-geomorphology investigations) you would see its edges marked by a combination of stepped shorelines and long sand ridges. These show that the water levels of the lake varied considerably over time and that it was occasionally as high as 950 metres above sea level, and as much as 300 to 400 metres deep.

So this was a phenomenally large expanse of water, and in its heyday it was simply teeming with life – similar to that found in the lakes, such as Turkana, of the East African Rift Valley. Gargantuan mammals thundered around its edges – and stayed right until the end days of its slow demise, about 50 000 to 100 000 years ago, when it would still have been a rich wetland area. Archaeologists have found evidence of almost every mammal species you can imagine living off the bountiful lake – only many of these were much, much larger than the ones we know now. The giant zebra, for instance, was about a third larger than its modern equivalents, and the giant buffalo had a horn span in the order of 2.8 metres. Indeed even the human beings who lived there in the Middle Stone Age were giants, averaging about 6½ feet. Interestingly, no fish fossils have yet been found, but archaeological exploration of the area has, to date, been superficial.

The Zambezi, Chobe and Okavango rivers fed the lake for thousands of years, but widespread faulting followed its formation – in part triggered by the weight of the water on the earth's crust. About 100 000 to 500 000 years ago the continent tilted,

Sowa's 'modern' shoreline

land levels changed and the rivers either reversed their flow or changed their course. Sediment began to collect in the lake's bowl, its waters slowly shrunk and evaporated, became progressively salty and therefore less hospitable to the life forms they had previously supported. Eventually a hard crust formed over the floor of the lake and the sterile, saline environment that developed upon it killed off not only the lake but all life forms that could not migrate or adapt to new 'homes'. The extent to which the lake's death was caused by climate changes we don't know, but there is some evidence that the Makgadikgadi Pans still held substantial quantities of water as recently as 1 500 years ago – perhaps because of higher rainfall and lower temperatures prevailing at the time.

All in all, it's a dramatic story and that it should take place in the arid areas of modern Botswana through which I was walking makes it all the more so. As Mike Main says, again in his book *Kalahari* (Southern Books, Johannesburg 1987):

'To me it is amazing and a source of endless fascination that the dry, hot, dusty Kalahari of today has been the scene of such remarkable events. It has borne upon its sands great rivers and vast lakes. It has heard the sound of crashing waves and witnessed wild storms, and it has seen rivers, swollen beyond their banks, coursing in untamed floods across its thirsty sands. Now, it is a thirstland, without rivers or lakes and the only sound in the distant bush is the soft sighing of the wind.'

A heart-melting sight – even for a Victorian gentleman

Kokonje camp

Traversing a lunar landscape

Two days before, Franci had phoned to say that she had come down with a bad bout of 'flu and would not be able to film this section of the walk. After a panicked search, she and Karin managed to engage the services of an adventure cameraman by the name of Phil Vail. He was to come in convoy with some of Sue's friends (Carol van der Linde, Mandy Momberg, Aileen Guest and Philippa Meldrum) who were joining us for the week. We waited and waited for them to arrive – 7pm came and went, as did 8, then 9… until we eventually saw their cars coming towards us across the blue sands like hovercraft on a sci-fi lunarscape. They'd been delayed trying to get Phil's saloon car through some of the rough terrain on the outskirts of the pans.

Bang goes my midnight stroll, damn it. Not enough time for Phil to rest and get ready before the walk, but John says the moon will be big for a few nights more, so I must be content with a postponement.

I rose extra early the next morning so that the dogs could have a walk on the island before being left with John while Phil and I set off on our first trans-pan odyssey. And it turned out to be 15 kilometres' worth of pure elation. *The surface is the colour of cement – and level enough to be the pride of any builder. It encourages introspection, despite the fact that I had a camera in my face for most of the day! Lots of wind, lots of fun until a complete screw-up spoilt the day. Had arranged to meet Sue at a GPS waypoint on the next spit that she could get to around the edges of the pan. But John had given us the coordinates for a point in the middle of the bush, so Phil and I spent an agonising afternoon crashing through the thorns trying to find the rendezvous. Felt like Hansel and Gretel – and arrived at our destination to find no Sue, no vehicle and no gingerbread house! So we trudged back to the edge of the island where she was standing on top of the vehicle scanning the horizon with a very worried frown! We've done 8*

A landscape that encourages introspection

kilometres' extra walking in a completely futile loop. Phil's exhausted and I must take ultimate responsibility for the mess. John worked hard at this but it's easy to make mistakes, and I should have checked his waypoints.

The next day we were once again to pay dearly for our errors. Our new camp was 70 kilometres further north on a game reserve owned by the local Soda Ash Plant. In the morning, it took four hours' driving around the edges of the pan to get back to my starting point where John and Phil dropped me off for a solo lumber through the same, dreaded mopane forest that had so frustrated us the previous day. Two hours later, I popped out the other side at our agreed meeting point – to find nothing but nothingness to greet me. I waited and wondered, waited and wondered – until I assumed the worst and phoned Sue who had the second satellite phone with her in camp.

'Something's happened to the boys – I think they might be stuck. You need to drop everything and come and get me please.'

Sue unloaded the water tanks from the roof of the Isuzu, along with everything else that would make the vehicle too heavy to pull off a rescue, and after several hours, arrived with Mandy to pick me up. We drove southwards around the spit and a little later came across John, walking forlornly towards the rendezvous point with a backpack containing food and water. He looked like a lugubrious ghost, covered in white clay.

'What's happened?' I said through clenched teeth.

'We were getting some 4x4 shots for the movie and got stuck on the pan,' he replied sheepishly.

Soon enough we came upon their tracks and it became clear what had happened. Instead of winding their way along the edges of the pan to the pick-up point, they'd decided (as boys will) to play while teacher's away.

I snapped at John with barely contained anger. 'But you've been told, you've been warned, you've been advised to follow old tracks and *never leave the shoreline unless you've tested the surface of the pan*. It's the first golden rule out here!'

What a forlorn sight greeted us when we got to the 'crash' site. The boys had sped out onto the clay tennis court of Sowa Pan, only to find that its foundations

The beached whale

were made of black, soapy, cloying mud. There lay the Isuzu, like a beached whale surrounded by evidence of their frantic but futile attempts to dig it out of trouble. Stuck. Badly stuck – a full 140 metres from the edge. Steven Spielberg and Michael Schumacher with their belly in the pan. Like John, Phil looked like a phantom, covered from head to toe in black mud and fine grey dust, and while I might see the humour of the situation now, I certainly didn't then. I erupted in volcanic fury at the two cowering miscreants.

'The second golden rule is *never try and dig yourself out of the pan*. You're meant to follow the "jack-and-pack" technique of winching up the vehicle and placing logs, grass, whatever you can find under the wheels until you've created a firm enough surface along your tracks to reverse back out. We're going to have an enormous battle getting you out now.'

I foresaw a ripple of unfortunate consequences about to unfold. The timetable determined that I must continue the walk, but I would now be unsupported until such time as Sue had managed to get John's vehicle out of its predicament. Phil would be needed for that job, so I would have no one to record this spectacular place on film, and most irritatingly of all I would again not be able to do a night walk because it was just too risky without back-up. What an unholy mess! Our tow straps weren't long enough to pull John's Isuzu out while keeping the second vehicle on safe ground, and Sue would have to go back to the Soda Ash Plant to borrow more. So we left the kamikaze kings to their grim fate with a couple of peanut-butter sandwiches, some cold tea and the aftertaste of a world-class wigging.

I set off alone across the grey desert landscape while Sue and Mandy drove home to our camp. A few hours later I arrived at the edge of the next spit – to find nothing but nothingness to greet me – yet again. Where was she? The sun went down and I began to get very cold. 'What's going *on*, Sue?' I bellowed down the sat phone. 'Sorry, Tricia, we got stuck!'

'I don't believe it! How much more of this crap are we going to put up with?'

Eventually, I heard the vehicle crashing through the undergrowth, followed by the sad story of the afternoon's events. Sue and Mandy had got wedged in a donga and, having given John their spade, spent hours digging their vehicle out of trouble with a hammer and some spanners. By the time they got back to camp and found some tow straps (from Julian Stewart and Shorne Darlow, two hugely helpful employees of the Plant) it was too late to get back out to the boys – the third golden rule being *never drive on the pans after dark*.

Girl Power: The rescue team

John and Phil would have to spend the night in their vehicle. *I'm worried about them alone out there – it gets so cold at night and Phil is an epileptic. Phoned his brother Sean Wisedale in Durban who says P is likely to have his pills with him, but that with his condition it's critical he gets enough sleep. Fat chance of that tonight!*

Morning came and the rescue effort swung into action while I headed out across the pan alone. And if it hadn't have been for Sue's friends I doubt that the exercise would have been successful that day. Philippa volunteered to stay in camp and look after the dogs while Sue, Mandy, Carol and Aileen drove back to the boys and their marooned vehicle. Several kilometres from the accident site they found a bare-chested cameraman walking towards them 'looking for cellphone reception'. It was a potentially life-threatening thing to do. Rule Number Four: *Never leave the place where you were last known to be.* Bad decisions in this ruthless environment can have ghastly consequences, as we'd heard from Julian the night before.

John and Phil had passed a tranquil night, watching the changing colours of the pan as the wind slowly abated and the moon inched up the sky. Every now and then they started the engine to warm themselves between their shivering excavations under the chassis of the vehicle and sorties to collect wood in the mopane forest on the spit nearby. By dawn it was clear that there was no way the vehicle was going to budge. They waited for a while until Phil, despite John's pleas, left on foot to find help. *Did he imagine we'd just leave them out there forever, I wonder?*

The girls swung into action. Measuring the distance from John's vehicle to the shoreline, they threaded seven tow straps together, linked up the Isuzus and Mandy gently inched the rescue vehicle up the embankment. The whale shuddered and started rolling out of the ditch. But John, no doubt as a result of his complete exhaustion, hit the brakes by mistake. A tow rope snapped and down fell the whale, back into its large plug-hole. 'Let's try again,' said Sue, 'but this time I'm going to drive your vehicle, John. You're just too tired to handle this.'

So with Aileen on signal duty between the cars, John and Carol wedging tree stumps under the wheels to prevent backslide and Phil filming the whole operation, they tried again. Success! The whale popped out like a cork from a champagne bottle and was dragged to the safety of the shoreline. Viva Suzi and Da Sisters!

Meanwhile, the flip side of the pan's Janus face was giving me the time of my life. Out here alone on this vast, flat plate, I am having one of the most euphoric, peaceful experiences I can remember. Everything is put into perspective and context. You learn that you are insignificant, fragile and expendable. You are taught what extinction looks like. You realise that nothing is as important as treading lightly on the earth and dealing gently with her peoples (even back-up!). You stare into your own soul.

The yoga mat on which you're contemplating your past and future conduct is slightly springy and covered in an ever-changing series of patterns. As the summer waters of the pan dry and recede, they leave beautiful textures and formations behind them. The colour is a subtle variation on cement grey, but one minute you're on an old elephant hide, the next a lizard skin. Then you're a gallinule, skipping over giant lily leaves or a child crunching over cornflakes. The pad, pad of your feet throws up little puffs of fine, grey dust in their driest parts and when the wind picks up you are covered in clouds of steely talcum powder. Nothing is as it seems in this magical desert of trompe l'oeils and mirages. Large objects are rendered tiny, and specks become monsters in a topsy-turvy world that taunts and deceives. You walk for hours towards a cow that turns out to be a branch, you head for a grassy knoll that shimmers and evaporates to nothingness. Eventually, I came across a pink feather or two, then more and more of them, followed by footprints and bird smells until I was in sight of thousands and thousands of flamingos swirling above an ice-blue mirror on the horizon.

Dealing with the beached whale

I am so proud of the fact that I am now competent enough in GPS navigation not to worry about getting lost, so I relaxed and had a little one-woman party – taking photos of my shadow and self-portraits of my little picnic in the middle of nowhere. Danced and sang from the depths of my being. Joy. Untrammelled joy and freedom. I am given to think that I even found God's address. Believers will no doubt be furious that it was given to a vociferous sceptic like me, but here it is: 20 22 45S / 26 10 25E, Sowa Pan, Makgadikgadi.

You reach it after 55 kilometres alone on foot through an ocean of post-apocalyptic stillness. When you get there, you take off your backpack and sit cross-legged on an utterly featureless landscape under a dome of bright sky. There is no shore in sight, no object to break the cut-line of the horizon. There is no life here. No trees, no birds, no animals. But there is all life here. The story of the earth told through the sands of this ancient lake, the story of your own past told through your quietened mind and enchanted heart.

Mike Main

There is a particularly beautiful description of the Makgadikgadi's duplicity in Mike Main's book *Kalahari* (Southern Book Publishers, Johannesburg, 1987): 'Early-morning mirages build clear, distant mountain ranges, which melt away in the rising sun. If you look about you, just after dawn, you will see on every horizon forbidding, blue-black walls of rock that seem to rise precipitously and encircle you completely... But as the temperature rises, it is the mountains whose confidence crumbles. First they begin to tremble, as if in fearful anticipation of the coming day, whose early light has revealed the barren wastes and lifeless plains they are to command. The burning heat and the endless emptiness seem too daunting a prospect. The first deserters waver and flee. The ranks broken, the army of hills and rocks turns tail. By eight o'clock there is nothing left but the sky and the grass and you.'

Surely this was the most remarkable place of my journey so far, and later in the day I was delighted to have a visit from the author of that tribute to its treacherous beauty. Mike and I huddled around a crackling fire with the cold

winds of the desert-like landscape ballooning our jerseys while he told me of the demise of the ancient sea and the animals that populated it. The next day, Izak Barnard spent time with us and related some of his many tales about the Bushmen people that populated the pans' peripheries in more recent times – people who had been scorned by my ancestors and their ilk and who continue to battle for their rights in modern Botswana:

> 22nd. Trekked as usual, leaving the salt pan, outspanned by a large Masarwa kraal (the Masarwas are the lowest cast of savages in these parts) but the people all bolted in the woods at our approach. And as we could not catch any, so failed to find out where they drank and had to go on without water.

By the end of the week I had completed all but a few kilometres of my magical walk up the eastern edge of Sowa Pan and, like the rest of the team, I was heartsore at the thought of leaving its flat horizons and gorgeous sunrises and sunsets. On Sunday, Izak drove me in his old Mercedes Benz to see something of the terrain I would face during the next section of the walk. We roared through the sand on the banks of the Nata River, then sped northwards on the tarred road towards Kasane before turning around at the vet fence control gate. The guard struck up a conversation with Izak, who regaled him with the story of my walk.

'Aren't you scared?' he asked with his head through the window and his eyes wide with disbelief. 'We have a lot of lions around here!'

The 'lowest class of savages'?

Hundreds of books and movies have been produced about the Bushmen, their remarkable survival techniques and sad struggles to maintain their lifestyle in 21st-century Africa. And while the influences of these earliest of Africa's inhabitants is widespread across the southern subcontinent, I was just as intrigued to hear the anecdotal descriptions of the effect these astounding aboriginal people have had on the life and worldview of one Izak Barnard.

For 22 years, starting in the early 1960s, Izak spent at least one month a year with different groups of Bushmen living around Phuduhudu, Kweneng, Metsiamonong and Molapo in the Kalahari. Because many of them speak Tswana and Izak too is fluent in that language, he was able to learn much about their social dynamics, spiritual practices and symbiotic lifestyle. He hunted with the men, gossiped with the women and played with the children. When they moved their grass-domed homes, when they treated the sick, when they danced and sang and fell into trances, he was there – quietly observing the ways of these most gentle and decent people. And that they in turn loved Izak is clear from the fact that there are between 40 and 50 Bushman songs about him and the times he shared with his Kalahari soul-mates.

As Izak is wont to say, for the Bushmen the land is their newspaper – a document they 'read' every morning for an update on what has happened in their world the night before. That they are phenomenal trackers is well known, but Izak attests to their almost telepathic ability to understand the mind of their prey. They can tell merely by the way an animal stands and moves whether it is territorial or migratory – whether it's, say, looking for its group or the next salt lick. Interestingly, though, while most Bushmen can find their way home across the most featureless landscape by day they become completely lost after dark – which is quite contrary to frequently published claims about their purported skills in stellar navigation.

Regarding their mysticism, Izak tells me that the strange and very powerful energy attendant on their trance dances can be felt even by observers of the ceremony. He's seen Bushmen bark like dogs and crow like chickens when in an exalted state, sometimes falling into the fire with no apparent damage to their skin. And when they return from their journeys into the spirit world, they bring important and

Izak Barnard and his soul-mates

valuable messages for their families. Each group has its own particular music to induce the trance state – and, most importantly, to end it too. One or two 'medicine men' are always in attendance during these ceremonies and should they, or the music, fail to bring the 'entranced' back to this world, he or she will die – and Izak has seen it happen.

The Bushmen's ability to access the bountiful but hidden 'pantry' of the Kalahari has already been described (see page 222), but Izak tells of their joyful feasting when fruits or game are abundant and their tendency to gorge themselves at these times, because tomorrow might bring nothing. Everything is shared, everyone is consulted in decision-making (including the children) and every task is undertaken cooperatively. 'They understand so much more about death than we do,' says Izak, 'because while we develop the science of technology, they develop the science of the soul. They leave their elderly to die with no apparent signs of grief, because they know that death is not an end but a transition. And because the survival of the group is dependent on everyone being strong, the weak or sick are also left behind.' One day, however, Izak came across a poignant exception to that rule. A little group comprising an adult man, his wife and their child had made the tiny grass shelter in which the elderly are traditionally left to die and placed their mother in it because she was blind and struggling to keep up. But she was still strong, so after much debate it was decided to make some animal skin patches for the old lady and to strap these to her knees and elbows as 'guards'. Thus protected and led by the small child, the old woman slowly crawled away across the hot sands, while the adults foraged for food in the surrounding bush – all three of them now extremely vulnerable to attack by the predators of the Kalahari. Eight days later, Izak drove into a settlement called Kang where he was astounded to see the family alive and in one piece. The old woman had crawled 25 kilometres to get there.

After many years with the Bushmen, Izak's services as a guide became much sought after by anthropologists, authors, tourists and film-makers wanting to observe and document their fast-disappearing world. Many of these visitors have witnessed, among other things, the Bushmen diviners' astounding (and unnerving) abilities. One of a German party's womenfolk insisted on having a psychic tell her fortune by 'reading' the skins – small discs of animal hide that are 'thrown' in much the same way as a Zulu *sangoma's* 'bones'. The diviner was reluctant to do so, but after much insistence said: 'You and your husband walk very far from each other. Your one child is with you, but not with you. And the other child is far, far away on another path.' Izak reports that the woman became quite hysterical and it emerged that she and her spouse were going through a divorce, their one child was mentally retarded and the second, a drug abuser.

For Izak, the Bushmen hold the key to contentment and peace – a key that has been long lost by modern 'civilisation'. 'They are the most polished, intuitive, graceful people I've met,' he says. 'They have time for each other – unike us – and they've taught me the most valuable lesson of my life: to deal honestly and decently with all people you come across.'

Sowa Pan to Tamafupa Pan

Wild, virgin Africa

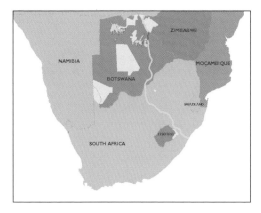

Sowa Pan to Tamafupa Pan
119 kilometres
Total: 1 912
Week 16
27June – 3 July

Soon after our exit from the Makgadikgadi Pans, we got intimations that we were entering the 'grown-up' part of our journey. 'Keep an eye on your dogs,' said the owner of Elephant Sands, the first public camp site we'd been in for months. 'The resident leopard around here has just had my two Jack Russells for dinner.' Suddenly none of us was quite so keen on the privacy afforded by having our tents far away from each other. We laagered the camp as best we could before nightfall, leaving an exposed flank to the chaotic protection of some beer-bellied *Sowf Effriken* 4x4 cowboys and their full-throated progeny. Oh, that a discerning leopard should wander through and pick out these barefoot pollutants of the gene pool.

Karin and Steve

It was all too much of a reminder of the world we'd be returning to after weeks of unpeopled landscapes and we (selfishly) resented the company the camp site provided, notwithstanding its very hospitable owners and piping-hot showers. Elephant Sands is situated just off the main road between Nata and Kasane and it was our home for three nights while I walked the last leg of Sowa Pan before heading north along the tarred road.

Once again, our little band of gypsies had changed. Phil Vail left us to return home with Aileen and Carol, and Karin and her American boyfriend Steven Bartlo arrived to film the last month of my walk. Karin loped after me for the final few kilometres of my pan trek, then jumped into the vehicle with Sue while I bundu-bashed into Nata town. K works so hard and so creatively. Loved having her around for the last of the meditative and uncluttered beauty of Sowa. She was lucky to get a lift into town, though, because I had a perfectly shitty afternoon battling through the thorn trees to Nata.

June 26th: Next morning we came to some fine pools and good grass very near the Shova River along whose banks we travelled some miles northeast. We had been advised to follow this river to the east, till we came to its higher branches, the Nata and the Tsebanane, but the natives told us that road was very dry, and promised to show us a better one, leaving the river at once. We trusted them for indeed we had little choice.

The last of Sowa Pan – this time with plenty of company

I too 'had little choice' now but to make some more navigational compromises. None of the pans and vleis mentioned after this entry in Richard's diary could be found on our maps and I had to assume that he and his party travelled further east than was feasible for us because we needed a road – however bad – for the vehicles. But Richard had mentioned 'Tamafupa Pan' and, again, thanks to Mike Main, I knew exactly where that was, so I reconciled myself to the fact that I would have to rejoin his tracks at that place about 70 kilometres further north. In the meantime, I would try to make fast progress along the tarred road I assumed ran parallel to his route.

Wednesday, 29 June. 35ks on hot tar and I'm broken tonight. Definitely feel worse after tar than any other surface. Started again in Nata town and left Sue and Karin there to do some filming. They walked the dogs along the river and Mpho had her first unexpected swim – thought she could walk on water and promptly sank! It is one of my regrets about this expedition that I hardly ever get time to enjoy those moments – I seem to spend my

Lion road

The Nata River – venue of Mpho's walk-on-water experiment

days walking, writing or washing. The girls eventually got to me after I'd had five hours alone on the road and I bit Sue's head off for leaving me so long without resupply. Felt like such a jerk. It must be hard for these people, having to deal with my sugar lows, but my temper was also the aftermath of fear. Several people had stopped to speak to me (one of them a guy who worked for National Parks) and all said I was mad to walk alone on the road because it's crawling with lions. But there will be similar dangers ahead for the next four weeks and I must get used to the prospect of walking into 'nasties'.

Thursday, 30 June. After yesterday's warnings, Sue and Mandy spent the day alternating the task of sitting on top of the vehicle to keep guard over me. Very touched, but got a little tired of the constant engine drone. Sue is clearly very nervous about me being out here unprotected, but I'll have to work on her to let things be because I can't have the Isuzu up my bum all day. After all, if a lion gets me, it's tickets (hopefully) and her only problem will be to clean up the mess and phone my mother!

In the late afternoon I was somewhat less full of bravado. Some 60 kilometres north of Nata I left the tarred road and walked eastward towards what is known as The Old Hunters' Road – a deep sand track (again) that snakes up the border between Zimbabwe and Botswana. Within metres of stepping onto it, I encountered signs of the 'big guys', followed by lion spoor the size of a soup plate. I froze. 'Please confirm for me, Mandy, that it's not going my way?' I whined to my roof-top guardian. 'Nope – relax,' she assured me. The harbingers in the sand seemed to send a very clear message: *Know your place!* In fact, to a townie alone on foot without any form of protection other than a pepper spray and a boat flare, it sent an even clearer message: *Know your limitations!* I gulped and soldiered on towards the finish of the day's walk.

My trek ended at a small water hole where three bull elephants were sucking their fill after a hot day in the bundu. They reminded me of old codgers having a natter over a G&T at their club, giving the lady visitor a cursory nod before resuming their tusk-tusking about the modern decline in water levels. (That's a fact, by the way. Botswana is drying up and Richard's diary confirms how much fuller the pans along this road were in the 1860s.) I enjoyed their quiet,

Roof-top guardian

lumbering company for a short while before one of them got too close for comfort and I leapt into the vehicle, called it quits and headed back to camp.

Quite enough for one day, thank you very much. Am I nervous about the next leg? Definitely. John did a recce of some of the old road today and confirms that it is wild, virgin Africa, almost untouched since R and R came through. Great privilege to be out here, but I will pay a high price emotionally trying to get everyone through it unscathed. And now we have only one satellite phone. The charlatan in Johannesburg who sold them to us is refusing to give us more airtime, as he promised to do, so until such time as Discovery can sort this out, we will have no e-mail contact and John will be able to receive calls but not make them. What he's to do in the event of something happening to him is anyone's guess. All rather scary.

Signs of company

An old gent at his club

The next morning we said goodbye to Mandy, Philippa and the throng of holidaymakers at Elephant Sands and our gypsy caravan moved off into 'wild, virgin Africa'. There was no sign of my big friends at the water hole where I resumed my walk, save their large footprints in the sand. Just as I was about to depart, a 4x4 pulled up containing a good-looking young professional hunter by the name of Tim Frayne. In the cab with him were his two Spanish clients.

'What are you doing here?' he enquired.

Yet again we told the story of the walk while the foreigners' eyes bored into me as if I were an asylum inmate. I quizzed Tim about what lay ahead.

'Plenty of leopard and lion for the next 10 to 15 kilometres – after that not too much to worry about,' he said. 'But if you get into trouble, these are the coordinates of our camp and you're welcome to pop in. We're pretty much the only folk out here.'

Meanwhile the three wise men's tracks were being closely studied by the Spaniards. *They were almost salivating as they pored over the telltale signs of the old gents' departure, all sparky in their anticipation of a kill.*

I felt sick. Made the stupid mistake of saying that one of the elephants had good tusks and am now tortured that I signed his death warrant.

Little did I know that a few days later I would get grizzly confirmation that The Ivory Club had an obituary posted at the door for one of its wisest members…

Further east, Richard too was keeping a beady eye out for local wildlife and in particular for the elephant he had come such a long way to hunt but had yet to see. Again he bemoaned the rampant plunder of his predecessors, and again I was alarmed to read of the devastating effect these early hunters had had on the area's herds.

June 29th: We strained our eyes to look for gemsbok, as we longed to have a gallop after those beautiful long horns over such ground; this is their country, but we could discover none. The late marks of a troop of elephants by the water was however an excitement, but as we knew that this herd had a choice of many fountains to drink at, and that therefore their whereabouts were very uncertain, we did not think it worth the loss of time after them, but still pushed on for our goal, the Zambezi. At Ombi we came on the tracks of wagons going south, and learnt from the natives that they were Chapman's (Messers Chapman and Baines) who we had hoped to have found near the Victoria Falls, below which they had been engaged in trying to launch a boat; but fever and other misfortunes had obliged the party to go south about January.

July 1st. We came to two pools in the sand, called Jurea, a place where Baldwin had great sport with elephants, buffalo and rhinoceros, but great was our disappointment on going round the pools to see no spoor of either of the former, and only one fresh of the latter animals; though the bleaching skulls of elephants will long bear witness to the sport of days gone by.

Five kilometres further along the road I found something my somewhat neurotic imagination thought to be evidence of someone else who'd tried to do this road on foot, alone and unarmed. Half buried in the dusty track was the vestige of a khaki shirt. Its edges were shredded, a lone button hung by a thread, and it was covered in puncture marks. 'Talk to me,' I implored while gazing at it over another of our wonderful picnic lunches in the bush.

Boat-building on the Zambezi

Arguably the most ambitious expedition ever underatken to the Zambezi River was that of James Chapman and Thomas Baines between 1860 and 1863. It was Chapman's dream (just as it had been Livingstone's) to prove the navigability of the river in order to foster commerce in the interior, so he and Baines hatched a brave but flawed plan to cart two copper boats there, which they hoped to launch below the Falls and 'sail' to the mouth of the river. Baines set about designing and constructing the boats in Cape Town, each of them comprising six watertight compartments, which weighed no more than what one man could easily carry and which could be separated for transport by wagon and for portage through the Zambezi's rapids. The idea was that, during calm sections of the river, the two hulls could be joined by parallel supports – catamaran style – and covered in canvas to give some protection against sun and wind. The boats would be sailed to Walvis Bay in what is now Namibia, then trekked by ox-wagon across that country and the Kalahari. But the expedition was so beset by trouble that it took *two years* to get only the ends of the boats to Logier Hill near the Batoka Gorge on the river – the party's oxen having died in their dozens of lung sickness, their horses stolen and 'Hottentots' having tried to prevent the group from travelling through their land. Baines set about trying to build the middle sections of the boat, while Chapman hunted to feed the camp, which included three white assistants and Chapman's brother Henry. Six months later only one boat was half finished and it was decided to abort

Boat-building at Logier Hill

the plan. By now the men had endured repeated bouts of malaria and were running out of medicine; they had suffered heatstroke, semi-starvation, accidents, deaths, nagana and bitter friction in camp. Leaving the copper boat-tips behind, they turned for home in March 1863 (their wagon tracks still visible when Richard and Robert came through here many months later and their boat-building yard still in evidence for many decades to come). But the return trip was also horrendous. On the way to Lake Ngami they found the countryside devastated by smallpox and ravaged by a war between the Damaras and the 'Hottentots' and they eventually limped into Walvis Bay and returned to Cape Town.

James Chapman's journal of his time at Logier Hill, published in *Travels in the Interior of South Africa*, Part II (AA Balkema, Cape Town, 1971) makes for poignant reading. It relates his battle with the burdens of leadership, constant headaches, loneliness and homesickness. His letters to his friend Sir George Grey are similarly moving, one of 20 September 1863 saying: 'My present state of health [is] much enfeebled and shattered [and] after an absence of nearly three years I have returned to find myself ruined in a pecuniary sense as well.'

But the men were not to know that the world would ultimately benefit from their trying time at the Zambezi – in the form of 11 beautiful paintings of the Victoria Falls and its environs by Thomas Baines and some pioneering photographs by James Chapman.

'Tell me what happened to you!' Sue looked at me as if I'd gone quite crazy. Perhaps I am losing it out here – I must get a grip. She spent the rest of the afternoon driving in close proximity (too close for my liking – I can't hear anything over the roar of the engine), but the terrain was open enough not to cause too much concern about something springing upon me unannounced, and by dusk we were safely ensconced in our new camp. Altogether, it had been a much easier passage than the old party had endured to this point.

July 1st: A very fine white grass growing about here works itself into your socks and trousers, so that you are driven wild unless you wear gaiters. We had indeed to give up light clothing altogether and wear nothing but heavy moleskin or leather, even on the hottest day, for nothing else has any chance amongst the wait-a-bit thorns, which never miss an opportunity of laying hold of you, and then it is simply a trial of strength between your coat and the fish-hook thorns.

The voorlopers' and oxen's legs were in a dreadful state, bleeding after every trek, and it was very often hard to make the oxen face the thorns at all, and quite impossible to keep the span straight, which in this heavy sand and thick trees makes driving very hard work, and the axe had now often to be produced to cut down a tree against which the wheel had struck.

Two ancient leadwoods (*Combretum imberbe*) guarded our tents on the edges of the completely dry Tamafupa Pan. It seemed, from the size of their girths, that they could have been easily 1 000 years old and I was, once again, deeply moved by the notion that my ancestors had also stood beneath them, gazing up at their delicate pods and grey mosaic bark. Indeed, the trees had the height and gravitas of Acropolis columns

A camp like a colander

and they were sure to have observed agonies and ecstasies along this pioneering ribbon equal to any Greek drama. They certainly witnessed behaviour befitting an Aristophanes comedy while we were there. My neurosis about the safety of Tapiwa and Mpho had us plugging every pinhole until our camp made Piet Retief's laager look like a colander. We had tents, vehicles, shade cloth and thorn bushes combined in an intricate barricade against the beasties. Truth be told, any leopard worth his salt could have strolled in for snacks if he'd so desired, but I was more anxious about keeping the dogs in than the predators out. At whiskey time, the 'kids' were summonsed from the camp peripheries and the 'door' in the laager closed for the night. At lights out, they were relegated to the car for fear that their scent would attract unwanted visitors to my tent. And you haven't seen relief until you've seen them being let out of their Isuzu kennel in the morning!

Bedding down in the Isuzu kennel

Saturday, 2 July. I think this walk is beginning to take its toll on my body because I am completely wiped out today. Got up at dawn to let two (hysterically relieved) dogs out of the car, fed them, took them for a little stroll, then collapsed back into bed until 11am. After a lazy day, I watched the sun go down over the inky-black dry soil of the pan as the guinea fowl found their roosts and the nightjars began their plaintive cries: 'Good Lord, Deliver Us.' Well, Good Lord deliver me from a city skyline for the rest of my days.

Dwarfed by an African Acropolis

Tamafupa Pan to Pandamatenga

Beauty beyond telling

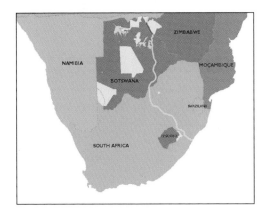

Tamafupa Pan to Pandamatenga
141 kilometres
Total: 2 053
Week 17
4–10 July

'Welcome to Hwange National Park,' said John, rushing into Tamafupa camp after another of his forays around the area. 'My Garmin says we're inside Zimbabwe right now and that The Old Hunters' Road weaves back and forth across the border all the way to Pandamatenga.'

He was right – without a GPS there was indeed no way of knowing which country we were in at any point along the road because a few hundred metres of sagging wire cable and the odd orange fence post were all that remained of the boundary fence between the two countries. When we first came across what remained of the demarcation, Sue and I took schoolgirl delight in an illegal crossing onto 'That Man's' turf. I wonder if anyone has ever been arrested on this road by Robert Mugabe's henchmen?

A border without a borderline

The sandy path I was now walking became known as The Old Hunters' Road subsequent to Richard, Robert and Henry's visit because it developed into something of a wagon highway to Central Africa during the last few decades of the 19th century. Increasing numbers of traders, hunters and even tourists to the Victoria Falls used the road because it was outside the tsetse belt and was linked by a chain of pans rather like pearls on a necklace or (as the Batswana describe it) vertebrae on a backbone. In those days most of the pans retained water until well into the winter, but it was to become a matter of increasing alarm to us as we travelled northwards alongside them to see that global warming and other climatic changes had resulted in not one of the pans having so much as a drop for our passage. When the time came to demarcate a border between what was then Rhodesia and Bechuanaland, colonial officials took the easiest option and declared this road to be the boundary and it was fairly well used until the parallel road between Francistown and Kasane was built. Slowly, The Old Hunter's Road fell into disuse – to the point

Pans as dry as old bones

at which, in 2005, the surrounding bush was in much the same state as it had been in 1863, but with a far more consistent track running through it than my ancestors had had to follow – as their *voorlopers* and oxen had learned to the cost of their lower limbs.

The Old Hunters' Road

The cost to me of walking this road was both emotional and psychological because for the first time on my journey I was in very real danger of

encountering some very dangerous animals and I had to concentrate hard with every step. It made the days long and harrowing. Gone are my musings and meditations as I power through triumphant mornings. Gone are my music and mutterings as I trudge through pain-filled afternoons. Now my mind is alert and my eyes are up, scanning the bush from left to right

Plenty of gadgets but no weapon

in a perpetual search for movement and form. I try to remember my bush lessons: check shady spots for lion, look for legs under trees, listen for alarm calls.

Suzi's Protection Services

But I know enough to know that I know nothing. I can feel how miserably inadequate my faculties have become after years of urban assault. Sure, I've done a fair bit of walking in 'Big Five' country – that was one of the privileges of growing up in Zambia and Zimbabwe – but it has always been with people who know what they're doing out here (where are you cousin John Dabbs when I need you most!) And despite the fact that Sue does a vehicle sweep of the road ahead and regularly climbs on top of our Isuzu's roof to look for trouble, this mopane forest is so thick in places that it could hide a dinosaur with ease, let alone an elephant. Not a comforting feeling.

And hardly a great time for the hounds. I'm so paranoid about them being munched that they're only allowed out of the vehicle when the terrain is open enough for us to see far ahead. They're bored out of their minds.

Waiting for 'Mum'

The brothers Glyn and Henry Osborne were now on the eve of becoming the fourth foreign party to reach the Victoria Falls since Livingstone had 'discovered' them eight years previously. The party had penetrated far into the 'Dark Continent' and was now in territory known to a mere handful of outsiders. As mentioned, they came across wagon tracks left by James Chapman and Thomas Baines after their expedition to the Falls the year before, but apart from this brief confirmation of their route, they were travelling blind. Even their local guides eventually confessed to having no idea where to find the legendary 'Smoke That Thunders'. At one point, the men found themselves well on their

A welcome leg-stretch for 'Pluto'

way to Mzilikazi's seat at Bulawayo before realising their navigational blunder. Venturing there without the chief having 'given the road' (in other words, permission to enter) would incur the kind of wrath that Zimbabwe's current head honcho would have visited upon me should I have attempted that diversion.

4 July. Got to camp nice and early after 26 ks, had a hot shower, but not before being told that we'd run out of water! Damn it! You know if teacher doesn't keep an eye on absolutely everything there's trouble. I haven't had a shower for two days in an effort to keep supplies up, but it seems John et al have been using it with abandon. Either that or the tanks weren't properly full when we left Elephant Sands, which I suspect is the case.

Running out of water was logistically problematic – to put it mildly – because we were now in the middle of nowhere. I would have to go to Tim Frayne's hunting camp to ask for assistance and I felt deeply humiliated at the prospect of letting them in on our incompetence.

But it was a visit that was to change my life…

Tim greeted me with bloodied hands, which he wiped on the sides of his shorts before shaking mine. I explained our problem and he quickly agreed to let us have some water from his borehole. Sue, Karin and I let the dogs out of the Isuzu and they rushed towards a pile of unidentifiable debris next to the kitchen. Oh no, I thought, I bet that's the remains of a carcass. Next they disappeared around a corner and I made the mistake of following them to a wire cage at the back of the staff quarters. There, tossed and toppled on

Staring at my ancestors' conduct

a concrete slab like barstools after a drunken brawl, were four grey, bloodied feet. Their treads were worn and their toenails scuffed and they'd clearly served one of Africa's great elephants for 50 or 60 years. Nearby were his dentures, smooth and creamy, but topped by the mushy remains of his skull flesh. On one of them the butchers had left an eye – a sad, accusing eye that shall haunt me forever. I was silenced and profoundly shaken by the ignominious death facing me. Is this one of the old chaps I saw at the water hole a couple of days ago? What kind of people enjoy doing this? My ancestors – that's what kind of people. How can my flesh and blood be so different from me?

Whether it was trauma or four months' party deprivation I can't say, but I proceeded to get absolutely motherless on the hunters' gin and asthmatic on their Cuban cigars. Sue and Karin reported the next morning that I spent eight drunken hours casting aspersions on their manhood, slandering their bloodthirsty Spanish nation and insisting that they apologise to the elephant for what they'd perpetrated. But their host, Tim Frayne, said one thing that temporarily silenced my tipply tirade and that shall also haunt me forever.

'Patricia,' he said in response to my asking him how he could slaughter for a living, 'if I hunted every day for the rest of my life, I wouldn't kill as many animals as I did in the name of conservation for KwaZulu-Natal Parks Department.'

We drove home well after dark to a very relieved John who'd sat by the fire worrying about what could have happened to us. I felt awful – it was the kind of inconsiderate and potentially dangerous behaviour for which I had often berated him and now I'd been guilty of it too. The next morning I was hungover and still sheepish.

Wednesday, 6 July. 15.67ks! Well, my drunkenness last night surely put paid to an early start. Got up at about 8am, had fried eggs and bacon, then promptly went back to bed. Dozed fitfully and eventually started walking at 1.15 – almost exactly the time I finished yesterday! It was hot and still and I struggled, but that's my fault I reckon! But the day provided me with lots of time to think and, having consumed bacon with my breakfast, I have come to the conclusion that I have no right to criticise those who hunt. It's gross hypocrisy to lambaste people like them while I support the abattoir industry through what I eat. Millions of head of livestock live and die in far worse circumstances than the old ellie I

Tim Frayne and some unruly visitors

saw yesterday, and I have decided to forgo meat and chicken once I get home – and for the rest of my life. Patricia The Vegetarian – who would have thought?

At this stage of their journey, my ancestors were still living in great hope that they'd bring down an elephant, not only because its ivory would help pay for their expedition but because of the tremendous kudos accorded to those who killed these mighty behemoths. But after what I'd witnessed in Tim's camp, I felt more than a little relieved that the 'brutes' were still eluding Richard and his party.

Jul 3rd. We trekked and soon saw that a troop of cow and calf elephants had passed along the road during the night. If we had known then how few we were destined to see, we should certainly have mounted and pursued.

There can be little doubt that the animals that fell to the old party's guns died horrible, agonising deaths because the weapons of the time were so inaccurate, and while my ancestors may have regarded hunting as being as innocuous as a game of cricket, I had many hours on the road to contemplate how they felt about the slow deaths they witnessed. My good friend Ivor Sander did some valuable research for me at the Brenthurst Library on the 'jolly good fun' that 19th-century hunters had at the expense of Africa's game, the gist of which I had in my tin-trunk library on the road. Some of it made for nauseating reading over my evening whiskey – Richard's diary included. Gordon Cumming, for instance, describes an elephant hunt thus in his book *A Hunter's life in South Africa* (John Murray, 1850):

'I hit a great bull in the shoulder and lamed him… I resolved to devote a short time in contemplation of this noble elephant before I should lay him low. I off-saddled the horses under a shady tree, made a fire and put on a kettle and made coffee. There I sat in my forest home, cooling sipping coffee, with one of the finest elephants in Africa awaiting my pleasure behind a neighbouring tree.

I then decided to make experiments for vulnerable points and, approaching very near, I fired several bullets at different parts of his enormous skull. This did not seem to affect him in the slightest; he only acknowledged the shots by a "salaam-like" movement of his trunk with the point of which he gently touched the wound with a striking and peculiar action. Surprised and shocked to find that I was only tormenting and prolonging the suffering of the noble beast, which bore his suffering with such dignified composure, I resolved to finish the proceedings with all possible despatch. Accordingly I opened fire upon him from the left side, aiming behind the shoulder, but even then it was long before the bullets seemed to take effect. I fired six shots with the two-grooved, then three shots at the same spot with the Dutch six-pounder. Large tears now trickled from his eyes, which slowly shut and opened; his colossal frame quivered convulsively and, falling on his side, he expired.'

It's quite disgusting. Disgusting and deplorable and unforgivable, but I have to ask myself how my conduct is going to be viewed many years from now. Are subsequent generations going to question why I was silent about the agony of animals in abattoirs, zoos, laboratories, canned-hunting operations and selective-breeding programmes? Are they going to demand an explanation as to why I contributed wilfully and knowingly to the demise of the planet? I suspect so. It's time to change.

Getting plastered with Tim's clients may have cost me my dignity, but it cost one Christoffel Schinderhutte his life. Several of the pans along The Old Hunters' Road are named after early pioneers in the area, one of whom was the aforementioned Stoffel, a man in the employ of George Westbeech, the trader founder of what is now the border town of Pandamatenga. In July 1875, Stoffel headed south down this road in his wagon but broke down – presumably at the pan named after him. So he reached for his bottle of home-brewed brandy and, while under its evil influence, took to the road again and promptly mowed down one of his servants. He then shot another hapless helper, as well as several of his oxen, and then fled into the bush, never to be seen again. Legend has it that all that was found to identify him was a piece of his beard and his *veldskoen*. It is not reported why his killer resisted the shoes, but I have some pet theories.

Before our alcoholic marathons, both Stoffel and I could have done with some other information, which John found in our travelling library while waiting for us in camp. Bartle Bull's *Safari: A Chronicle of Adventure* (Penguin, 1988) has a chapter about Karamojo Bell, who was named after the Karamojan hunting

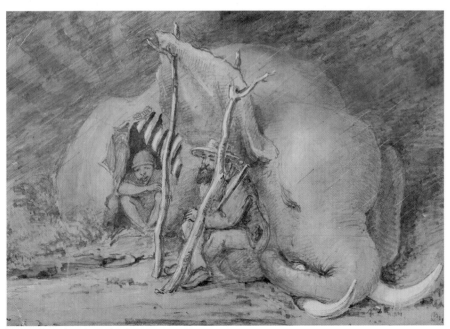

Unusual use for an elephant

The baker at work in his baobab kitchen

Still hard at the damned diary

grounds of northeastern Uganda and considered the greatest elephant hunter of his time (the early 1900s). Bell shot over 800 elephant in another of Africa's wild, remote wonderlands, which he's said to have loved because 'there a man could still slit a throat or grab a native girl without being badgered by alien law'. His Belgian clients taught him to handle post-slaughter drinking bouts by glugging a dozen raw eggs combined with lots of raw buffalo flesh before imbibing their liquid rot-gut. So now I know where I went wrong! Wonder what response I'd get from Sue (as a vegetarian of 20 years' standing) if I asked her to bring minced buffalo for my lunch on the road. 'Suzie's Snack Bar' is doubling as 'Suzie's Protection Services' at the moment and we are more than slightly smug that, after 17 weeks on the road, standards are still high. Our picnic table has a relatively clean cloth on it and we're still lunching on fine cheeses and fresh, crunchy salads. Dear Gilly and Taffy Walters sent us a huge sack of their famous, fabulous ODB bread mix (as in Our Daily Bread), which John bakes to perfection in our Cobb oven. Dinners still comprise lip-smackers like Thai beef stirfry, roast chicken (will miss those in my 'new' life!) and Greek-style couscous, so despite having walked 2 000 kilometres, I am still the substantial woman I was when I left. Maybe I should continue walking to Cairo, unsupported, in order to lose weight.

On Thursday, 7 July, I reached the last of the big milestones before the end of my journey – my 2 000th kilometre. The Victoria Falls were now hardly more than 140 kilometres away and my long walk would soon be at an end. I clocked up 'The Big Two' at Jolley's Pan, which is named after another early trader who died on the road – this time of malaria. For us, though, the place was indeed jolly, and the dogs and I did Olympic-style laps of honour around the pan to mark the occasion, while Sue applauded and Karin filmed my feat. The girls had spent the morning surreptitiously designing prizes for me, which included a garland made of mopane leaves and awards like 'The Soft Sand Award for Perseverance' (an envelope filled with Kalahari sand) and 'The Footing Award for Put-Foot Glyn' (a gnarled piece of mopane trunk). I shall treasure them always, just as I will the people who conceived them. Sue Oxborrow is quite one of the nicest people I know. She takes such good care of my dogs that I'm humbled. Taps is getting a tad fat from not walking enough during the past couple of weeks, poor dear, and he must wonder what he's done to deserve such slothfulness. Call me anthropomorphic, but I do believe that he knew we were celebrating something special and Karin has often remarked how sensitive he is to my moods. Mpho brought me a smelly old piece of dead vulture as her contribution to the festivities. Karin says that many indigenous guides and poachers in Africa believe that vultures symbolise foresight and knowledge and that I should be most grateful for the gift! How do I feel about doing 2 000ks? Well, for me this kind of challenge is much easier than handling my life back home and I'm dreading going back to its drudgery. I have self-discipline from Mum's genes, a high threshold of pain and a touch of masochism for good measure, so this task has been easy by comparison with dealing with Johannesburg's demands.

The 2 000ks Awards Luncheon

Got back to camp to find that John too had been furtively busy - baking a chocolate cake! It was light, creamy and a quite stupendous credit both to our little Cobb oven and the large baobab that sheltered it from the strong winds of the day. Steve provided his usual mix of eccentric music over the Isuzu's stereo and we partied late into the night. Karin's boyfriend is a beaut - so calm and unruffled by the hectic goings-on around him and always willing to help out with cooking. He's spent the past couple of weeks getting lost or stuck in a Mercedes Benz saloon car that is totally unsuited to this kind of terrain. But somehow, just when we think he's become lion lunch, he pitches up none the worse for wear. After 15 years meditating in some Indian ashram, he's got to be the most laid-back person I've ever met and he's just what we need in our manic camp.

As Richard's diary forewarned me, after a week of paying my dues through bands of dense, adrenaline-firing mopane forest (where I had come across plenty of spoor but nothing scarier than my own imaginings), I entered delightfully different terrain.

9th. The weary woods ended at last, sand changed to gravel, and from a rising ground we got a fine view over a broken, undulating, woody country, with high hills towards the East, most refreshing to the eyes after weeks of nothing but dead flat sand. 'There must be rivers there,' were everyone's words, and we were right, for in the afternoon we came to a real running clear stream such as we had not seen since we left Marico two months ago, called Deka... Our unaccustomed bodies had a swim in the river... In many places about here are hollows in the hills, bare, splintered and black, with quantities of fine dust, and ashes at the bottom, which look as if it could not be long since they were thrown out by volcanic action.

Richard had called the sight 'most refreshing to the eyes'. I would describe it as positively mind-altering. Beauty beyond telling – black, basaltic ridges

A big home for a small inhabitant

alternating with swathes of grasses that boasted every shade of a hairdresser's blond palette: strawberry, corn, platinum. Our new camp was on the side of a hill on which, once again, we had two arboreal sentinels – this time in the form of gnarled baobabs marking the slow passage of time. Mike Main's notes on the area suggested that it had been the site of an army base at the time of Rhodesia's guerrilla war and it certainly provided a wonderful lookout for activity on the plains below. Roan antelope, zebra and tsessebe hoofed around us by day and predators patrolled the area by night. At dusk we sat on top of the vehicle with the dogs and watched a sedate line of elephants, 100 strong, moving in single file through this giant landscape like hematite beads on a golden carpet.

Beauty beyond telling

Hyenas very close as I write this so the dogs are in the car. Shame - they're spending their whole lives there now. Despite the manifold gifts of the past four months, we are ready to end this great adventure now. Did a long interview with Karin, which always forces me to think about what I'm feeling. She says I often use the phrase 'I beat myself up out there today'. Well, that's how it feels. Every day is a slog - albeit a far-from-boring one - but I think I've hammered my old bod enough now, and John and Sue are mighty tired of repetitive camp chores and unconquerable grime. They've bashed in and pulled out literally thousands of tent pegs, struck and made camp 137 times, cooked hundreds of meals and washed dishes in difficult circumstances. For them, this trip must have been like being on army manoeuvre. One final push left.

Hurrying now

Relentless washing in a laundry with a view

That 'final push' would entail a mere 80 or 90 kilometres through the Matetsi Safari Area of Zimbabwe, and I decided to head as fast as I could towards the border town of Pandamatenga, where we'd be in cellphone range to sort out the logistics of the last leg of the journey. After covering 39 kilometres in thick sand and record speed, I arrived at the fence of the border post to an angry reception from an off-duty customs official chatting to a friend over tea. Why is it I always manage to approach international border posts via the back door?

'You are in a sensitive area and must leave immediately,' she said.

So we did, heading back to our magical 'baobab camp' where we sat out the weekend on its hill top watching more of the wildlife movie that had been our live entertainment for the past few days – puny, gobsmacked humans in the midst of a passing parade. On Sunday, however, the film reels changed and we found ourselves caught up in the midst of a spaghetti Western as shots zinged past our ears from poachers' guns and animals ran for cover. The hunters' car sported the somewhat ironic sign: 'Orphan Relief and Care.'

As usual, the ancestors' party was providing a mirror for our trials, but theirs were of a far more serious nature:

> Going home, the servant sighted some of Sekeletu's men, his enemies, dodging him through the bush, and was in mortal fear. It was lucky for him that we were there, as they had come on purpose to kill or carry off as slaves all the people of his kraal.

One of Richard's dogs, a 'cur' named Bass, disgraced himself with a gemsbok (whatever that might mean) and had been sold to a passing local for 40 pounds' worth of ivory, Osborne fell into a donga and Robert lost yet another mount:

> Sunday, 12th. Another evil also beset us, the horsesickness, the time and country for which we thought we had long ago passed, and carried off Colesberg, a shooting horse of Bob's in a few hours. This was a severe loss to him, as he had now lost his two steadiest horses, and his arm being still very weak, he could only use a light rifle.

Bob, then, was still paying heavily for his riding accident in the races at Pietermaritzburg all those months before, and the subsequent fall soon after he entered Botswana. He was not to know then that these injuries – or ones very similar to them – would cost him his life.

Hunting for humans

Richard's diary contains several references to slaving around the Victoria Falls:

July 13th. Found a deserted kraal, and dead body of a black man, who had been murdered the day before by the marauding party from Sekeletu's that had dodged us about at Deka and which, seeing the white men, had come to the Matetse kraal.

14th. A lot of locals came in from Deka and other kraals, as they thought we would protect them against Sekeletu's party.

20th. Several Makololos volunteered to go with us [to the Falls] and carry the little we wanted, as they thought they were only safe along with us.

Aug 11th. An armed party of Sekeletu's men came to carry at day-break. The natives were in great consternation; many bolted into the woods or came to our fires, but we told the warriors we should not suffer them to be traded, so at length they departed to hunt up other wretched makololo's.

The fact that this ghastly trade was still being conducted in 1863 is sad testimony to the inabilities of both the British government and David Livingstone to put a stop to the practice in the heart of Africa, so far from their influence. Despite abolition having been declared in 1833, and the Royal Navy having tightened their blockades of Africa's coastline, slaves continued to be used to carry ivory, copper, iron and other products to coastal towns such as Zanzibar until well into the 1880s – chiefly because humans were not susceptible to *nagana*, as oxen were. And having got

to the coast, those 'beasts of burden' who survived the trek were shipped off to plantations and mines across the Atlantic seaboard – and at a rate some historians estimate to have been about 60 000 per year at the time of my ancestors' visit to this continent.

In the Zambezi area, the industry was controlled and managed by the Portuguese and their half-caste cohorts, the Mambaris, who had travelled up the river and made strongholds for themselves on its banks and islands. And, under their control, human trafficking had been eagerly practised since the 1830s by the Makololo, the 'tribe' Livingstone hoped would host the Helmore/Price party of missionaries (see page 229). In fact, one of Livingstone's reasons for pressing his superiors for Christian occupation of the region was the hope that their influence would stop the trade. But it must be regarded as grand naivety on his part to assume that this lucrative business would be abandoned in favour of prayers, education and legitimate trade in non-human goods. As Tim Holmes states in 'The History of Zambia' (www.thezambian.com): 'Domestic slavery was part of the social order of... central African states... Very rarely did the Portuguese have to go raiding to capture slaves: by selling the rulers goods such as cloth, rum, jewellery and firearms they drew the rulers into their colonial economy as suppliers of slave labour.' And if African chiefs were utterly debased by this ignominious trade, so too were their foreign partners, as Frederick Courtenay Selous and his companion LM Owen found during a hunting trip to the Zambezi in 1877. In his book *To the Banks of the Zambezi*, TV Bulpin gives an account of what the hunters encountered on Kasoko Island below the Kariba gorge:

'The incongruity of the slave trade was always that its participants could simply see no wrong in it. While the slavers made their visitors comfortable with an excellent meal in a clean home, and talked wistfully of the civilised world, they were surrounded by unhappy people. Bands of women were chained together from iron rings around their necks. On the veranda where the traders sat and yarned, hung three raw hippopotamus-hide *sjamboks*, the lower part of each stained black with blood. There was constant coming and going of raiders bringing in slaves who were secured on the island in a variety of stocks made from large logs about one foot in diameter. Through these logs, holes were bored sufficiently large as to allow a slave's foot to be pushed through. Other holes carried pegs that clamped the legs into position and prevented escape. Half a dozen slaves were fixed to each log.'

Elsewhere on the subcontinent, slavery was also still practised during my ancestors' visit, but mostly in the guise of serfdom or domestic vassalage. Both the Matabele and the Bamangwato used Bushmen or Masarwas as 'servants' who worked in their kraals, herded or hunted for them for no pay or benefits. Known as *batlhanka*, the slaves were absolute property, and in *Travels in the Interior of Africa* (AA Balkema, Cape Town, 1971) James Chapman described the effect that

Slaving – a blight on all our consciences

this had on the minds of the enslaved: 'They call themselves dogs, pack oxen and horses of Sekgomi and never think of aspiring to any other position. Dogs because they hunt and kill game for their masters (the Ngwato), pack oxen because they must carry home the proceeds of the hunt for hundreds of miles, and horses because they must act as spies for their masters and run from one post to another with information.'

As to the extent of slaving in South Africa at the time of the Glyns' visit, John Mackenzie, the missionary stationed at Shoshong (see page 199), wrote in 1879 about his 'sad lot' at having to witness slaves passing through the town on their way to the Transvaal, having been bought in the interior by Boers. But, according to Andrew Anderson, who travelled the region at much the same time as Richard and Robert and published a book called *Twenty Five Years in an Ox Wagon* (Chapman & Hall, 1888), slavery in Natal and the Cape was extinct by 1864 and was 'rapidly becoming so in the Boer States'. And while he claims that relations between the Boers and their 'servants' were much more cordial than those between the British and theirs because 'they treat them more familiarly than we do', he describes his shock at being served coffee in a Natal Boer's household by a Zulu girl wearing not a stitch of clothing:

'The Zulu girls, as a general rule, wear some little bit of rag at their kraals, but his one had nothing. I found the Boers do this on purpose to show them they are an inferior race, and to keep them under. At many of the Boers' houses I found their female servants were in the same way, as they have a wonderful prejudice against the black races, and treat them as dogs; and I found out afterwards that all the Boers' servants were slaves, and received no pay, their food being mealie, Indian corn, and milk. And as the boys and girls grew old enough to marry, any number of children would be seen on a farm.'

Whether or not slavery has been abolished worldwide is moot. Certainly, the 20th century heralded freedom for all in South Africa, but many of our farmhands, miners and domestic workers continue to eke out a meagre existence on our 'liberated' soil. In the East, windowless basements house garment workers who churn out designer gear in pitiless conditions and children are sold into prostitution by their parents. In North Africa – particularly the Sudan – we're told that human trafficking is still rife – so when exactly will the scourge of our ancestors finally be eradicated?

Pandamatenga to Panda Masui Forest, Zimbabwe

Wanderings through Isiah's corner of Eden

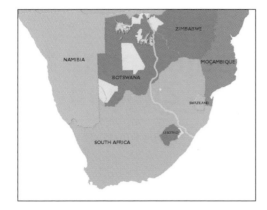

Pandamatenga to Panda
Masui Forest, Zimbabwe
55 kilometres
Total: 2 108
Week 18
11–17July

13ᵗʰ July. Trekked to another stream, Matetse. Here we found a strong cattle kraal, and the natives said it was not safe for oxen to go farther as the tsetse fly was very close all round us, so we made ready to leave our wagons and walk to the Zambezi, but in the first place it was necessary to lay in a store of meat for the people at the wagons during our absence, and the country did not seem very promising for big game.

So at last we were even. From a point just north of Pandamatenga, Richard, Robert and Henry would now be 'footing' to the Falls like me, and I calculated from our maps that the distances I would have to cover each day were less than half those that their wagons had forced me to do during the previous four months. I couldn't help feeling smug.

Camp of the Long Wait

But I was also grateful for a pause in the old party's progress because, while they hunted to feed their staff, we needed to obtain permits to traverse the territory ahead. We moved camp to the outskirts of Pandamatenga and set up our tents under a grove of statuesque *Acacia polyacantha* trees, which were home to three different types of owl. They whooped and whistled above our heads while the dogs romped in the grass, freed at last from the confines of the vehicles. It was another simply gorgeous camp, but it was the scene of many logistical challenges as I spent hours on the phone and e-mail trying to get permission to traverse the northwestern corner of Mr Mugabe's country. Despite having started the process weeks before, we still awaited permission from a bevy of bureaucrats before proceeding through the border.

Battling with bureaucrats

The Matetsi Safari Area in Zimbabwe falls under the auspices of that country's Departments of Forestry and National Parks, and those areas that are not preserved as indigenous forests are leased to commercial hunters. I had been assured by my contacts in Zimbabwe that the good publicity my quest would bring this pariah state would guarantee official sanction for our expedition and our movie, but I was reluctant to cross the border without those essential pieces of paper in hand. Day after day they proved to be elusive. After an initially positive response to my request, it now seemed as if the Parks authorities didn't want a lone white woman moseying about in their hunting concessions. And the Department of Home Affairs seemed to be similarly reluctant to have us record the process. I couldn't decide whether political paranoia or bureaucratic bungling were the cause of their reluctance.

What are they afraid of? Or what are they trying to hide? After all, I'm not about to do a political exposé. Ndaipanenyi Mukwena of the Zimbabwe Tourist Authority in Johannesburg has been marvellous to deal with, as has her counterpart in Harare, Stanley Banda. They assure me that they'll finalise their decision to let us film the journey soon – whatever 'soon' means. This is far more of a worry than getting the go-ahead to walk through the national parks. I could perhaps do the latter without being spotted, but should Karin pull out a camera at Vic Falls without the necessary permission, I'm told we'll have our gear confiscated, never to be returned, and we might even be chucked in tjoekie. Ed and Pat Cumming, who farm just outside Pandamatenga, have been helping us a great deal with advice about the walk ahead. They are refugees from Zim so they know what it's like to incur the wrath of the Mugabe regime and they tell me that the area near the Falls is crawling with so-called 'war veterans', so I must err on the side of caution and wait as long as I possibly can for the documents. Feel so alone now with all these headaches and responsibilities.

Days passed as 'yes', 'no', 'yes' answers came to appeals by several influential intermediaries (like Yvonne Christian of Wilderness Safaris' office at Victoria Falls) who were petitioning the authorities on my behalf. Time was beginning to run out and my stress levels rose by the hour. I *had* to reach the Falls on 22 July as per The Diary, and *nothing* was going to stop me seeing the faces of my loved ones gathered there to welcome me. I'm getting increasingly pissed off with these shenanigans. We've all tried so hard, we've come such a long way and I'm damned if we're going to get stopped now.

Plotting some felonious 'footing'

Heading for Bob's Border Post

There was nothing else for it but to plot a fast, felonious hoof to the Falls. But we needed to suss out both the lie of the land and the hunters operating in the Matetsi area, so John, Karin and I did a one-day recce into Zimbabwe to glean what we could about the feasibility of my plan. The guys at the border were great – nothing like telling people you've walked 2 000ks to get them interested in your journey! Things have tightened up a lot since John left his home country four months ago. We'll only be allowed a certain amount of groceries and there's a limit on the fuel we can carry.

I regret that I'm not able to give the names of the hunters in the area who offered me their help, but their security demands that I cannot do so here – suffice to say that they were, to a man, enthusiastically supportive of my mission. We agreed that as long as I stayed away from their leopard baits and told them exactly where I was going to be at any given hour, they'd turn a blind eye to me walking through their areas illegally. But spending time in their camps proved to be an even greater trial than it had been at Tim Frayne's operation...

Had another grizzly day with dead animals. X camp was hosting nine client hunters, two of them Spanish women (what is it about this nation?). The place was awash with blood and gore, along with an upturned elephant head balanced in some tractor tyres, ready for butchery. The animal's great neck had been brutally severed and its gentle bottom lip had hairs protruding from it just like Mpho's – such a pathetic end to a noble life. And *all the while the hunters gorged themselves on lunch while congratulating each other on their exploits – revolting people.*

Two days later, great news came in the form of a filming permit from the Department of Home Affairs, thanks to more persistent lobbying, this time from Vanessa Nucci and her colleagues at The Grace Group (who were to host our end-of-walk celebrations at the Victoria Falls Hotel). But we still had no thumbs-up from National Parks and I really didn't fancy being hosted by one of Mr Mugabe's less-salubrious establishments. Eventually, two of my octogenarian relatives saved the day and I was effusively proud of their efforts. Val and Doug Dabbs (my mother's sister and her husband) dragged their polite but adamant forms into the Harare office of the Director General of National Parks, where they patiently explained their mad niece's desire to walk through the Matetsi area. Fortunately for me (as sexist as this sounds), the individual they petitioned was a woman, Tessa Chikaponya, and she was so impressed by my feat that she agreed to grant permission for the walk. Four hours later, Val and Doug had the all-important permit in their arthritic hands and quickly faxed it through to a garage at Pandamatenga, where I picked it up.

'Best you don't mention that you have dogs with you, though,' warned Val. 'They are prohibited from entering any of our national parks. And you have to be accompanied by an armed game ranger.' *Suits me, frankly, I'm tired of battling through Big Five Turf unarmed.* We were on our way.

Well, not quite. We still needed to get permits for the dogs to go through the border, and that entailed a 100-kilometre drive to the more northerly town of Kasane, where a tall, highly personable vet by the name of Dr Babiyana inspected the dogs and stamped their papers. *Legal – we're all legal at last – even little Mpho. Let the Zim games begin!*

Well, again, not quite. A rather worried John greeted us back in 'Owl camp'.

'I've just had a visit from a Botswana customs guy, who says we're camped on the wrong side of The Old Hunters' Road and that we're in fact inside Zimbabwe here. He reckons that we'd better move before we're arrested for entering the country illegally.'

'What bureaucratic nonsense,' I thought to myself. 'Botswana is all of 300 metres away.' Because we were scheduled to move off the next day, I toyed with taking a chance on us remaining undetected for one more night, but soon decided that it was stupid to risk everything we'd achieved by staying put. So on an afternoon when we all desperately needed to rest and relax prior to

The bribe box

the next leg of our adventure, we packed up and moved to a much less salubrious site on the other side of the road. John filled the vehicles with diesel and water, while Sue and I (to our shame) filled a box with cigarettes, sweets and food in case we needed to bribe our way through any ugly encounters in Zimbabwe. Now we were well and truly ready, as were Richard, Robert and Henry. But they were already considerably further north than me and after the delays of the past week, I would have to work – and walk – hard to 'catch up' with them.

20th. Camp being now provisioned, we were ready to walk to the Zambezi. Several locals volunteered to go with us and carry the little we wanted, as they thought they were only safe along with us. Kean and Guy we left with the wagons in charge of all the livestock except three donkeys and three dogs. One wagon, however, we thought we might safely take with us for one day, and then send it back, so we trekked down the river, crossed it, and got to a more stony country with several streams running E, going ourselves NNE.

Friday 15 July. Walked precisely 1.54 kilometres – what an astounding accomplishment! We crossed the border, again without incident, found a nice camp site in the park, but decided it was foolish for me to continue walking without the ranger – hence this ridiculously short distance! Left the dogs with John while Sue, Karin and I drove to the local National Parks office. The warden is a woman, yay yay, Mrs Silvia Maladze. She was slow but polite – very, very polite – and she's given me the guide who Yvonne Christian recommended: a chap called Isiah Tshuma. He's supposed to be the best in the area – renowned for the bush skills he's acquired after 28 years in this wilderness.

At the staff compound, Isiah was waiting for us outside his neat little house and he was exactly as I hoped he would be – fluent in English, well mannered, old fashioned and meticulously turned out in his Parks uniform. He put his FN rifle and camping gear in the back of the vehicle, waved goodbye to his family and we headed for our camp. At dusk we pulled up to the tents, nestled far into the bush, and two dogs rushed out to us in the beam of the headlights. Isiah was silent but bug-eyed with shock. Dogs are strictly banned in National Parks areas and the rangers are instructed to shoot them on sight. I had put him in a most invidious position, but he handled it with the kind of grace and diplomacy from which his country's politicians could well learn. Isiah erected his worn old tent next to mine and over supper we explained our dilemma – sending the 'kids' home to South Africa was unfeasible, as was sending them ahead to the Falls. If they stayed in the vehicles by day and within the confines of the camp by night, would he please keep our secret? He agreed to do so – no doubt in part because he knew he'd be generously rewarded for his silence.

Isiah Tshuma, guide and companion

Getting sad now it's nearly over

The next day, Isiah and I walked 33 kilometres along the banks of the Matetsi River in the footsteps (I liked to think) of my ancestors. And this jet-black Ndebele man proved to be just the company I needed for my last, very emotional, week on foot – observant, calm, quaintly humorous and still awed by the beauty that surrounded us. But he had clearly been misinformed by his employers about the nature of my mission.

'They told me there was some woman who wanted to do a little walking. I have brought the wrong shoes!' I looked down at his highly polished, thin-soled lace-ups while he winced in pain. Sure enough, they were of the kind suited to the short strolls before breakfast that most tourists seek. 'And you walk so fast. You should have been born a man, Patty!' I assumed that was meant as a compliment.

Creatures of Isiah's Eden

John drove to Isiah's home to collect some stouter boots for the task in hand and we continued our wanderings through his corner of Eden over the next few days, choosing routes that would sometimes mimic those of my ancestors and sometimes suit my craving for spectacular sights and big game. And we had both in abundance – stomping armies of buffalo, 300 strong, and shy families of sable. Bossy elephant mums and grumpfing gangs of wildebeest. Belts of deep sand alternated with black-rocked ridges, all covered with a grey fur of bushveld trees, quite still and dead but waiting for the first rains when they would explode with impossible greens and golds. Our long hours of wordless companionship alternated with low-voiced stories of what Isiah had witnessed on this soil. Stories like that of the enraged buffalo that broke the spine of a poacher and spent four days lying next to his victim before leaving when rescue came. Sad tales about the stupendous herds of

Long, low conversations between master and pupil

game that roamed this area in the 1970s before the hunters came and decimated them. Disgusting accounts of blood seekers, one of them an American paraplegic who was determined to 'down' an elephant from his wheelchair.

'But that's OK,' declared Isiah, who is also a part-time preacher in the Apostolic Church. 'Man has dominion

We walked while the dogs did game drives

over the earth and God told Noah that he could kill whatever animals his heart desired.' Evidently God also told Isiah that it was sinful to use his knowledge of the medicinal properties of local flora when prayer can cure anything. Well, God save me from that kind of philosophy.

The Matetsi – dry as a bone

Isiah's tracking is amazing – turns out he was trained by a Bushman tracker. He can tell how old an elephant is from the depth of its tread and where a buck has gone over seemingly solid rock. His round eyes miss absolutely none of the signs out here and he's trying to teach me the basics, but I fear I'm a hopeless student. Apparently, the word matetsi is a corruption of the Ndebele word matetje, which means slippery. The river was so named because of the algae on the rocks, which became treacherous for those crossing the river in the rainy season. Oh that it should have a drop in it now. Today we saw lion spoor that was positively Jurassic. Even Isiah stopped and gawked – and when he says 'fuck', you gotta believe it's big.

Our last camp of the week was on a sandy hill in the forests of Panda Masui, outside National Parks territory but still very much among the abundant wildlife of this region. Isiah thought it safer to stay there in view of the fact that we had the dogs with us and needed to avoid them being detected by other rangers and scouts patrolling the park area. Autumnal leaves crunched under our feet and pale sunlight filtered through the bare branches of the trees above our heads. Thousands of Africa's black bees swarmed around our tents and drowned in our washbasins. In the dead of night a lion grunted nearby, but I was too tired to stay awake and listen to his courtship rituals. With a cursory, 'Hello, big boy,' I turned over and fell asleep again. Perhaps I would have forced myself to tarry awhile with him if I'd known then that we were in the last wilderness camp of our trip and that he was the last lion I would hear on my extraordinary journey.

Tinder-dry forests waiting for the rain

Big George of Pandamatenga

The border town of Pandamatenga was originally named Mpanda Mutenga after an African ivory hunter called Mutenga who was killed by Lobengula as punishment for trading illegally in ivory with white people, and a grove of mpanda, or rain, trees (*Philenoptera violacea*) where he based himself. But in the late 1800s, the settlement became synonymous with an Englishman by the name of George Westbeech who arrived in Africa in the same year as Richard and Robert Glyn and eventually established a firm British foothold in the area around the Falls. George was a gifted entrepreneur and negotiator who won the trust of several of the kings, chiefs and headmen living in the heart of Africa. Both Mzilikazi and his successor Lobengula allowed him to hunt and trade in Matabeleland for about six years, after which he decided to try his luck further north,

in Barotseland. The Lozi chief, Sepopa, took such a liking to Westbeech that he detained the trader for 18 months at his kraal on the junction of the Chobe and Zambezi rivers where the two men developed a deep and lasting friendship. And it was a friendship that turned out to be very lucrative for Westbeech because when he was 'released' by Sepopa, the chief bestowed upon him £12,000 worth of ivory – an enormous sum in those days. With the proceeds of the sale of the ivory, Westbeech bought three wagonloads of goods, and after marrying the daughter of a Boer from the Transvaal, set up a trading operation with her at Pandamatenga in 1875. He also began capitalising on Sepopa's greater 'gift' – the only hunting licence granted to a white man in Barotseland. Over the next decade and a half, Westbeech's shop, storerooms and cattle kraals

George Westbeech's settlement at Pandamatenga

became something of an institution – famed throughout the subcontinent for the facilities they offered to travellers wanting to leave their oxen and horses outside the tsetse belt before walking to the Falls. And George became legendary for his honest, generous nature, his bravery and intelligence. The local people nicknamed him *Georosiana Umtunya*, meaning Big George (to distinguish him from his assistant, George Blockley who was called Little George), and he was famed for his ability to consume large quantities of alcohol and to survive numerous bouts of malaria – in fact, he is alleged to have been stricken with the disease 30 times in seven years. While he lived at Pandamatenga, Westbeech assisted no fewer than five Barotse kings, became a member of the Barotse Council of State and did much to lessen Portuguese control of the area. That he managed these interactions without alienating any of the region's leaders is remarkable, because power struggles between them were endemic and extremely bloodthirsty – with human sacrifices and witchcraft being common.

But the monopoly George Westbeech had on hunting in the Falls area took a terrible toll on local wildlife. Because the tsetse fly prevented ivory being transported by oxen and hunting being done on horseback, Westbeech employed 'armies' of local Africans to do his hunting for him in the fly belts. And their effect on the game was quite devastating – indeed some commentators believe that Westbeech and his employees were responsible for exterminating white rhino here by 1882 and, even by the late 1870s, hardly a single elephant with good-sized tusks could be found.

George Westbeech died in the Transvaal while on a trip to the Cape Colony in 1888 – somewhat predictably of liver disease.

Panda Masui Forest to the Victoria Falls

Puny and insignificant in the face of such a force

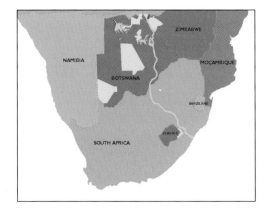

Panda Masui Forest to
Victoria Falls
44 kilometres
Grand Total: 2 152
Week 19
18–22 July

July 21ˢᵗ. Next morning, after sending back the wagon, we packed the three donkeys with our blankets, biscuit etc., not without difficulty, for while everything else had got thin on the sapless grass, these brutes had grown quite fat and very bumptious. We marched four hours over a country studded with small igneous hills of black rock, and crossed several small streams... Two hours' more walking and we left the stony ground and got on a high sand flat. We toiled on till dark, hoping to reach water, but had at last to encamp in the forest without any. We had only about 1½ pints with us, so passed a thirsty night. The natives soon got their supper by digging some fine roots there, as large as very large parsnips.

Where were you in this forest, Richard and Robert? Still taunting me, I see, after all these months together! The end is so close now. Were you feeling the same as me: expectant, humbled, unsure? I now had five days in which to cover the mere 44 kilometres left to the Falls, so after a relatively short morning walk through the tinder-dry forest, Isiah, Karin and I called it a day and the team travelled by car to one of Isiah's favourite spots – a slow bend in the Katshetshete River where hundreds of antelope and giraffe paraded on ink-black soil and drank from the stream's still, ice-blue waters. We sipped cold beers and chatted desultorily, feeling melancholic and reflective as the end of our trip approached. Not a squeak from Tapiwa when he came upon all this game and sometimes at very close quarters. Mpho is getting braver and braver, albeit from the inside of a vehicle! They are so dirty now that they make my clothing and hands black within minutes. I wonder how they'll adjust to the walled property they're about to return to in Johannesburg.

And those would be?

Tuesday, 19 July, was the last day I'd have in the company of Isiah because I wouldn't need him once I reached the peripheries of Victoria Falls town and was outside the national park. But before we parted I had one, all-important task for him: to find the sight I'd dreamt of since leaving Durban and which would be the ghost-like harbinger of my labours' end – the spume of the world's most spectacular waterfall. I knew that without Isiah's help I could very easily miss it in the dense forests through which we were travelling, so despite the fact that Richard was to see the Falls' vapour 'three days hence', I challenged my guide to find it for me now. We walked and talked, walked and talked, always searching for these puffs from Gargantua's pipe, Isiah thrilled by the challenge of locating them. Finally (about 15 kilometres from the gorge) he took me to the top of a rise in the quiet forest and said: 'Look, Patty, there it is.'

And there indeed it was – The Smoke That Sounds, as Chief Sebitwane first described it to David Livingstone.

> July 22ⁿᵈ. Started with the first light, and soon heard a distant roar, which we knew must be the falls. Three hours toiling over thirsty sand, through forest... brought us to the edge of the plateau, and far away to the NE we could see the tall pillars of vapour rising over the forest trees and marking the spot we had come so many thousand miles to see.

Richard had told me to look out for 'tall pillars'. Livingstone informed me that there would be 'five columns of vapour, white below, darker up above, so as to simulate smoke very closely'. But perhaps because we'd approached the Falls from a slightly different angle, I saw a meringue-like topping on a pudding bowl – a cottonwool crust over a dip in the hills. I wept. Isiah whooped. Karin unobtrusively filmed. I phoned those with whom I wanted to share this great moment in my life – mother, sister, friends – and saluted my forebears – Richard, Robert and my late father, John, all three my mentors and guides through both the most horrible and the most wonderful moments of this journey. And I felt a rush of conflicting emotions, which would assault me again when I stood at

The legendary 'Smoke', but from a different angle than the one from where I first saw it

the Falls. *A happy/sad moment and I am not entirely sure how I feel about the end. I know that I'm ready to go home now but I'm also sure that I'll face dark days ahead.*

But the finish was still three days hence. Isiah and I had deliberately walked further than necessary each day so as to have some 'catch-up time' in hand should we run into trouble and find ourselves battling to meet The Diary deadline of reaching the Falls on the 22 July. Now that the Zimbabwe leg had gone so smoothly we could afford to spend a couple of days on the outskirts of town, cleaning our persons, our kit and the vehicles before launching ourselves into polite society. It should have been a joyous time, but instead it became a heart-breaking introduction to the realities of Zimbabwe's land invasions.

Before he left us Isiah arranged for us to stay with some friends who were running a hunting operation on a private farm not far from Victoria Falls town. While John went ahead to set up our final camp, Sue, Karin and I drove Isiah home. Outside his house we handed a bucket filled with groceries and a generous tip to this remarkable, bush-wise man and I hugged and thanked him for the wonderful things he'd brought to my journey. *He was thrilled and insisted on a formal 'goodbye' for the benefit of those who would eventually see our TV documentary. It's been amusing to see how much he's enjoyed being filmed and Jesus comes into virtually every statement he makes to camera!*

The last few kilometres of the 19th-century wagon trails into Victoria Falls were where the railway line is now

But within hours of our arrival at Woodlands Farm later that day, Sue and I decided that our new 'home' was definitely spooked. Our tents were erected on the front lawn of an all-but-empty farmhouse, overlooking a broad valley and a busy little water hole. Before us lay an archetypal swathe of Central Africa from which sounds of animal feuds, bird courtships and even the odd steam train drifted up to us. The valley was beguiling and contemplative at sunset, and bustling and fresh at dawn. But when we turned to face the family home built to enjoy these delights at tea- and toot-time for generations to come, the place was silent and sad. The swimming pool was bleached and dry, the tennis court weedy. An old tractor shed nearby was being used to crank up and butcher the animals shot on the farm by wealthy clients. Tapiwa rushed onto the lawn sporting a bloody waterbuck foreleg, Mpho was playing with its ear. The kitchen of the house had been hastily gutted of its custom-made cupboards and the telephone socket down the passage was still surrounded with the sticky residue of the family's scribbled notes and reminders. Muscled surfers and sweaty rock stars leered down from a bedroom door – haphazard posters of a child fan. Poignant reminders of happy times.

But they weren't always happy. We soon learnt that the house had witnessed a triple tragedy. Its owner had lost his brother in a 'terrorist' attack during the Rhodesian bush war, then his child burnt to death when a candle fell into its cot, and finally his wife hanged herself when the 'war veterans' invaded their haven. *It feels as if we're trespassers here, squatting on other people's*

grief – we're all very anxious to be moving on. But it's fitting that we're here because it means that we can experience at least some of the pain of this country. Zimbabwe's political realities would have been denied us if we'd only had a pleasant romp with Isiah. Our hosts on the farm are rumoured to be the war vets who evicted this family but I have to say they're unfailingly hospitable and warm towards us. Maybe that's Isiah's influence. I gather that the invaders have cut a deal with some commercial hunters who utilise 'their' land in exchange for a cut of the profits. Some rumours have it that they're exceeding their game quotas to the point of rampant slaughter. How true that is I can't say, but certainly some South African hunters have recently been banned for their shamelessly unethical conduct in the Matetsi region. End games by people who smell the end days of this ruined nation.

Waiting in a sad place for a happy end

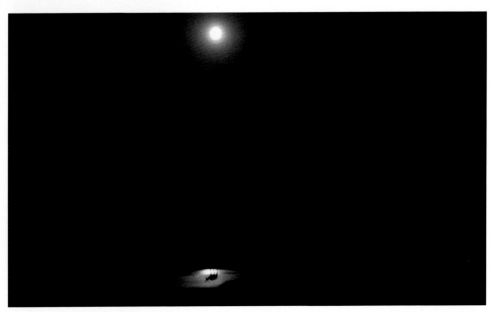

Last full moon of the incredible journey

But I had another end to think about, and just as had happened at the start of the walk in Durban, I struggled to feel anything at all as I approached it. Was it all too huge again? Was numbness the lid with which I clamped a box full of messy emotions? *Only seven kilometres left now. Had a call from Mum to say that friends and family are ready and waiting at The Victoria Falls Hotel, but there are some problems about getting the journalists to the reception on time so I will have to wait for the green flag before entering town. Karin and I have decided that it would be best to go to the actual Falls the following morning so that we can be there when the light is at its best and when my team can have some quiet time together without the crowds. Sue and John did a manic spring-clean today while I washed the dogs, gave myself a leg-wax and plucked my eyebrows. Nothing like attention to detail for the Grand Arrival! Sue performed a touching little ceremony for the wounded souls who once occupied this place – threw some petals around the garden and said a silent prayer that they're at peace now. Sweet girl. John is excited to be home in Zim and will not be returning to SA with us, so I will have to drive his Isuzu back to Johannesburg. We watched the moon come up over the little dam, with waterbuck silhouetted in its shaft of silver light. Special wine reserved for the occasion – our last little dinner together as a team. I wish I could do this journey all over again, with more time to stop and reflect on what has happened to us along the way.*

So close now

Late the next morning, I slowly approached town along the tarred road, becoming more resentful by the minute at the bustling activity of shoppers and tourists along the route. Steve went ahead to the hotel, armed with Karin's other camera so that we'd have two capturing the event on film, while the rest of my team lurked in the car park at the end of the hotel's pathway until we got word that everyone had gathered. After what seemed to be a long wait for the go-ahead, I began the final few hundred metres of my odyssey. I crawled through the (switched-off) electric fence of the hotel's grounds, topped a gentle rise on its manicured lawns with Karin, Sue and John following me and my two panting hounds straining on their leashes. Before me lay a long red carpet leading up to the stone steps of this gracious hotel, and lining its Victorian veranda were my nearest and dearest. When their first shouts of welcome reached me I

Waiting for the 'get-go'

knew that the greatest adventure of my life was at last over. I stormed up the carpet, draped in a South African flag courtesy of Sue, and fell into the midst of the smiling, clapping, crying people who had come to share this moment in a gesture of solidarity that left me humbled. Even Isiah and his wife Evelyn were there, all dressed up in their Sunday best. My sister Shirley had arranged for the carpet, some cocktails and a blackboard crowded with messages of welcome – I felt like royalty.

At the helm of the reception party were my mother, Norma, and the senior member of the Glyn family in South Africa – my father's 93-year-old brother Ronald. Isiah opened the proceedings with a prayer of thanks for my safe delivery to the end of my long walk, and Mum and Ronald made heartfelt speeches that made my throat constrict and my eyes smart. Uncle Ron presented me with a one-of-a-kind, hand-crafted medal engraved with the words 'The Victoria Falls Cross'. It had been designed and commissioned by him in total secrecy and, given his advanced years, I was immensely flattered by the effort it had taken for him to bring it to Zimbabwe in person and pin it on the swollen chest of his wilful niece. The medal glints at me now as I write at my little desk back in Johannesburg – a memento of our happy get-together in the moist, balmy air of the Falls. I shall wear it whenever I need reminding that, with determination, self-discipline, support and a little luck, *anything* is possible.

Looking back, that weekend was a jumble of confusing, contradictory emotions. I feel disorientated and disconnected somehow. Seem to have lost the art of conversation after all these months on the road. Too many people, too much noise, too much luxury. Can't sleep in my big, comfy bed, can't see the moon and can't hear the night sounds I've grown to love so much.

A Royal Reception

We made it – and they made it special

There is a large troupe of aggressive baboons in the hotel's grounds and I'm more paranoid about Taps' and Mpho's safety than I've been since we left Durban. I've been warned not to take them to the Falls because the rocks on the edge of the precipice are so slippery. Sad that they won't be there for the very, very end of the journey tomorrow.

In the midst of the festivities there was a moment of both great calm and great internal chaos for me – and it happened when I made my way to the Falls the next day, 23 July. John, Sue, Karin and I rose before dawn and were the first visitors through the national park's gates at 6am. We walked along the winding path, catching occasional glimpses through the trees of the massive curtain of water that awaited us, and at the end of the path were confronted by the entrancing cascade that many believe to be the pulsating heart of Africa.

How to describe what I saw? And what I felt. The Victoria Falls are by now such an iconic image, such a well-known feature in travel brochures and postcards that it hardly seems necessary to describe them here, but as I stood in their swirling mists I thought of early travellers like Richard, faced with the big question as to what geological trauma could possibly have given birth to this zigzagged rent in the earth's crust, and with the equally daunting task of describing this staggering display of natural power to the folk back home in tame ol' England – without the benefit of photography. I was gratified

One-of-a-kind medal for a one-of-a-kind odyssey

to note that Richard had been as much impressed by the magnificent forests on the banks of the Zambezi as he was by the Falls themselves, because of all the things I would miss about my journey, it was Africa's trees I would yearn for most. But here is his account – albeit less than lyrical – of this overwhelming spectacle of power and beauty.

Thursday 23ʳᵈ. We started down the river for the Falls. The stream, 'whose full breadth from the quantity of islands you can scarcely even see', soon becomes full of rapids... Bursting through the thicket we came on the end of a chasm running at right angles across the bed of the river, a vast split in the surface of the earth, which literally swallows up the river, for all you see of it again is a little boiling brook forcing its way along the bottom of another chasm, which runs from the first at nearly right angles. It is no broken fall, for the water comes sheer from top to bottom in one single bound. Two islands divide the principal falls, and the chasm is so filled with vapour, 'which falls on you in the form of soaking rain that you can see nothing of the depth, except when the wind blows from the East.' The best view is from the angle, where the two chasms meet. The rocks there are rather lower than the side from which the water falls, so you face a vast wall of water falling into a chasm filled with spray, on which the bright hues of the tropical rainbow play in every

How did they happen?

As is well known, the Victoria Falls is the widest curtain of falling water in the world, measuring 1 708 metres across, with an average drop of 92 metres. When the Zambezi River is in full flood (usually in February or March), 500 million litres of water cascades over the precipice every minute, but that reduces to a mere 10 million litres per minute in the dry months of the year.

Standing on the lip of the gorge, facing the torrent, one is consumed by many questions, chief among them 'What geological phenomenon caused this?' Experts appear to agree on the genesis of the Falls having been when Africa was still part of the supercontinent, Gondwana. At that time (about 200 million years ago), molten lava started seeping from the earth's core along fault lines in its crust – one of which followed what is now roughly the course of the Zambezi River. The lava is called basalt and it formed a table-top covering of the surrounding areas, gradually eroding in exposed areas but remaining protected from the elements in low-lying areas like the one through which the river eventually flowed. When the paleo-Makgadikgadi Lake (see page 239) started overflowing about three to five million years ago, its waters emptied over this basalt table and eventually cut a swathe through it. But there was a series of faults in the basalt, caused by the inconsistent cooling of the lava, and they lie perpendicular to the course of the river. These were filled with softer material and the river began exploiting and eroding them, creating steep falls from the hard rock on top. But, as Mike Main says in his book *Zambezi, Journey of a River* (Southern Book Publishers, 1990), because 'there is a limit to how far the river can cut down into the soft rock... When that limit is reached, the only direction for further erosion is backwards, along the course of the river. In the case of the Zambezi the cutting back process carved out the present gorge...vertically... and the resulting feature [is] remarkable because of its relatively smooth face and its perpendicular sides.' Over the last half a million years, the Zambezi has repeated this pattern no fewer than eight times, each time creating the series of sharp bends below the Falls and each time causing a spectacular waterfall. The water always found a weak spot somewhere along the lip (like the Devil's Cataract now), concentrated on it, worked it away, until the whole current flowed through it. Eventually the waterfall vanished and we got one more 'leg' of the zigzagged series of gorges below the site of the Victoria Falls now, all of which mark its earlier sites.

The widest curtain of falling water in the world

First to the Falls?

During the many decades since David Livingstone 'discovered' the Victoria Falls in 1855, claims have often surfaced that he was not, in fact, the first white man to see the astounding cascade at the heart of Africa. Few, if any, of these have been adequately substantiated – largely because of the paucity of written accounts by early travellers to the interior. Seventeenth-century maps of the continent suggest that the Falls were known to very early explorers, and the 'Clouet' map of 1727 shows a great cataract on the Zambezi River, but this was later shown to be Cahora Bassa in Mozambique. Arab and Portuguese traders had been in control of slaving in the region for centuries prior to Livingstone's arrival, but they had employed 'half-caste managers' who did their dirty work on the ground. Nonetheless it is not unfeasible that one or two Europeans reached the Falls before 1855 – but none of them left records of their visit, or certainly no records that have survived. Descendants of a coterie of early Boer hunters such as Jan Viljoen, Willem Pretorius, Martinus Swartz and Stoffel Snyman have laid claim to the Falls' 'discovery' for their ancestors, but none can provide incontrovertible proof to support their contentions. Certainly, if Jan Viljoen had been to the Falls, it seems highly likely that he would have mentioned the fact to the Glyns but, as mentioned on page 149, he did not. The *Voortrekker* Carolus (Carel) Johannes Trichardt has also been put forward as a Falls pioneer, but despite his feats being quite remarkable (he travelled inland from the coast of what is now Mozambique many times from the 1830s and reached places as far flung as Ethiopia and Madagascar),

he is known to have reached the Cahora Bassa Falls on the Zambezi, and not the river's more impressive cascade further inland.

As for Englishmen, we know that James Chapman came within a whisker of becoming the first of that country's explorers to see the Victoria Falls (see page 135). The hunter Henry Hartley is sometimes claimed to have reached them in about 1849 and to have subsequently given David Livingstone directions to the Falls in exchange for two mugs. Given that Hartley later undertook famous expeditions with men like Thomas Baines, it seems inconceivable that his feat is not mentioned in any of the explorers' journals, notwithstanding the reluctance of some of them to aggrandise other travellers of the time. Major-General Baden-Powell asserted that his ancestor, William Cotton Oswell, preceded Livingstone to the Falls, but the claim was never made by the man himself. Oswell, who accompanied the famous missionary to Linyanti in 1851, noted the cascade in a map, and mentioned them in his journal, but did not ever claim to have visited them. When James Chapman was returning from the Deka river region in 1852, he came across one J Simpson near Shoshong who had been hunting in Sebitwane's domain and had lost all his oxen to the fly. Whether or not Simpson saw the Falls, however, has never been substantiated.

Early sightings of the Falls by foreigners being the coup they were, there is also much dispute among contenders for the positions of runners-up in the race, although it seems to be generally accepted that William Baldwin was the second white man to see them, having found them almost by accident and by means of a pocket compass in 1860 (see page 38). Servaas le Roux makes the claim in his book *Pioneers and Sportsmen of South Africa 1760–1890* (published by the author, Salisbury, 1939) that the Boer elephant hunter Martinus Swartz was the third foreign visitor, and that he saw the Falls in 1861, but I have found no sources that can corroborate this assertion. There is little doubt that Boer elephant hunters were active in the northern parts of what is now Botswana for much of the early 19th century, but none of them left journals or reports. In fact, Richard mentions having met a man called John Sniman [Snyman?] in the Matetsi River area who'd been there for at least 18 months.

David Livingstone – definitely the first?

[He] had lost most of his oxen, and had fever, and had only shot eleven elephants. Our [blacks] knew him, said he had murdered his wife in Marico, ran away to Sekeletu, stole a horse, and went to Tekornie, changed the horse for a wife and came up here, where he rules over some [black] kraals, frequently tying men to his wagon wheels and cutting their throats. We therefore fought rather shy of this gentleman, and did not buy his ivory, not caring to weight our wagons with it.

James Chapman and Thomas Baines are widely accepted as having 'come in' third, with a sighting of the Falls between 23 and 30 July 1862, leaving the Glyns the fourth foreign party to get there almost exactly a year later. However, an enterprising hunter/ trader by the name of Henry Reader was on the Zambezi at the same time as Chapman in 1862 and he might well hold claim to fourth 'prize'. If indeed he did see the Falls in that year, then his wife – who travelled with him – was certainly the first white woman to see them. If not, then there are a couple of distaff contenders – among them George Westbeech's young wife, who was reportedly taken there on her honeymoon in 1875, along with the wife of Westbeech's colleague, William Francis. Little did they know how many millions of newlyweds would follow their precedent.

direction, while on your right hand flows away a stream that you can hardly believe to be the same that falls in such breadth in front of you, so great is the depth of the precipice. A stone thrown from this point took 5½ seconds to reach the water, and none of us could quite throw to the top of the fall. The stream comes from the falls with a bend south, but soon turns again at more than right angles to the NE.

Victoria Falls' famous rainbow

David Livingstone, of course, was the first to tell the Victorian world about the Falls, and he started his description with a subtle acknowledgement of the challenge he faced: 'No one can imagine the beauty of the view from anything witnessed in England.' But then, to my mind, he makes a critical error that compromises his account somewhat – he embarks on a contorted comparison between the mighty Zambezi and the puny Thames:

'If one imagines the Thames filled with low tree-covered hills immediately beyond the tunnel, extending as far as Gravesend; the bed of black basaltic rock instead of London mud... the pathway being 100 feet down from the bed of the river... the fissure from 80 to 100 feet apart...'

Figures and numbers, measurements and guesstimates – all so typical of the manly 19th-century explorer. Livingstone had duties to fulfil towards his Royal Geographical Society sponsors, of course, so his account is largely a matter-of-fact medley of scientific assessments and factual descriptions. But it is almost completely devoid of emotion – barring that one, now famous line that redeems his dry prose: 'Scenes so lovely must have been gazed upon by angels in their flight.'

For a really moving account of an early visit to the navel of Africa, one must look to the German explorer Eduard Mohr, who arrived there seven years after the Glyns. In his book *To the Victoria Falls of the Zambezi* (facsimile reproduction of the 1876 edition by Books of Rhodesia, Bulawayo, 1973) he talks of 'indescribably beautiful draperies' over a 'great altar of water'. And he gets very close to articulating the effect of standing in the midst of that swirling spray:

'After looking down for some time into this raging, leaping, foaming, heaving chaos, deafened by the terrible noise of the maddened waters, and shaken by the menacing howl rising up continuously from the depths, which seems to pierce through bone and marrow, one wonders how the rocks, those hard ribs of the earth, can withstand the shock of such a mighty onset!'

And Mohr has the courage to share his *feelings* – feelings that reverberated in me so hard that I shook and sobbed uncontrollably on the edge of the fissure the Makololo people call the 'pestle of the Gods':

'It seemed to me as if my own small ego had become part of the power which raged about me; as if my own identity were swallowed up in the surrounding glory, the voice of which rolled on for ever, like the waves of eternity. But I throw down my pen. No human being can describe the infinite; and what I saw was a part of infinity made visible and framed in beauty.'

One is so puny and insignificant in the face of such a force that I can't help wondering what this thing called life is all about. What does it matter that I've just walked 2 152 kilometres to get here? What is the point of my efforts? What's the point of any effort at all? Here I am at the mid-point of my life and the last 45 years seem to have passed in a futile flash. Will the next half be the same? I'm deeply grateful for getting here alive and for the efforts of my team in helping me do so, but I can see no greater purpose in the journey. Elation and triumph are mixed with emptiness and loneliness. The peace of a dream fulfilled is equalled by the tumult of those still unrealised. Is all of humankind driven by my quest not to 'go gentle into that dark night'? And why am I suddenly so obsessed with the notion that I cannot die after consuming more of this planet than I have replenished?

My shoulders shook with emotion as Karin quietly recorded my turmoil. K is her usual wonderful self, allowing me to express exactly what I'm feeling without any judgement or interference. It's as if her camera has become my confessional during the past months and I shall miss its insistence on introspection and self-analysis. Nearby John took photos of the tumbling waters while

Conflicting emotions at the end of the journey

Support Services – bar none

Sue tried to comfort her fractured friend. Months of self-control unravelled in alternating bouts of shuddering tears and delirious laughter as we sipped champagne and toasted our journey.

And the ancestors seemed to be close by. Or at least their conduct consumed my thoughts. My extreme emotion at the Victoria Falls was, in part, a reaction to Richard's thoughts as he arrived at this awesome spectacle. Like me, its majesty had inspired in him as much regret as it had awe – but his regret was that he had not as yet brought down an elephant. I simply could not understand his lip-smacking reaction to seeing these creatures as mere trophies in a scene so befitting their magnificence:

July 23rd: As we stood to admire, lo! 6 bull elephants appeared on the opposite cliffs. Quietly they tore up a great tree and fed on the leaves. As if they knew that they had chosen the only place in South Africa where they would not be made to feel the weight of our bullets for, for 40 miles or more down, nothing without wings can scale the cliffs and cross the stream of the boiling Zambezi. Gifford, however, went along the edge in the vain hope of getting over, while we watched the monsters. Presently we heard him fire; the elephants raised their trunks and walked off, while we went to see if he had shot a buck, but found instead an old bull buffalo roaring out his last on the ground. He had fallen at the third shot, after chasing Gifford to the edge of the precipice.

One by one, I threw my shells into the water, along with the *sangoma's* silver coins and a walking stick I'd found with Isiah, which seemed to symbolise my father's wise guidance. And I cried and cried for all the 'monsters' we kill-clever apes have destroyed, each of us in our own way. With each fling of these precious talismans into the foaming river below, I vowed to try to live by the resolutions I had made in the bleak landscape of the Makgadikgadi Pans – to tread lightly on the earth and deal gently with her people. I resolved to become a vegetarian and to learn an African language. I apologised for the hurts I'd caused and celebrated the contributions I had made. I gave thanks for the love of two dogs, for our safe delivery to the Falls and for the many, many people who had supported my efforts – chief among them those standing at the precipice with me – Sue Oxborrow, Karin Slater and John Kerr. I thought about what I should do with the second half of my life on the continent I adore, and the walks across her glorious terrains that I hoped still lay ahead. I picked up some rocks from the oily, black cliff before turning from the water and heading home.

The dawn on the second half of my life

The Journey Home

My journey back to 'civilisation' was to be as difficult, in its own way, as Richard's, Robert's and Henry's was to be. Within an hour of my family and friends catching their flights from Victoria Falls' airport, I was in my Isuzu, ready to start the two-day drive back to Johannesburg. Sue and I would take the vehicles home because John lives in Zimbabwe, and Karin and Steve were staying on to enjoy a short break there. We hugged our team-mates stiffly and said hurried, contained goodbyes – each of us awkward in the knowledge that we'd never again share such an intense experience together, nor get such intimate insights into our different psychologies. During the past four and a half months, we'd seen one another at our best and our worst. We'd argued and laughed, impressed and disappointed each other by turn. At times, we'd sought deep conversations by the fire; at others, we'd shunned contact altogether, secluding ourselves in the privacy of our little Oztents. This, I'm sure, is the way of all self-contained, travelling bands, faced with the hard tasks and personal growth inherent in tough expeditions. One thing I knew for sure as I drove down the driveway of the hotel was that the trip had changed us all irrevocably. I hoped for the better.

Like some of my crew, Richard and Robert also tarried at the Falls, but for less benign reasons. They had still not shot an elephant and stayed on the river for a week, endlessly searching its banks for their quarry. When not out hunting they enjoyed the hospitality of the Makololo people and Richard handed over the precious letter from John Mackenzie to a headman who could forward it to Sekeletu. The hunters also spent a day visiting David Livingstone's famous island:

> June 27th: Livingstone's garden, though strongly fenced, has been breached in many places by the seacows [hippos], and is now nothing but a mass of rank grass. I could only find the stump of one peach tree. We found his and Baldwin's initials nearly grown out, so recut them, and inscribed Glyn 1863 by their side.

Fearing that their staff at Pandamatenga were going hungry, they turned back on 7 August. But they got to the wagons, to discover that Guy and Kean had shot a black rhino and, with the larder thus well stocked, Richard and Gifford were tempted back into the 'fly' on foot for one last try for elephant, particularly as Richard's right arm had at last healed sufficiently for him to lift a heavy gun again. They were not to be disappointed – but Richard came close to losing his life:

16th August. Crept up to the last bush and fired at a bull's shoulder. The herd was off at once, but after following them for about 400 yards [366 metres], I came on the bull on his knees and head, quite dead. Went on after the others, but only got a long shot, and then a long chase after one that turned back by itself. Till quite beat, I lost sight of him, and went towards where I had heard Gifford firing. Directly I saw four elephants coming towards me, the last with trunk in air, trumpeting wildly. I fired at her; she turned at once and chased me. I ran for my life, but she kept sight of me, and got most unpleasantly close, till I felt like a mouse before a cat. There was no real cover, only mopane trees the size of hazels scattered about on stony ground. At last I gave her the slip by dodging round some bushes and, much to my joy, she left me.

Gifford, I found, had killed a calf in hopes of stopping the mother, but she had only chased him well and left him. The hunt was not over yet, the blacks reported some of the troop still below us. We found two elephants under charge of a great toothless cow. The skin of her ear now binds this book. We fired at her and at the next biggest. They charged in line and drove us back to the blacks. This was repeated over and over again, the charges getting shorter and shorter, till at last, sorely wounded, the old cow stood under a tree with the others by her. One of the young bulls fell dead, and with our last rounds... we shot the cow through the heart. She fell, but the tough old brute got on her legs again. It was, however, all over, and she fell nearly on the other... It was now about 1.30 and we had been on the run since 5am but we sat enthroned on the elephants, too overjoyed by our success to feel hunger.

So, the elephant ear that binds my ancestor's precious diary once belonged to a brave but toothless old cow. Why shoot her if she had no ivory? And why celebrate her ignominious end by *sitting* on her still-warm flank? I try not to judge. I try not to condemn – but it is difficult to remain uncritical of these sad events so long ago.

It appears that, in his diary, Richard downplayed the great service that James Gifford did him that day, because according to a letter written by James' father, Alexander – once again to his half-brother Patrick Gifford in Scotland – the young expedition manager saved his skin that day:

'20 July 1867. Sir Richard Glyn writes him regularly, sends presents through the book post to him, he wishes to get to England (his rental is £37,000 per annum and at his Uncle's death will be £80,000). He does not seem to forget that James saved his life at the risk of his own – he galloped down a hill till within ten yards, fired, its trunk was up to strike, but in place of striking the horse's back (the latter at full speed), it dropped perpendicular, and the huge bull Elephant fell dead. Sir Richard had wounded him, but not in a vital place, or he could not have gained on the horse, for he was a very fine one. James took him with him this trip.'

The trip to which Alexander refers was one to Matabeleland in June 1867, in which Gifford joined Henry Hartley on an elephant hunt. In fact, in the years subsequent to the Glyn expedition, James' services as manager, guide and hunter were sought several times by famous 19th-century gold- and ivory-seekers such as Thomas Leask, George Arthur Phillips, John Lee and the Finaughty brothers. And when his hunting days were over, he went to the Diamond Fields to try his luck and was last reported there in 1882. Clearly, James Gifford became a deservedly successful man.

On 21 August 1863, the hunters at last headed for home, nervous now that they'd be trapped in the dry interior until the rains came in December. Ten days later, while on the Old Hunters' Road, they came across the 'infamous' Solamanink, Peat and Kurtman, the staff who had deserted them over two months before and who had been sent back to find the Glyns under pain of death by an irate Jan Viljoen. The men were welcomed back by a very relieved party who'd battled without their expertise in the interim. And it was expertise that was sorely needed for the return journey, when the expedition faced desperate thirst time and time again, along with many other trials. They took the wrong route and found themselves between the two Makgadikgadi Pans, with no water for miles and the prospect of either retracing their steps or trying to cross the pan. The wagons sunk to their axles in the soft clay and, for several days, the party took the oxen in relays to wells on the other side of Sowa Pan. When at least some of the oxen were sufficiently strong to pull again, the wagons slowly lumbered around the northern 'lip' of the pan and eventually found firmer ground. But the 'sandy flat' both they and I had traversed on the eastern shore of the pan was now hotter than ever:

Sept 15th: The blacks were getting done and wanting to lay down under every bush. My two dogs also kept galloping from bush to bush, throwing themselves into any little shade they could find, the heat being now very great and the fine salt dust getting into everyone's mouth. Presently I missed Alp, a strong lurcher. Harry came up and handed me his collar, saying he had fallen dead in the path behind me. The horses now broke away, the chestnut pony leading them on to the water. I trotted on to stop them, and poor old Dot, my English pointer, became very bad, seeming to lose all power in his hind quarters, and howling with misery and thirst. He would soon have died if I had not made Mafume, one of our guides, carry him. I pushed on now for the water to save my dog, for it was still far away on some hill sides. Some Masarwas [Bushmen] met us with water in calabashes, but Dot could not drink out of them and got frantic, so I impounded a musical instrument made of a gourd, pulled out the iron keys, and gave him water in that, but he nearly tore it to bits, for he was mad with thirst.

So, once again, passing strangers had saved them, and late that afternoon, the party straggled in to a 'spring hole about three feet deep', which kept them going for another few days. And so they limped towards Shoshong and, finally, to safety.

After that point, the journey was characterised by terrible attrition among the horses. Old Batwing, the horse that had served both Baldwin and Richard so well, at last 'could not get up without help' and had to be shot. Nipper got a thorn in his eye and lost the sight of it, and horse sickness killed Bob's horse Harper. Next to go was Empress, Osborne's last and best horse, which died of 'inflammation of the bowels'.

When the party reached Jan Viljoen's farm, he was away, but they were warmly welcomed by his wife and family:

... for they had thought we must have come to grief when our servants bolted, and the last they had heard of us was from Boers who said we were such queer folk that we should never get to the Zambezi, for they had seen us put down blankets for our dogs to lay on at night.

No doubt the people of Durban were similarly surprised to see the Glyn party safely home, and Richard too was conscious that they'd been unusually lucky, given their inexperience in the interior:

Christmas Eve, 1863: Of our horses, five only remained out of 15, of dogs four out of 20. Of oxen we had only lost by death nine, but many more by chopping for fresh ones. Still we had been exceptionally lucky, particularly in oxen, and had gone through the whole trip without any serious misfortune or accidents of any kind, which was almost more than the most sanguine could have reckoned on. We were reprieved one day from the sea, but on Jan 2nd set sail for England, having been in the colony just ten months, during which time we had trekked some three thousand miles. Of course, trekking so far, to the Zambezi, interfered greatly with our shooting. No doubt we might have killed a greater number of head nearer Natal. But we killed enough for sport. All in fair daylight! Not one at night! And not one when the flesh could not be made use of.

The list at the end of Richard's diary details a total of 160 head of game killed, among them eight elephant, three black rhino, 21 giraffe, 15 buffalo, 22 springbok and one leopard. But the king of beasts had eluded them and they returned to England without having shot a lion. I am glad, at least, about that. For lion, to me, will always symbolise everything that is bold and wild about Africa – and everything we must work hard to preserve.

A large brown envelope lay on my kitchen table in Johannesburg. In it was a detailed account, drawn up by my house-sitter, about what had happened in my home during my absence. The electricity bill had, inexplicably, soared seven-fold, one of the cats had arthritis, the leaks in the roof had worsened and my gardener was 'cheeky'. The report had been written with good intentions, but it contained a litany of urban evils I had tried so hard to escape: petty-mindedness, mundanity and materialism. And it served to issue a clarion call that I was once more part of a society with which I was becoming increasingly disaffected. The cats ignored me for days – and I wished the world had too. Friends phoned to welcome me home and tell me their news. 'So, when can we see you?' I fudged my replies, not wanting to let on how little I felt like seeing them. All I wanted was to be left alone on my veranda, clutching at the few fragments I could find of the natural world through which I'd travelled. But the moon's nightly journey was not the slow creep across a giant sky I'd come to love. Here, its arc was broken up into short glimpses between walls and roofs – and, like the stars, its glow was tarnished by never-die street lights. The leaves that rustled on my suburb's hillside were largely those of alien trees and rampant weeds, and the birds in my garden competed against engine drone from the main road below. Our tents and camping gear, spread out on the lawn for a thorough cleaning, looked prosaic and tatty – utterly unlike the proud but humble home we'd come to cherish.

So I did what I usually do when I'm sad – I walked. The tiny, choked *spruit* that runs through Johannesburg provided some relief from my melancholy, and some make-believe games for my two dogs, used to adventure and excitement around every corner. Here, my (equally melancholic) little Tapiwa had his tail up once again, and held his head proud as he trotted ahead of me, mimicking what he'd done for so many kilometres across Africa. Here, Mpho could stage her ambushes in the long grass and sniff out old bones to gnaw on the run.

Eventually, I donned my city smile and set about slowly re-engaging with the folk of my 'town' – only to find that my mask was easily penetrated and that theirs hid nothing from my eyes, freshened as they were by months away from insincerity and idle distraction. 'How was your walk?' was a question I dreaded, knowing that I'd have two minutes to supply a summation of my wonderful trip before releasing the enquirer to pursue conversation about other matters. Friends I thought I could trust showed me brutally why I couldn't – but others dived into my soul-pool with me and shared my grieving. In the long and lonely months while I battled with the twin tortures of writing this book and reliving my walk through its lines, they quietly tolerated my depression and despair, phoning with words of encouragement and reinforcing the imperatives of completing this last, all-important, leg of the journey.

Once I got onto the speaker circuit with my talk about the walk, fresh assaults awaited my still-tender epiphany out in the arid bushveld. The road through Botswana had provided a quite unexpected 'road to Damascus' experience, which would alter my conduct forever – a transcendent awareness in which I saw myself as part of a much, much bigger picture. And it had resulted in my decision not to eat meat or chicken for the rest of my life. Since my return, I had done some research into the devastating effect meat-eating is having on our planet, as well as the way in which livestock is 'grown' on our factory-farms and slaughtered in our abattoirs. It not only made for nauseating and deeply disturbing insights into humankind's moral and physical demise, but it confirmed my resolution to have no part in that process as far as I could possibly help it. But for some people in my audiences (thankfully the minority), it was not information they welcomed – despite the fact that it occupies a very brief section of my presentation. As far as these people were (and are) concerned, I should be the 'brave, inspiring, motivational woman' who walked solo through rural Africa, not the bearer of sad tidings on animal abuse in which we are all complicit. I should be the compassionate heroine who rescued two starving dogs, not the heartless monster I had found myself to be by inflicting untold torture on livestock through what I consume. And those who were not ready for the message tried hard to shoot the messenger. I have had to get used to their invocations to delete this aspect of my talk. I have had to watch the faint-hearted in my audiences lower their heads and close their eyes as I show how a cow faces its ugly end in a killing house, only to see them pile into their steaks at dinner. I have had to lunch with people who raise funds for chimpanzee sanctuaries, watching them consume the flesh of equally intelligent creatures, such as pigs, that spend their lives in ignominious confinement. I have had to commune with well-meaning friends who fight for wetlands, game reserves and forests while the land they seek to save is ravaged through what they put into their mouths. In short, I have had to get used to the fact that, in trying to effect a change in what we eat and how we 'harvest' it, I have taken on a battle that is going to be neither popular nor winnable. And that it is likely to entail the hardest journey of my life.

So, one road has led to another – as most roads do – and who knows how many more are left for me to travel? I trust more than were left for Robert when he returned home from his expedition across Africa. Information about him is scant to say the least, but he is on record as having registered for a degree at Cambridge University in June 1866. Within 10 months he was dead. I have stared at his death certificate many times, willing it to tell me more of the circumstances in which he died, but the pale green document only reveals that he breathed his last on 9 April 1867, at Blacklands House, Chelsea, London. He was 33 years old. John R Hill was 'present at death'. I hope John was a close friend. And the cause of Robert's demise? 'Pyemia. Inflammation of the veins of the right leg and arm – one week. Exhaustion – one week.' Pyemia is what we would call septicaemia today, or a bacterial infection of the blood, often resulting from open wounds. What had happened? We think that Blacklands House was an army barracks at the time and, as a former officer, Robert would have had ready access to horses which he could exercise or race in nearby Hyde Park. Did he have another riding accident? Fall on a spike or fence? Get jabbed by someone's sword? And were these injuries the last straw after the falls that had so weakened him during his trip through Africa? I'll never know.

Henry St George Osborne's post-expedition life remains similarly ungenerous in its detail, owing to a massive fire in Dublin's central records office in 1922, which destroyed most of Ireland's personal and family records. But we know that he married and had at least two children – a daughter named Geraldine and a son, Henry Ralph, who went on to become a councillor for County Meath. The family Osborne remained at Dardistown Castle, Drogheda, until 1969 – so perhaps 'my' Henry lived out his days there in relative luxury and continued developing his father's prestigious racehorse stable.

About Richard George Glyn there is no shortage of information because he lived a long, productive and high-profile life. When he returned from Africa he received news that he had inherited the baronetcy from his uncle

Sir Richard Plumtree Glyn who had died childless. But because Richard Plumtree had also left no will, his money was divided up between nine heirs, leaving 'my' Richard with insufficient funds to run Gaunts estate. Well, that is what I assume to have been the case because he let out the house for 18 years before he finally occupied it in 1884. But while living at Lewiston House, another Glyn residence nearby, the 'new' Sir Richard led an active, community-minded life. He married Frances Geraldine Fitzgerald about five years after his Africa odyssey and they produced a girl, Mary Geraldine, and a boy to continue the Glyn line, Richard Fitzgerald. Over a period of many years' service in the County, Richard George held offices such as Justice of the Peace, Deputy Lieutenant of Dorset, High Sheriff, Chairman of the Wimborne Bench of Magistrates and Captain of the Yeomanry. He was also active in local politics and was instrumental in founding the local hospital, grammar school and the Dorset Field Club. Indeed an extract from his obituary, published in the *Dorset County Chronicle* on 15 August 1918, gives one an idea of how much his contribution was valued:

'Though not of commanding stature, he was a man of fine parts and resolute and enterprising nature, with considerable power of leadership and public spirit. As a soldier, a traveller, a sportsman, a remarkably successful master of hounds, and again as a county magistrate and public man, embued with a fine spirit both of patriotism and philanthropy, he served his day and generation right well, doing thoroughly and whole heartedly everything he set his hand to do. His firm but kindly face will be greatly missed, and his death make a sore gap in East Dorset society and public life.'

In time, Gaunts was built up by this indefatigable man into a thriving county estate, its lands extended and planted with hundreds of trees, and its manor house enlarged and improved. Some of the people who gave Richard loyal service on his farm are buried near him in the graveyard at Stanbridge Church, their gravestones – and those of other family members – somewhat dwarfed by the huge cross that marks Richard's resting place. It notes that he died on 9 August 1918, at the grand old age of 86.

But it seems that the pursuit that brought Richard to Africa – sport hunting – is the one activity for which he'll best be remembered. Mention his name in Dorset today and people in the know will invariably say of him: 'Oh yes, he was Master of the Blackmore Vale Hounds for years and years, of course. Outstanding horseman and hunter.' In fact, Richard was Master of the Vale for nearly 20 years, from 1865 to 1884, and during that time he killed 2 340 foxes, averaging 61 brace a year – a 'very notable kill rate', according to experts. The issue of fox hunting being so divisive in rural England at present, I have no doubt that there are those who would regard that tally as 'disgusting' and an equal number who would laud it.

Am I fanciful in wondering, however, if he found fox hunting a poor and tame substitute for the wild chase and high excitement he'd had on our continent? Did the mournful cry of his country's tiny predators on white winter nights always bring to mind the bigger, deeper howls of Africa's great beasts? Did he lie in his grand bedroom upstairs at Gaunts House, watching ice crystals form on its windowpanes and yearn for the intimacy of a little canvas 'penthouse'? Did he look back on the Africa odyssey as his last fling at freedom before taking on a long life of duty? And did he think of our plains and our peoples when he lay dying?

I know I shall. And I know that every time I hear the shy *chirrup* of a scops-owl or smell the dust in crisp, white grass; when I lie under an old tree or feel the late afternoon sun on my throat, I shall be filled with the sense of peace and purpose that was mine for four and a half months on our glorious subcontinent. And I shall do what I have done every day since I returned from the Victoria Falls – I shall celebrate being an African.

Photographic Credits

210 At the fireside. Baldwin, WC: op cit

223 Hippopotamus trap. Lord, WB & Baines, T: op cit

223 Female elephant, pursued with javelins, protecting her young. Livingstone, David: *Missionary Travels and Researches in South Africa*, John Murray, London, 1857

229 Holloway Helmore, 1858. Kilby, S: *No Cross Marks the Spot*, Galamena Press, Southend-on-Sea, 2001.

230 Anne Helmore, 1858: LMS/Council for World Mission Archives, London

231 Roger and Isabella Price. Kilby, S: ibid

251 Izak Barnard and the Bushmen: *Getaway Magazine* Photo Access, Patrick Wagner 1995

261 Boat Building on the Logier River. Lord, WB & Baines, T: op cit

273 *Rainy Afternoon*. Charles D Bell. Library of Parliament, Cape Town

281 *Famishing Slaves Deserted*. Wash drawing by Johann Baptist Zwecker, c. 1859. ART. 396/14, Brenthurst Library, Johannesburg

293 Pandamatenga: Zimbabwe National Archive

295 Victoria Falls: photograph courtesy Jeremy Glyn

305 Victoria Falls: photograph courtesy Jeremy Glyn

307 David Livingstone: MuseuMAfricA

All photographs of Sir Richard George Glyn, his brother Robert, Gaunts House and The Diary are reproduced courtesy of Sir Richard Lindsay Glyn, to whom the author is grateful. Photographs of the 2005 expedition were taken by Karin Slater, Franci Cronjé, Sue Oxborrow, John Kerr and Patricia Glyn.

Internet Sources

www.1837online.com
www.nationalarchivist.com
www.ancestry.com
www.regiments.org
www.householdcavalry.co.uk
www.crimeanwar.org
www.rdgmuseum.org.uk
www.familyrecords.gov.uk
www.meathroots.com
www.irishorigins.com
www.ancestryireland.com
www.familysearch.com
www.cabi-publishing.org
www.originsnetwork.com
www.rootsweb.
www.ancestry.co.uk
www.harrowschool.org.uk
www.cam.ac.uk
www.energa.com/meathhc/meathlinks.shtml
www.shropshireregimental.org.uk
www.from-ireland.net/gene/churchrecrds.htm
www.parliament.thestationery-office.co.uk
www.endangeredspecieshandbook.org

www.lib.cam.ac.uk
www.nationalarchives.gov.za
www.ukzn.ac.za
www.cai.cam.ac.uk
www.genealogyworld.net
www.unep-wcmc.org
www.cons-dev.org
www.ubh.tripod.com
www.historyworld.net
www.thezambian.com
www.eyewitnesshistory.com
www.site.mweb.co.zw
www.quaggaproject.org
www.sacip.org.za
www.cinetecadelfriuli.org
www.thinkexist.com
www.silentera.com
www.sandiegohistory.org

www.encyclopedia-titanica.org
www.trin.cam.ac.uk
www.booksofzimbabwe.com
www.cfsph.iastate.edu
www.awf.org
www.krugerpark.co.za
www.sanparks.org
www.wildwatch.com
www.addistribune.com
www.africaguide.com
www.planetark.org
www.lonker.net
www.ntz.info
www.ralphmag.org
www.columbia.edu
www.comrades.com
www.ciwf.org
www.national-army-museum.ac.uk

Bibliography

- Abdy, Charles. *The Glyns of Ewell – The story of a family from 1736 to 1946*, published by the author, 1994.
- Anderson, Andrew A. *Twenty-Five Years in a Waggon*, Chapman & Hall, 1888.
- Baldwin, WC. *African Hunting & Adventure from Natal to the Zambesi*, 3rd Edition, Richard Bentley & Son, 1894.
- Barrett, CRB. *The 85th King's Light Infantry*, Spottiswoode & Co, 1913.
- Becker, Peter. *The Pathfinders*, Viking, 1985.
- Bensusan, Dr AD. '19th Century Photographers in South Africa', *Africana Notes and News*, Africana Society, June 1963, Vol. 15, No. 6.
- Bensusan, Dr AD. *Silver Images. History of Photography in Africa*, Howard Timmins Publishers, 1966.
- Bentley, Nicolas (ed.). *Russell's Despatches from the Crimea 1854–1856*, André Deutsch, 1966.
- Bosman, Herman Charles. *Idle Talk: Voorkamer Series (I)*, The Anniversary Edition, Human & Rousseau, 1999.
- Boucher, Maurice (ed.). *Livingstone Letters 1843 to 1872*, The Brenthurst Press, 1985.
- Breutz, PL. *The Tribes of Mafeking District*, Ethnological Publications, No. 32, Department of Native Affairs, Government Printer, 1955.
- Breutz, PL. *A History of the Batswana and Origin of Bophuthatswana*, published by the author, 1989.
- Broadbent, GA. *Narrative of the first introduction of Christianity amongst the Barolong tribe of Bechuanas*, Wesleyan Mission House, 1865.
- Brown, JT. *Among the Bantu Nomads*, Seeley, Service & Co. Ltd, 1926.
- Burke, EE (ed.). *The Journals of Carl Mauch – His Travels in the Transvaal and Rhodesia 1869—1872*, National Archives of Rhodesia, 1969.
- Bull, Bartle. *Safari – A Chronicle of Adventure*, Penguin, 1988.
- Bulpin, TV. *To the Shores of Natal*, Citadel Press, 1954.
- Bulpin, TV. *To the Banks of the Zambezi*, Books of Africa, 1968.
- Burman, Jose. *Towards the Far Horizon – The story of the ox-wagon in South Africa*, Human & Rousseau, 1988.
- Callender, MP. *A Thesis on the Diary of RC Glyn*, unpublished research conducted for Patricia Glyn, 2005.
- Cameron-Dow, John. *Comrades Marathon – The Official History*, Don Nelson Publishers, 2006.
- Campbell, Alec and Main, Mike. *Guide to Greater Gaborone*, published by the authors in association with The Botswana Society, 2003.
- Campbell, John. *Travels in South Africa undertaken at the request of the London Missionary Society. Being a narrative of a second journey in the interior of that country*, Francis Westley, 1822.
- Chapman, James. *Travels in the Interior of Africa*, Vol I & II, AA Balkema, 1971.
- Chapman, James. *Travels into the Interior of South Africa*, Bell & Daldy, London, 1868.
- 'Chatty'. *There's Peace in Baobabwe*, published by the author, Zimbabwe, 1987.
- Child, Daphne. *A Merchant Family in Early Natal*, AA Balkema, 1979.
- Coates Palgrave, Keith: *Trees of Southern Africa*, New Edition revised and updated by Meg Coates Palgrave, Struik Publishers, 2002.
- Cornwallis Harris, Captain William. *The Wild Sports of Southern Africa*, Pelham Richardson, 1844.
- Cornwallis Harris, Captain William. *Portraits of the Game and Wild Animals of Southern Africa*, first published by the author 1840, this edition Galago Publishing, 1986.
- Couzens, Tim. *Battles of South Africa*, David Philip Publishers, 2004.
- Cumming, R Gordon. *A Hunter's Life in South Africa*, John Murray, 1850.
- Dachs, AJ (ed.). *The Papers of John Mackenzie*, Witwatersrand University Press, 1975.
- Da Costa Leal, Fernando. *Journal about a Journey from Transvaal to Lourenco Marques in 1870*, Geographic Society of Lisbon, 1943.
- Davson, Sir Christopher. Tape recording of Glyn family history, Private Collection.
- De la Harpe, Roger and Pat, Leitch, Barry and Derwent, Sue. *Zulu*, Struik Publishers, 1998.
- Denbow, Prof. Jim. Personal communication with Patricia Glyn by e-mail, March 2006.
- Dominy, Graham. *The Imperial Garrison in Natal with special reference to Fort Napier 1843–1914, its social, cultural and economic impact*, Thesis for DPhil, University of London, 1995.
- Duminy, Linda. *The Royal Hotel – History in the Making*, Three Cities Hotels, 1995.
- Du Preez, Max. *Of Warriors, Lovers and Prophets*, Zebra Press, 2004.
- Fulford, Roger. *Glyn's 1753–1953. Six Generations in Lombard Street*, Macmillan & Co Ltd, 1953.
- Gibson, RL and Reimold, WU. *Meteorite Impact!* Chris van Rensburg Publications, 2005.
- Glyn, Dr John St George. *The Genealogy of the Families of Glyn and St George*, published by the author, 1979.
- Glyn, Elinor. *Romantic Adventure*, EP Dutton & Co., Inc. Publishers, 1937.
- Glyn, Michael. *Footnotes to a Family History*, published by the author, 1994.
- Glyn, Ronald St George. *Reminiscences*, published by the author, 1990.
- Glyn, Sir Richard George. *Diary of Ten Months in South Africa 1863*, unpublished.
- Gold, Mark. *The Global Benefits of Eating Less Meat – A Report for Compassion in World Farming Trust*, www.ciwf.org, 2004.
- Gordon, Ruth. *The Place of the Elephant – A History of Pietermaritzburg*, Shuter & Shooter in association with The Simon van der Stel Foundation, 1981.
- Gowing, Sergeant Timothy (Royal Fusiliers). *A Personal Narrative of the Crimean Campaign*, William Heinemann, 1954.

- Green, Lawrence G. *Karroo*, Howard Timmins Publishers,
- Grobler, JEH. *Jan Viljoen (1812–1893) – A Pioneer on the Western Border of Transvaal*, MA Thesis, University of Pretoria, 1976.
- Hall, Sian. *Dogs of Africa*, Alpine Blue Ribbon Books, 2003.
- Hall, Sian and Marsh, Rob. *Beyond Belief – Murders and Mysteries of Southern Africa*, Struik Publishers, 1996.
- Hibbert, Christopher. *The Destruction of Lord Raglan – A tragedy of the Crimean War*, Longman, 1961.
- Hochschild, Adam. *King Leopold's Ghost – A Story of Greed, Terror and Heroism in Colonial Africa*, Pan Books, 2002.
- Holmes, Timothy. *Journey to Livingstone – Exploration of an Imperial Myth*, Canongate Press, 1993.
- Hopkins, Pat. *Eccentric South Africa*, Zebra Press, 2001.
- Hughes, Nigel. *The Paintings of the Bay of Natal*, Mertrade, 2001.
- Hyatt, Stanley Porter. *The Old Transport Road*, Andrew Melrose Ltd, 1914.
- Jeal, Tim. *Livingstone*, Pimlico, 1993.
- Kilby, Stella E. *No Cross Marks the Spot*, Galamena Press, 2001.
- Knightly, Phillip. *The First Casualty – The War Correspondent as Hero, Propagandist and Myth Maker from the Crimea to Vietnam*, André Deutsch, 1975.
- Koopman, Adrian. 'Unpacking Jamludi – Zulu Names in Language, Culture and Communication', Inaugural lecture, University of Natal, unpublished, 28 May 2003.
- Laband, J and Haswell, R (eds). *Pietermaritzburg, 1838–1988. A New Portrait of an African City*, University of Natal Press in association with Shuter & Shooter, 1988.
- Le Roux, Servaas D. *Pioneers and Sportsmen of South Africa*, The Art Printing Works Ltd, 1939.
- Livingstone, David. *Missionary Travels and Researches in South Africa*, John Murray, 1857.
- Lord, WB and Baines, T. *Shifts and Expedients of Camp Life, Travel and Exploration*, Horace Cox, 1871.
- Mackenzie, Rev. John. *Day-Dawn in Dark Places – A Story of Wanderings and Work in Bechuanaland*, Cassel & Co. Ltd, 1883.
- Mackenzie, Rev. John. *Ten Years North of the Orange River – A story of everyday life and work among the South African tribes from 1859 to 1869*, Edmonston & Douglas, 1871.
- Mackenzie, W Douglas. *John Mackenzie – South African Missionary and Statesman*, Hodder & Stoughton, 1902.
- Main, Michael. *African Adventurer's Guide to Botswana*, Struik Publishers, 2001.
- Main, Michael. *Kalahari – Life's Variety in Dune and Delta*, Southern Books, 1987.
- Main, Michael. *The Hunters' Road*, unpublished, 1993.
- Main, Michael. *Zambezi – Journey of a River*, Southern Books, 1990.
- Meredith, Martin. *Africa's Elephant – A Biography*, Hodder & Stoughton, 2001.
- Mohr, Eduard. *To The Victoria Falls of the Zambezi*, Facsimile reproduction of the English edition of 1876, Books of Rhodesia, 1973.
- Morton, Fred, Murray, Andrew and Ramsay, Jeff. *Historical Dictionary of Botswana*, The Scarecrow Press, Inc., 1989.
- Nicholls, CS. *David Livingstone – A Concise Biography*, Isis Audio Books.
- O'Keefe, Bob (ed.). *Pioneers' Progress. Early Natal*, Hilltop Publications.
- Oswell, William Edward. *William Cotton Oswell – Hunter and Explorer*, Heinemann, 1900.
- Pakenham, Thomas. *Remarkable Trees of the World*, Jonathan Ball Publishers, 1995.
- Pearse, RO. *Barrier of Spears*, Howard Timmins Publishers, 1973.
- Pinnock, Don. *African Journeys*, Double Storey, 2003.
- Sandeman, EF. *Eight Months in an Ox-Waggon*, Africana Book Society, 1975.
- Schapera, I. *A Handbook of Tswana Law and Custom*, Published for the International Institute of African Languages and Cultures, Oxford University Press, 1938.
- Schapera, I. *The Tswana*, KPI Ltd, 1984.
- Scott Shaw, C. *Stories from the Karkloof Hills*, Shuter & Shooter, 1971.
- Selous, FC. *African Nature Notes and Reminiscences*, Macmillan, 1908.
- Sigmund, Otto H and Fraser, Clarence M (eds.). *The Merck Veterinary Manual*, Merck & Co., Inc., 1979.
- Sillery, Anthony. *John Mackenzie of Bechuanaland – A Study in Humanitarian Imperialism, 1835-1899*, AA Balkema, 1971.
- Spencer, Shelagh O'Byrne. *British Settlers – A Biographical Register in Natal 1824–1857*, Vol 7, Natal University Press, 2001.
- Tabler, Edward C. *Pioneers of Rhodesia*, Struik Publishers, 1966.
- Tabler, Edward C. *The Far Interior*, AA Balkema, 1955.
- Tabler, Edward C (ed.). *Trade and Travel in Early Barotseland – The Diaries of George Westbeech 1885-1888 and Captain Norman MacLeod 1875–1876*, The Robins Series, Vol 12, Chatto & Windus, 1963.
- Taylor, Stephen. *Livingstone's Tribe – A Journey from Zanzibar to the Cape*, HarperCollins Publishers, 1999.
- Wallis, JPR (ed.). *The Matabele Journals of Robert Moffat*, Vols I & II, Chatto & Windus, 1945.
- Wannenburgh, Alf, Johnson, Peter and Bannister, Anthony. *The Bushmen*, C Struik Publishers, 1979.
- Webster, Roger. *At The Fireside*, Spearhead, 2001.
- Webster, Roger. *At The Fireside*, Vol 2, Spearhead, 2002.
- Webster, Roger. *At The Fireside*, Vol 3, Spearhead, 2005.
- Webster, Roger. *The Illustrated 'At The Fireside'*, Spearhead, 2002.

Credits

I am deeply indebted to the following people for their help in making my walk – and this account of it – possible. If I have omitted to mention anyone, I apologise unreservedly. Many other friends who gave their support are not mentioned here because they were not directly involved in my journey – but I am nonetheless deeply grateful for their love and tolerance while I took to the road and then secluded myself during the writing of this book.

Claire Adderley, Graeme Addison, Brian Agar, the staff of the Alan Paton Museum, Mike Aldous, Nick Allen, Cora Bailey, Stanley Banda, Izak Barnard, Steve Bartlo, Andrew and Cathy Bean, Micky Bean, AD Bensusan, Lee Berger, Bill Bizley, Gary Boswell, Ren Brecht, the staff of the Brenthurst Library, Delyse Brown, Una and Eduard Bruwer, Barney Buchan, Iain and Carol Buchan, Robbie Buck, Michael and Vivienne Callender, John Cameron-Dow, Alec Campbell, Eugene Campher, Wessel Campher, the staff of Cape Union Mart, Jane and Vincent Carruthers, Oscar Chalupsky, Louis Changuion, Helen and Martin Charteris, Tessa Chikaponya, Yvonne Christian, Johann Coetzee, Rowena and Jan Coetzee, Mark Coghlan, Pat Colby, Candice Coleman, Lorraine Collen, Ashley Cooper, Tom and Day Coulter, Tim Couzens, Franci Cronjé, Ed and Pat Cumming, Graham and Ruth Dabbs, Val and Doug Dabbs, Shorne Darlow, Karen Davies, Angela de Waal, Rhiana Delport, Isaac Dlamini, Graham Dominy, Noo Dominy, Christine Driewes, Ruth Drinn, Linda Duminy, Malcolm and Yolande Falconnier, Louise Ford, Bruce Fordyce, Sean Fraser, the staff of Front Runner, Mike Fynn, Johan Gallant, Alan Garlick, the staff of Garmin, Roger Gibson, Jeremy Glyn, Norma Glyn, Patrick and Margot Glyn, Ronald and Mevagh Glyn, Shirley Glyn, Sir Richard Lindsay Glyn, Claude Goddard, Marcelle Graham, Andrew and Mel Greene, Amanda Greene, RW Green-Thompson, Aileen Guest, Ken Hardman, Lew and Maria Harris, Ferdie and Judy Hartzenberg, Peter Hayward, Mec Heart, Tim Hendon, Hennie Heydenrych, Stuart Hillcove, Zann Hoad, Alastair Hodgson, Amanda Holroyd, Nigel Hughes, Alan Jeffrey, Beverly and Derek Joubert, Mark Karam, John Kerr, Kgosi Sediegeng Harrigan Kgamane, His Excellency Lieutenant-General Ian Khama, Steven Khosa, Lindiwe Khuzwayo, the staff of Killie Campbell Museum, Leona Kleynhans, Adrian and Jewel Koopman, Uri le Roux, Scobie Lekhutile, Kgosi Edwin Lentswe, Terri Leppan, Robert and Helen Levitt, Estelle Liebenberg-Barkhuizen, Nimrod Mabaso, Godfrey Mabi, Sally MacRoberts, Mike and Kirsten Main, Miss Maladze, Ginny and Garry Marx, Eve and Roland Mazery, Mick and Gloria McConnell, Graham McCullogh, Fylyppa Meyer, Graham Miller, Nkosi Mlaba, Kgosi Godfrey Moilwa, Mandy Momberg, Ingrid Moss, Joyce Mthembu, Makhosi Mthembu, Ndaipaneyi Mukwena, Ruth Muller, Louis and Pietrou Naudé, Elliot Ndlovu, Vanessa Nucci, David O'Sullivan, Alison Oates, Adrian Odendaal, Sue Oxborrow, Derik Pelser, Philippa Meldrum, Ian Player, Chris Plewman, Marguerite Poland, Christina Pretorius, Roy Pringle, Franz Prins, David Rattray, Diana Robertson, Philip and Megan Romeyn, the staff of the Royal Hotel, Sheila and Stratford Russell, Ivor and Heather Sander, Bruce Sawyer, GP Schoeman, Steve Schwarer, Jim Shannon, Karin Slater, Jackie and Mike Solomon, Mavis Sokhela, Hansie and Gerhard Snyman, Shelagh O'Byrne Spenser, Sendepe Spogte, Suzanne Stevens, Julian Stewart, Lindy Stiebel, Kgosi Suping, Adrian and Debbie Swales, Philippa Swan, Jerome Swan, Christo Swart, Barry and Cheryl Symons, Callum and Jenny Symons, the staff of Tala Gama Reserve, Stephen Taylor, Mathys Thompson, Paul Thompson, Mary Thrash, Arto Toivonen, Sue and Peter Topzand-Glyn, Evan Torrance, Tony and Jill Trail, Cole Tshipana, Isiah Tshuma, Johannes Tumane, Phil Vail, Egbert and Santa van Bart, Gert van der Berg, Carol van der Linde, Wouter van Hoven, Fanie van Rensburg, Guy Venter, Mark Verseput, Willie Viljoen, Leigh Voigt, Norma Watson, Steve Watt, Roger and Debbie Webster, Len Wigg, Paula Wilson, and Sean and Joy Wisedale.

Patricia Glyn
April 2006

Index of Historical References